THE BRUNEI REVOLT

Also by Nick van der Bijl

Pen & Sword Military Books
Nine Battles to Stanley
5th Infantry Brigade in the Falklands
Victory in the Falklands
Confrontation; the War with Indonesia 1962-1966
Commandos in Exile; The Story of 10 (Inter-Allied) Commando 1942-45
Operation Banner; The British Army in Northern Ireland 1969-2007

Osprey
Argentine Forces in the Falklands
Royal Marines 1939-1993
No. 10 (Inter-Allied) Commando 1942-1945

Hawk Editions
Brean Down Fort and the Defence of the Bristol Channel

THE BRUNEI REVOLT

1962–1963

Nick van der Bijl

Pen & Sword
MILITARY

First published in Great Britain in 2012
By Pen and Sword Military
an imprint of
Pen and Sword Books Ltd
47 Church Street
Barnsley
South Yorkshire S70 2AS

ISBN 978 1 84884 640 1

A CIP record for this book is available from the British Library.

Printed and bound in England by
CPI Group (UK) Ltd, Croydon, CR0 4YY

Typeset in Times New Roman by
CHIC GRAPHICS

Pen & Sword Books Ltd incorporates the imprints of
Pen & Sword Aviation, Pen & Sword Family History, Pen & Sword Maritime,
Pen & Sword Military, Pen & Sword Discovery, Wharncliffe Local History,
Wharncliffe True Crime, Wharncliffe Transport, Pen & Sword Select,
Pen & Sword Military Classics, Leo Cooper, Remember When,
The Praetorian Press, Seaforth Publishing and Frontline Publishing

For a complete list of Pen and Sword titles please contact
Pen and Sword Books Limited
47 Church Street, Barnsley, South Yorkshire, S70 2AS, England
E-mail: enquiries@pen-and-sword.co.uk
Website: www.pen-and-sword.co.uk

Contents

Foreword

In 1979, while I was attending a Jungle Warfare Instructors' course in Brunei, two Royal Marines invited me to join them on a day out at Limbang. I had never heard of the town and, unaware of its connection with the Royal Marines, instead, after a week of rain in the jungle, I opted to dry out on a beach near the camp outside Tutong. It was a decision that I later regretted.

However, in retrospect, it was understandable because the 1962 Brunei Revolt was one of those lesser known operations in which the British played a key role in maintaining stability in the western South China Sea region during a period of considerable turbulence in South-East Asia. And when it does get remembered, it is usually associated with 1963–1966 Confrontation with Indonesia. They are, in fact, two separate operations. Brunei was largely to defuse an internal security threat while Confrontation was a counter-insurgency campaign against Indonesian-sponsored incursions.

Most of the material for this book was collected when I was researching the Brush Fire Films DVD *Return to Limbang*, directed by Martin Spirit, who was the inspiration behind the project. I am grateful to those who agreed to be interviewed for the DVD and also those who provided artefacts, maps and photographs. From the Royal Navy, this included Admiral Sir Jeremy Black, Peter Down JP, Laurie Johnson, 'Buck' Taylor and Tony Standish. My thanks go to the late Major General Jeremy Moore for his detailed account of 42 Commando at Limbang and also John Bailey, the late Peter Caress, John Coombes, Tony Daker, Brian Downey, Kenneth Fyffe, John Genge, Alan Jarvis, John Leahey, Derek Lloyd, Captain Derek Oakley and Richard Targett-Adams and Terry Clarke of the Royal Navy. I am indebted to Malcolm Macfarlane for sharing information about his brother Sergeant Walter Macfarlane who was killed at Limbang, as I am to Geraldine Bull and Adrian Morris who kindly gave us access to the papers of their parents, Richard and Dorothy Morris, two of the hostages at Limbang. From the Army, I am indebted to the late Colonel Charles McHardy for supplying information on the Queens Own Highlanders operation; and to the late Lieutenant Colonel Gordon Shakespear, the Commanding Officer of the 1/2 Gurkha Rifles. From the RAF, Squadron Leader Hubert Blanche shared information on the Seria hostages, which included his late father, Herbert Blanche. The late Alastair Ker-Lindsay MBE explained the role of British Shell Petroleum and his experiences as a hostage. Former Assistant District Officer John Parry MBE provided details of how the rebellion affected North Borneo, now known as Sabah. I am also indebted to the Museums of the Royal Marines, Queens Own Highlanders, Royal Green Jackets Museum and the Gurkha Museum for giving me access to records.

Thank you to those who helped with photographs. Images of the first days of the Brunei Revolt appear to be quite rare; however, Pen & Sword have done their very best with snapshots taken fifty years ago with such cameras as Instamatics. I am also uncertain of the origins of some photographs, however I would be happy to hear from anyone who has copyright.

As always, I am indebted to my wife, Penny, not only for her patience but also her contribution as a hostess to *Return to Limbang* and her proof reading of this book in a period when the pressure was on to complete another project. To Brigadier Henry Wood and Matt Jones, of Pen & Sword Books, for their work in producing this project. To Lynne Maxwell for her gentle editing. To Peter Wood, of GWR for producing the maps, and to John Noble for his meticulous indexing.

ANDUKI, SERIA, PANAGA AND KUALA BELAIT

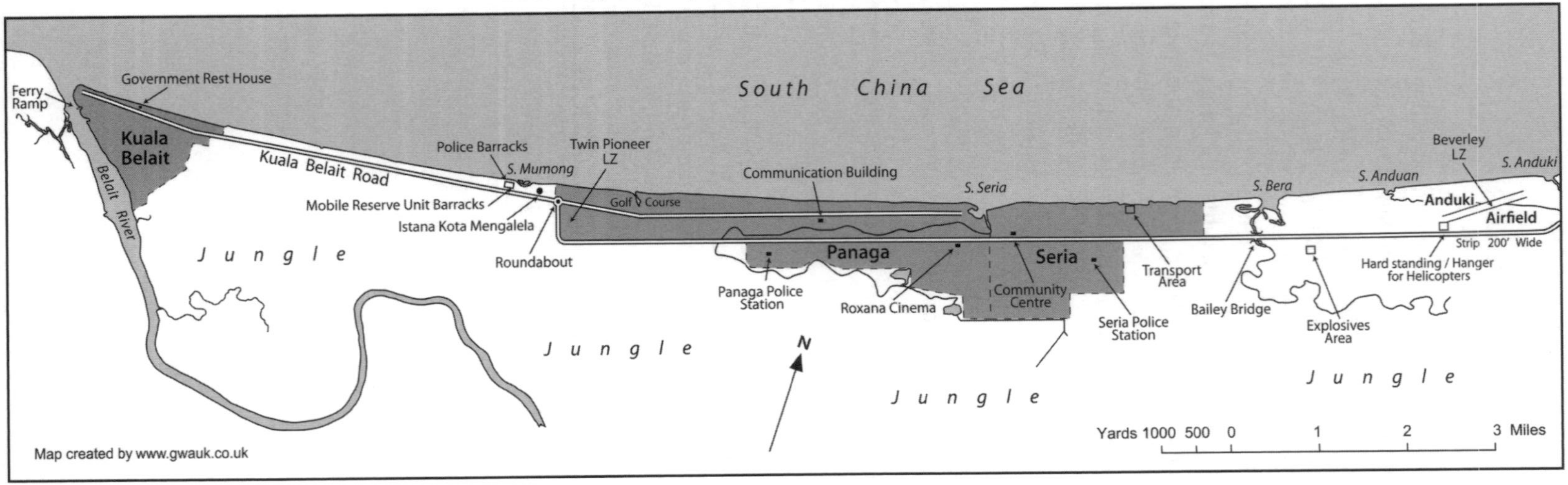

LIMBANG - 11/12 DECEMBER 1962

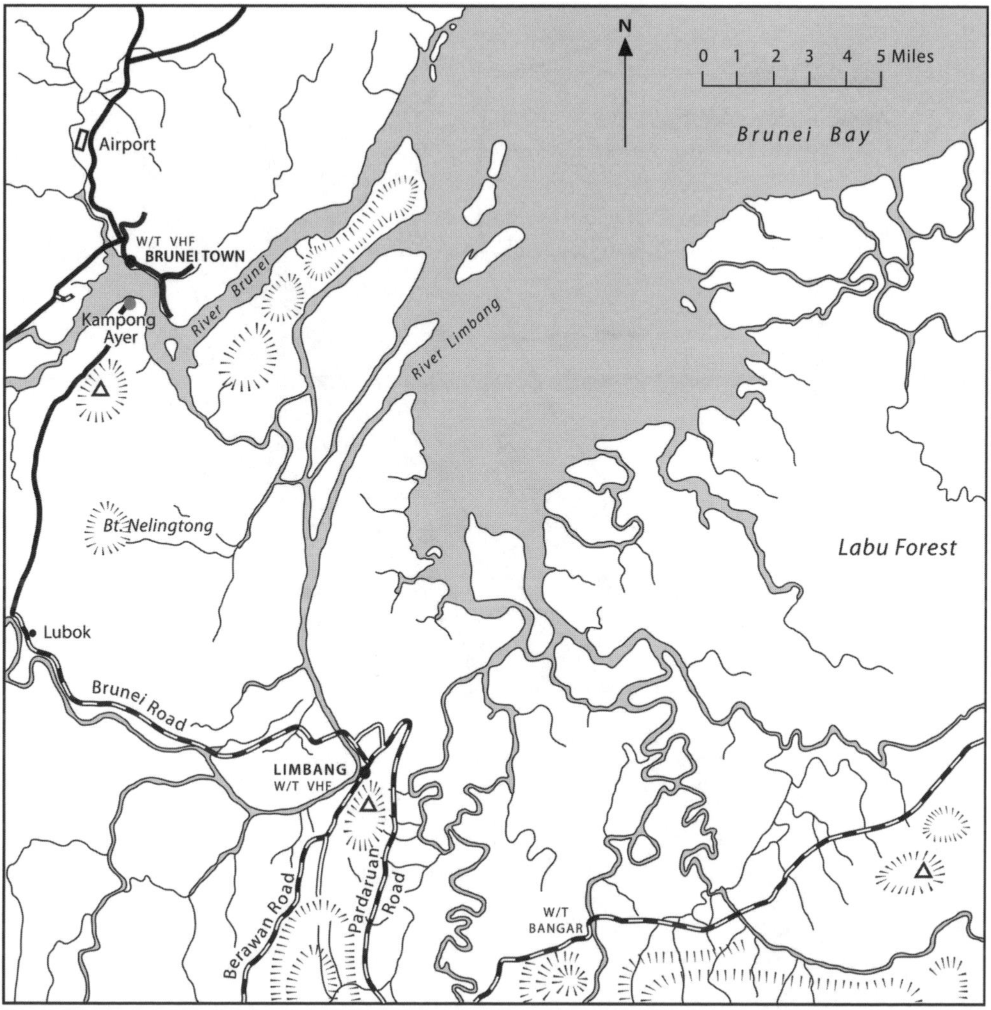

Map created by www.gwauk.co.uk

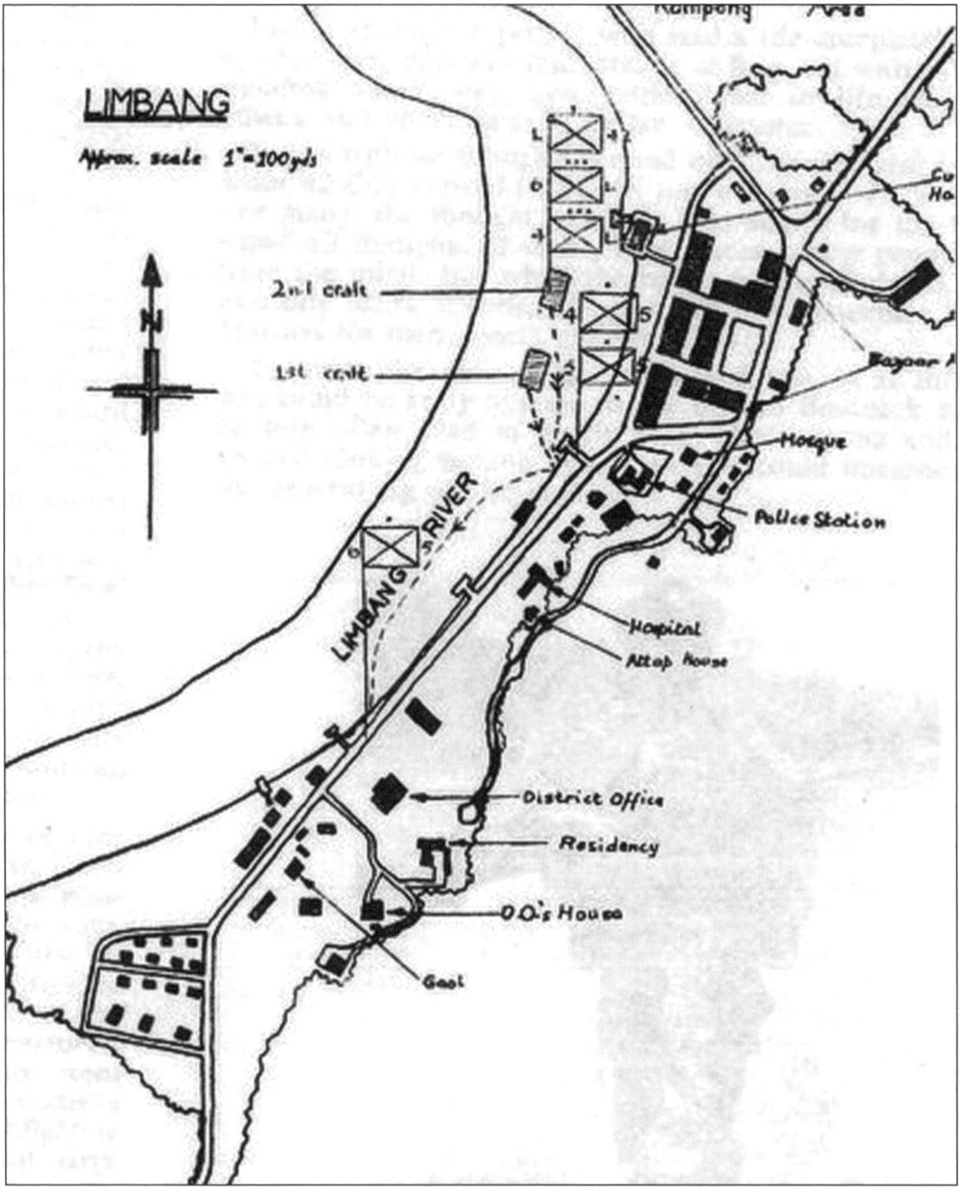
LIMBANG
Approx. scale 1" = 100 yds
N
Kampong Area
2nd craft
1st craft
LIMBANG RIVER
Mosque
Police Station
Hospital
Attap House
District Office
Residency
D.O.'s House
Gaol

CHAPTER ONE

Preamble

Arabic and Chinese records indicate that a trading sultanate at the mouth of the Brunei River existed as early as the seventh century. Regional trade from China and South Asia included stoneware, metals, silks and sandalwood, spices and gums tapped from the jungle. From this trade, the sultanate developed an empire of parts of Borneo, the southern islands of the Philippines and many adjacent islands. By the fifteenth century, Islam from the Middle East had been introduced. Between the late sixteenth and early seventeenth centuries, the reign of Sultan Bolkiah (1473–1521) is often described as Brunei's 'golden age' as he extended Brunei's influence over North Kalimantan, the Sulu archipelago, Java and Malacca and the Philippines, where he captured Manila. It was at the end of his reign that Ferdinand Magellan's fleet called in here during their search for the western route to the Spice Islands, otherwise known as Indonesia. Magellan had been killed in the Philippines. His officers found a city of sophistication and opulence. This first contact led to greater interest in regional trading by Portugal but this was an age of Spanish expansion and in 1571 the Spanish captured Manila and, over the next years, Sulu and Brunei itself.

The seventeenth Sultan, Sultan Omar Ali Saifuddin I, met the British sailor Admiral John Dalrymple in 1762, at the end of the Seven Years War in which the French had been ejected from India. Dalrymple agreed to contest French and Spanish encroachments into the region; however, the clashes led to Brunei and other south-east Asian sultanates descending into decline as trade routes and alliances were undermined. An attempt by the East Indies Company to succour Brunei failed in 1803 and by the mid 1800s, the once powerful nation of Brunei was in serious decline, its control confined to northern Borneo by rebellion and internal disagreements and its influence being overtaken by the development of Singapore. The region was ripe for exploitation by the early British imperialist adventurers.

The most influential was James Brooke. He arrived in Brunei in 1839 and helped Sultan Omar Ali Saifuddin II, the twenty-third ruler of Brunei, quell a rebellion and was awarded the governorship of Sarawak. Dubbed the 'White Rajah', Brooke fell out with the Sultan and, in 1843, defeated him. The British captured Brunei Town and the weakened Sultan signed a treaty with the British. When asked by Brooke if he should claim Brunei as part of Sarawak, London advised him that this would not be acceptable because it had a sense of national identity. An American offer in 1845 to protect Brunei was rejected and then two years later the island of Labuan was ceded to the British.

Largely empty except for a few Chinese shops and fishermen's rest huts on the beaches, on becoming the first governor, Brooke invited settlers. However, his efforts to entice Chinese and Brunei traders and shopkeepers failed and it was left to Chinese merchants from Singapore to exploit. The British had wanted to convert the island into a strategic naval base on a par with Singapore in the South China Sea region from which the rife piracy could be addressed. The discovery of coal at the north meant that the island could be developed as a shipping coal station. A year later, Labuan was declared a free port and Port Victoria grew into the commercial area, the location for Government House and government offices and the garrison, which, by 1881, consisted of three or four European officers, six guns and fifty police. By 1850, Brooke had imported Hong Kong convicts to mine the coal, build roads and clear the jungle. The population in 1867 was about 4000, the majority being Muruts, Dusuns and Kedayans, Malays from the Straits Settlements, 600 Chinese, Indian shopkeepers and 40 Europeans. The mining was supported by a light railway track to Port Victoria; however, frequent militancy and labour shortages saw poor results. It was also poorly administered largely because the Colonial Office insisted the island should be governed with the minimum of funds but revenue was low. In spite of initial interest from shipping companies, few vessels called because the quality of the coal was poor and within sixty years production had ceased. Malaria was rife. Labuan was not living up to its economic expectations and, by 1872, the British were seriously considering abandoning it. The British North Borneo Chartered Company then considered administering Labuan for prestige reasons.

North Borneo, with its capital at Jesselton (now Kota Kinabalu), covered 29,388 square miles. James Brooke had intended to acquire North Borneo in order to improve the safety of ships transiting through the South China Sea but the American adventurer Claude Lee Moses outwitted him. Formerly a member of the US Navy, during the early 1860s, Moses had persuaded the Sultan of Brunei to sell him the large tract of Brunei territory now known as Sabah (formerly North Borneo). He then sold the contracts to four Hong Kong merchants who set up the American Trading Company of North Borneo. When their attempt to develop Kimanis settlement failed, Moses became impecunious. One of the four, Joseph Torrey, convinced the Austrian Consul in Hong Kong, Baron von Overbeck, to speculate in North Borneo. In 1877 William Treacher, a young British civil servant based in Singapore, heard the bids and persuaded von Overbeck and his colleagues to bring the territory under British administrative and commercial control. Von Overbeck and his associates persuaded the Sultan of Brunei to cede the 28,000 miles of North Borneo. By 1881 the British North Borneo Chartered Company had been formed. Treacher initially established his office in Labuan but he clashed with the governor and moved to North Borneo to establish the capital at Kudah. Treacher rejected Spanish, Dutch and American claims and expanded the territory in the face of opposition from the Brookes family. After a period of instability and rashly planned projects, including the building of a railway line from Beaufort to Weston, by 1900, the company profits had improved as did the administration, economic development, health and education. Timber was an important resource but frequently ran into trouble when labour was short. Meanwhile, Sir Charles Brooke, nephew of James, was continuing to develop Sarawak into a prosperous and content multi-racial state, at the expense of Brunei.

Brunei was very weak and at risk of being swallowed up by Sarawak and North Borneo. However, the 1884 Weld Commission arrived from London and concluded Brunei was worth keeping and four years later Sultan Hashim Jalilul Alam Aqamaddin signed a treaty in which the sultanate became a British Protectorate with London controlling foreign affairs and defence while the reigning Sultan retained internal independence. The imposition of a Resident to exercise executive power and advise on all matters except local customs and religion was not agreed. Under the same treaty, the foreign affairs of Sarawak were also passed to London. Labuan's failures had become a regional embarrassment and the North Borneo Chartered Company agreed to take over the island in January 1890 but still its fortunes declined. But the treaty did not prevent further decline and, by 1895, the Sultan had ceded the Trusan Valley, Limbang and Lawas Districts to Sarawak. All seemed hopeless until several factors emerged: the discovery of oil in 1903, a British strategic decision to control the southern and western sectors of the South China Seas, the continued use of London to control the external affairs of the Sultanate, and the fact that the 1888 treaty was rehashed in 1905 to include a Resident. Two years later, Labuan was incorporated into the Straits Settlements colony that included Singapore, Penang and Malacca. The arrival of the Resident was followed by a Customs office, a land office and a police force seconded from Singapore. In 1911, Malay schools opened. In 1921, the Brunei Police Force was separated from the Straits Police Force and recruited former Indian Army soldiers as constables, commanded by a British inspector. In 1923, the responsibility of the Police was widened to include immigration and residential permits, the fire service, prisons and licensing for shops and stores. Plans were under way to incorporate Brunei into Sarawak when, in 1929, oil was discovered at Miri in Fifth Division of Sarawak and thirty miles to the west in Seria in Brunei. The find saved Brunei. Crude was pumped from the refinery at Lutong through floating loading lines to the tanker anchorage. Until then Miri had been a fishing village surrounded by dense, coastal jungle connected to Kuching by a weekly steamer en route from Singapore.

At 2,226 square miles, Brunei is one of the smallest countries in the world but one of the richest. At its widest in the west, it measures just 105 miles north to south. The climate is rain forest with December the wettest month and March the most dry. The two main rivers are the Belait and Tutong. Divided into the two enclaves of Brunei proper encompassing the administrative districts of Belait, Tutong, Brunei and Maura, Temburong district is separate west of the River Limbang. Most people lived in the coastal strip ten miles inland with most settlements located along the rivers. About sixty per cent of the population were of

Malay origin. The Bisayas claim to have founded the Sultanate. Living in big box houses, a cross between a house and a longhouse, they had developed transitional lifestyles between the coastal plain and the lower hills. Commerce was controlled almost entirely by the Chinese and yet they accounted for about twelve per cent of the population. While some dominated the bazaars, those living in rural communities were proficient rubber and pepper farmers. While most were influenced by the teachings of Confucius, their dialects indicated their origins from the southern Chinese provinces of Hooking and Teochew. Their faiths included Christian, Taoist and Buddhist but as Maoist Communism spread throughout the region, they were susceptible to subversion and these groupings became known to the Security Forces as the Clandestine Chinese Organization.

Also living in the coastal strip were the Kedayans. Formidable farmers, they were under-represented in the civil service and high places and regularly regarded as second class citizens. Their status originates from the legend of a cock fight between the Sultans of Brunei and Java, in which each bet fifty of their people. When the Sultan of Java lost, he paid with fifty Javanase, from whom the Kedayan emerged. These were vulnerable to subversion.

Inhabiting the lower reaches were the Iban or, as named by the first Europeans, Sea Dayaks. Planters of hill paddy fields and great users of boats, they were enterprising people and were thoroughly democratic with no presumption of hereditary. The Muruts and Kelabits are closely related and live in distinctive long houses, the former living between 500ft and 2,000ft above sea level and the latter living at 2,000ft to 3,500ft. Both had high living standards and had developed farming communities growing vegetables, raising fish in ponds, and raising cattle, buffalo, goats and chickens. Their hospitality was legendary.

Sarawak covers an area of 48,250 square miles, which is a little less than one-sixth of the island of Borneo. In 1962, it had a population of 776,990. The border between British North Borneo and Indonesian Kalimantan generally follows the watershed between the rivers flowing in a general north-westerly direction into the South China Sea and those flowing into the Celebes and Java Seas. The country is not particularly high but it is rugged with jungle-clad hills. Very little of the border had been surveyed.

Although Brunei, Sarawak and North Borneo were reliant upon Great Britain for military support, all three had paramilitary police forces with those in Sarawak and North Borneo following similar histories, traditions and organizations. The Sarawak Constabulary was formed in 1932 by the amalgamation of the military 612-strong Sarawak Rangers and the 1,007-strong armed Sarawak Police but had been reduced for economic reasons to 859. The Sarawak Auxiliary Constabulary raised in 1939 restricted its enlistment to anyone who had served in the Sarawak police, Colonial Police or Armed Forces. In 1940, legislation permitted the use of the Constabulary for military defence and the suppression of armed insurrection. The 900-strong police Force A emerged for use in law enforcement while the 100-strong Force B of three platoons of Dayaks was paramilitary.

At the 1940 Singapore Conference reviewing the defence of British interests in South-East Asia, Air Vice-Marshal Sir Robert Brooke-Popham, GOC Malaya Command, suggested that 200 RAF and Dutch aircraft were required to defend Borneo against the threat of attack, but his views were rejected on the grounds that the squadrons were simply not available. Without military and sea defence, the Denial Scheme was adopted to prevent an enemy using the oil installations by demolition. Kuching Airfield was to be held as long as possible. When Brooke-Popham was forced to honour the 1888 defence treaty in December 1940, he sent a company of the 2nd Battalion, 15th Punjab Regiment (2/15 Punjabs), commanded by Major Slater, from the III (Indian) Corps, primarily to defend the oil fields. The remainder of the 1,050-strong battalion followed in May 1941 with orders to defend Kuching airfield because its occupation by an enemy would give access to the Dutch airfield at Singkawang, but it was neither trained nor equipped for jungle warfare. The Hong Kong-Singapore Royal Artillery provided a coastal artillery battery of six 6in guns and troops from 35th Fortress Company, Royal Engineers, commanded by Lieutenant Hancock. By August, plans for the strategy assessed, Denial could reduce output by seventy per cent.

On paper, also available were:

The 1,115-strong Sarawak Rangers
Sarawak Volunteer Corps
The Sarawak Coastal Marine Service
The Sarawak Armed Police

The volunteers and police were to be used only for internal security. Collectively, the 2,565-strong 'SARFOR' (Sarawak Force) was commanded by Lieutenant Colonel Lane.

The Axis Pact between Germany, Japan and Italy benefited Japan in July 1941 when Germany forced Vichy France to cede French Indo-China to Japan, thereby giving her another regional front for access to China, where she had been engaged in military intervention since the mid-1930s, and a platform to threaten British interests in South-East Asia. Northern Borneo was important for several reasons:

- The island overlooked key sea routes between Java, Sumatra, Malaya and Celebes.
- The oilfields at Miri and Seria and the refinery at Lutong provided fuel.
- It provided a springboard and flank protection for attacking the Dutch East Indies and Singapore.

In November 1941, Lieutenant-General A.E. Percival, the new GOC Malaya Command, visited Sarawak and concluded that:

> Nobody could pretend that this was a satisfactory situation, but at least it would make the enemy deploy a larger force to capture Sarawak than would have been necessary if it had not been defended at all and that, I think, is the true way to look at it...the best I could do was to promise to send them a few anti-aircraft guns and to tell them of the arrival of *Prince of Wales* and *Repulse*, which were due at Singapore in a few days...not that I expected anti-aircraft guns to be of much practical value. But I felt that the moral effect of their presence there would more than counterbalance some slight dispersion of force.

Borneo was placed under the command of the embryonic and somewhat chaotic joint Allied American-British-Dutch-Australian Command formed in December 1941.

CHAPTER TWO

The Second World War

As part of the strategy to overrun the British in South-East Asia and the Dutch East Indies, the Japanese Southern Army was ordered to seize British North Borneo as a subsidiary operation to operations in Malaya and Burma. Singapore was the principal objective.

The Japanese Army pioneered modern amphibious landing techniques by training the 5th and 11th Infantry Divisions to conduct landings during the Sino-Japanese War (1937–1945) in northern China and around Shanghai. The Japanese were exponents of infiltration and formed elite landings units to seize beachheads and organize disembarkation of the subsequent assault waves. Unlike Allied operations in which navies predominated, the Japanese Navy reverted to supporting the Army once it was ashore. Japanese designers developed several types of landing craft, most fitted with bow ramps. (Find out more at www.encyclopedia.com/ and search for China Incident, Battle of Midway and Guadalcanal campaign.)

On 20 November 1941, Major General Kiyotake Kawaguchi commanded the 35 Infantry Brigade. Since Japanese units were generally named after their commanders, it and its attached components were known as the Kawaguchi Detachment. Raised in Tokyo, it consisted of units drawn from 18th Division then stationed at Canton in China:

HQ 35 Infantry Brigade
124th Infantry Regiment
2nd Yokosuka Naval Landing Force

4th Naval Construction Unit
1 platoon, 12th Engineer Regiment
1 unit from the 18th Division Signal Unit
1 unit from the 18th Division Medical Unit
4th Field Hospital
1 unit from the 11th Water Supply and Purification Unit

The landing force was reinforced by units usually based in Japan and Manchuria:

- 33rd Field Anti Aircraft Battalion
- One company of the 26th Independent Engineer Regiment (minus two platoons)
- 2nd Independent Engineer Company
- 80th Independent Radio Platoon
- 37th Fixed Radio Unit
- A unit from the Oil Drilling Section of the 21st Field Ordnance Depot
- 1st Field Well Drilling Company
- 2nd Field Well Drilling Company
- 3rd Field Well Drilling Company
- 4th Field Well Drilling Company
- 48th Anchorage Headquarters

At a planning meeting at HQ Southern Expeditionary Fleet at Hainan Island, at which Kawaguchi only had a small scale map of Borneo, the intelligence suggested the defending force was estimated to be approximately 1,000 regular soldiers and 2,500 native volunteers, with a probable further 5,600 Dutch soldiers in Dutch Borneo. The objectives were the oilfields and Kuching airfield.

As soon as the Sarawak Government was alerted to the Japanese attack on Pearl Harbour on 7 December and orders were received to deny the oilfields and refinery at Lutong, Lieutenant Hancock's sappers began wrecking drilling equipment, laboratories, subsidiary equipment and puncturing the sea-loading lines. Three days later, the demolition was complete. The same day, HMS *Prince of Wales* and *Repulse* were both sunk by Japanese aircraft.

The Kawaguchi Detachment and its naval escort left Cam Ramh Bay, Indo-China on 13 December. Two nights later, off the coast of Brunei, it divided into two task forces with the larger one heading west to Kuching, the remainder hovering north of Miri and Seria. At about 11.30pm in rising seas whipped up by increasing winds, the Left and Right Flanks, each of a Naval Landing Battalion, were lowered by cargo nets into landing barges. At 4.45am, Left Flank landed at Seria, seized the large copra plantations and prepared to advance to Brunei town. Right Flank landed at Miri half an hour later and captured government buildings and the airfield. Fifty armed police who fired a few shots were captured. After two companies had seized the refinery, the oil drilling units landed to survey and repair the damage. Japanese casualties amounted to several soldiers drowned.

Leaving a battalion to defend the oil fields, the two Naval Landing Force battalions were transferred from Miri and Brunei to join the main Kawaguchi Detachment on 22 December approaching the mouth of the River Santubong. At 4.00am the next morning, troops commanded by Colonel Akinosuke Oka, landed. When Lieutenant Colonel Lane reported the landings to Malaya Command and was instructed to proceed with the demolition of Kuching Airfield, this came as a shock because he and his officers had been led to believe that it was of strategic importance; the problem was that there were no aircraft to send. The out-numbered and inexperienced Punjabis retreated from Kuching (Colonel Oka was killed at Guadacanal in 1943). Reverting to his secondary orders of acting in the best interests of the defence of West Borneo by withdrawing into Dutch West Borneo to help defend the Anglo-Dutch air base Singkawang II, on Christmas Day Lane abandoned Kuching Airfield and set off for the border accompanied by some dependents and civilians. Some families, women and wounded had already been flown to Dutch airfields. Singkawang II was located at Sanggau, sixty miles inland and thirty miles from the Sarawak border and was already supported by a RAF wireless detachment relaying communications between Kuching and Singapore. It also had strategic significance in that it was about 300 miles from the Sunda Straits through which Allied seaborne reinforcements to Singapore would have to negotiate. When SARFOR and its dependents arrived at Krokong on the border, the route on the Dutch side was a jungle track and unsuitable for transport and, consequently, he had no alternative but to destroy his transport and the reserve ammunition and material that could not be carried, and march.

For two days, Dutch naval aircraft attacked the Japanese ships at anchor with a Dornier DO-24K sinking a destroyer and, on the third day, damaging a transport in a convoy heading west towards the Malayan Peninsula twenty miles west of Miri. Dutch submarines scored several successes. When the Japanese occupied Kuching Airfield, Singkawang II was bombed. Blenheims of 34 Squadron RAF flying from Singapore at extreme range also bombed the anchorage but did little damage. Meanwhile, the remnants of SARFOR joined Dutch troops retreating along jungle tracks toward Pangkalanbun until forced to surrender on 1 April.

At Miri on 28 December, Major General Kawaguchi ordered Lieutenant Colonel Watanabe, the naval landing force commander, to embark the battalion in landing barges and advance to Brunei in three days time and then requisition vessels to attack North Borneo. But when Watanabe arrived, the bigger ships had been scuttled and only *prahus* remained. A *prahu* is a small, open boat propelled either by sail or an outboard engine and used for inshore fishing and river transport. On 1 January 1942, two infantry platoons captured Labuan Island and Jesselton was occupied on 6 January. During the morning of 19 January, after Governor Charles Smith had surrendered British North Borneo, he and his staff, prisoners of war and civilian detainees were dispersed into prison camps, such as at Batu Lintang and Kuching. Several hundred prisoners and forced labour built the airfield on Labuan.

British North Borneo was divided into the five provinces and several Prefectures of Borumneo Kia. The new name translates into 'North Borneo' in Japanese and 'Our Borneo' in Malay – the first step in the occupation policy subverting British and Dutch colonial status. The Brunei Prefecture included Baram, Labuan, Lawas and Limbang. Responsibility for the operation and defence of Miri and Seria oilfields was retained by Army HQ in Tokyo. The Governor was also Commander of the Defence Force, the first being Lieutenant General Marquis Toshina Maeda, a liberal-minded aristocrat possessing a decent golf handicap and a fondness for ballroom dancing and Scotch whisky. He had served as military attaché in London between 1927 and 1930 and had retired from active service in 1939, before being recalled to active service in April 1942. Killed in September when his plane crashed on Labuan in a rainstorm, he was posthumously promoted to general and the island was renamed 'Pulau Maeda' in commemoration. His highly disciplined Chief of Staff, Major General Yoshinobu Manaki, was Governor until March 1945. Although he had little sympathy with Maeda's liberalism, he also was fond of golf, Scotch and dancing.

Maeda allowed Sultan Ahmad Tajuddin of Brunei to retain his throne and receive a pension and Japanese honours. In the event, the Sultan had little contact with the occupiers and moved to a temporary palace at Tantuya in Limbang. Inche Ibrahim (later Pehin Dato Perdana Menteri Dato Laila Utama Awang Haji Ibrahim), who had previously been Secretary to the British Resident, was appointed as the Chief Administrative Officer and managed to protect several important state documents, including those related to land titles. The Malays remained passive, although it was dangerous not to comply. The Kempei Tai were feared and internal security patrols dominated the coastal areas and riverine settlements. The Kempei Tai was formed in 1881 as military police more akin to gendarmes but evolved into a very powerful and influential combination of counter-intelligence service and Special Branch. It was equally feared in Japan, as it was in the occupied territories. The Japanese focused their favours on Malays because they had few ethnic and historical loyalties except to themselves and were thus easy targets for subversion, particularly those who had a grudge against the British. Public servants were paid their original salaries and usually spared forced labour and conscription into militias and home defence groups. Nevertheless, the administration collapsed because civil servants were relied on to collect revenues. Little attempt was made to maintain public works. Occupation currency was popularly known as *duit pisang* (banana money) because the $10 note depicted a banana tree, and had become worthless by 1943. Infrastructure development came to a near standstill, except for the airport runway at the Old Airport Government Buildings Complex. Using locally-employed civilians, the Army oil engineers repaired sixteen oil wells which, by 1943, were contributing to the Japanese war machine. In 1945 output had increased to half the pre-war productions.

Community councils and women's organizations were created. Several Bruneians were trained in Japan, including Pengiran Setia Negara Pengiran Haji Mohd Yusuf, who survived the Atom bomb on Hiroshima and later became the State Secretary and Chief Minister of Brunei. The

Education Department was re-aligned to extend its jurisdiction throughout the five provinces with the introduction of the Ejaan Fajar Asian vocabulary then being used in Japanese-sponsored Malay language periodicals in Singapore. Teachers and officials required to learn Japanese in night classes were usually taught by Japanese female teachers. One of those taught was Sheikh Azahari bin Sheikh Mahmud, born in Labuan in 1929 to an Arab father and a Brunei Malay mother. Azahari claimed he was born in Brunei Town. In 1943, an Army officer took direct control of education and instructed that Japanese classes be extended to two periods per day plus three periods of singing Japanese patriotic songs. The only Chinese school permitted was Brunei High School; however, this was only for Brunei students whose education in the English School in Labuan had been interrupted. A consequence of the Malays' favoured status was the growth of nationalism. This evolution was not new. During the 1930s, the Sultan Idris Teaching College in Tanjong Malim, Malaya, trained teachers influenced by the Indonesian nationalist movement to undermine Dutch colonialism. For many, it was the first time in their lives that they could exchange frank ideas and several had returned to Brunei fired up by the discussions of nationalist politics and freedom of expression. This led to the pre-occupation Brunei Malay Union emerging among the elite as a pressure group to raise education, health and welfare issues and needs of the local population with the British Resident. Its revival saw the militant Youth Association being encouraged by the Japanese shortly before the Allied landings in June 1945.

As early as 22 December 1941, the day the Japanese landed in Sarawak, Second Lieutenant Patrick Synge, an Intelligence Corps subaltern then at HQ Intelligence Corps in Oxford, used his experiences in the 1932 Oxford University Expedition undertaking ornithological and anthropological research in Sarawak, to write a paper to Commandant, Intelligence Corps. It was entitled Scheme for Guerrilla Activity – Sarawak, in which he proposed that:

> ...a force of 500 men or more if necessary, skilled in forest-craft, could be raised from the Long Houses of the Baram, Tinfar [Tinjar] and Niah rivers and organized into an effective guerrilla force.

Acknowledging that guerrillas could not defend oilfields, raids would 'do much destructive work' and therefore he proposed that guerrillas be employed 'to make periodic raids on the oilfields [namely at Miri] from the interior and prevent the Japanese from making effective use of them'. On 13 January 1942, he presented his proposals to Major Stoford-Adams at the War Office but learnt in mid-February that his ideas were considered 'impracticable'. Although Synge was regarded as not the 'right type' to lead such operations, the War Office had taken an interest and Tom Harrisson, who had been the expedition leader and was commissioned into the Reconnaissance Corps, was asked to submit his ideas. When he presented them in July, they did not differ markedly from Synge's, except that he placed more emphasis on the Seria oilfields and drew attention to the importance of 'face':

> The value on morale and confidence in the victory of Allied Nations would be immensely increased both throughout the Pacific and in China by the news that we were doing something even if slight in this area, that we were on the offensive as well as the defensive. The value of this question of 'face' cannot be over-emphasized.

Born in Argentina, Harrisson was educated at Harrow and Pembroke College. After the 1932 expedition he had been in the New Hebrides from 1933 to 1935. In 1937 he was co-founder of the Mass Observation project, which was the forerunner of commercial market research and targeted advertising. Instead of relying on the press for information it used anecdotal information, collected from interviews and comments after the abdication of King Edward VIII and during the coronation of King George VI, to gauge public opinion.

Captain D.L. Leech envisaged inserting expatriate Sarawak Civil Service officers, supported by medical and wireless teams, 'to establish wireless stations and to contact free Europeans and local natives likely to be still loyal'; organize the indigenous populations and Chinese to support Allied landings; raid Japanese outposts and construct temporary landing grounds. He selected three areas where resistance could be ignited – the Baram and Tinjar rivers inhabited by the Kayans and Kenyahs; the Rejang basin above Kapit peopled mostly by Ibans; and the Iban heartland of the Second Division along the Rejang River eastwards to the Sadong River. It was recognized that the Kempei Tai used informers and that it was impractical to insert Europeans into any locality unless they had local knowledge. Equally, it would be difficult to create an effective intelligence organization in Malay-speaking areas unless it was supported by Europeans who knew the area and could capitalize by contacting village chiefs and headmen nearer targets.

By 2 September, the War Office considered Harrisson's Borneo Oilfields Project to be 'a good thing, if only from a prestige point of view', and suggested that such expeditions should be organized in Australia with American assistance.

British North Borneo came within the scope of the South-West Pacific Area controlled by US General Douglas MacArthur. Although his principal aim was to occupy Japan, he assured the Dutch East Indies government-in-exile that he would conduct operations to liberate the Dutch East Indies. Selecting Borneo as a launch pad for his proposed offensive against Java, he entrusted operations to the 1st Australian Corps, which was commanded by Lieutenant General Sir Leslie Morshead. From their experiences in New Guinea and elsewhere, the Australians hated the Japanese with a vengeance, largely because of their treatment of prisoners and the wounded.

In March 1942, MacArthur approved the Australian proposal to form Special Operations Executive (SOE Australia) from several British officers linked to the Executive who had escaped from Malaya, Singapore and the Dutch East Indies. Among them was Major Egerton Mott, who had been Head of Mission in Java and, as a member of the Civil Component of the Far East Mission, had masqueraded in a civil capacity. The War Office agreed he should stay in Australia and in May he was appointed the principal advisor to the Director of Military Operations on Special Operations and then formed the Inter-Allied Services Department (I-ASD) with an operational remit to:

- Harass enemy lines of communications
- Attack enemy shipping and small craft in harbours and rivers
- Organize resistance
- Establish covert communications
- Spread propaganda against the Japanese and Germans
- Direct sabotage, subversion and fifth-column activity
- Administer the non-Australian members of SOE Australia. The Australians were administered by the holding unit, Z Special Operations

But the Americans became progressively unenthusiastic about having British and Dutch intelligence units in their theatre of war and in an effort to bring them under control formed the Allied Intelligence Bureau, with a US officer managing the budget. Allied relations became so toxic that, in 1943, the Australians formed the Services Reconnaissance Department (SRD); for administrative purposes, it was known as Z Force. The Borneo Project was revisited and on 6 October 1943, Z Force carried out the first of its eighty-one operations in the South West Pacific. Captain Francis Chester, in peacetime a planter and now a British Army officer, and six men landed from the submarine USS *Kingfisher* in Operation Python 1, with instructions to observe Japanese vessels in the Sibutu Passage and the Balabac Strait of the Sulu Sea. Supported by Filipino guerrillas under the command of an American officer, Chester conducted several visits to the east coast of North Borneo, not all covert.

Throughout their occupations, the Japanese treated the Chinese with hostility, in particular those raising money for the China Relief Fund. The Chinese were, after all, an enemy against whom they had been fighting for several years not only in China but also in Burma.

Albert Kwok was born in Kuching and after qualifying in Shanghai, he moved to North Borneo and established a medical practice in Jesselton, which proved a useful cover for his activities as a lieutenant in the nationalist Chinese Kuomintang Intelligence Service. As his plans to resist the Japanese took shape, he was given assurances of support from Tawi-Tawi in the southern Philippines. By mid-1943 Kwok and his deputy, Jules Stephens, had formed the Kinabalu Guerrillas in the Jesselton area, largely from Sikhs of the former North Borneo Constabulary, Chinese youth clubs, and former volunteers. Several offshore fishing communities off the west coast also formed groups, including one started by the headman Orang Tua Panglima Ali on Sulug Island.

By late 1943 the Imperial Japanese Army had suffered considerable casualties as the Americans island-hopped towards Japan and in Burma, where imminent offensives into India, if successful, would require reinforcements. But the Army was short of troops and orders were sent to establish local defence forces throughout its occupied territories to take over some occupation duties, such as guarding installations and some patrolling. When it was announced that the 3,000-strong North Borneo Defence Force militia would be raised under command of 37th Army to be led by Japanese officers supported by NCOs drawn mainly from the Malay elite, companies were established at Kuching (350 all ranks), Sibu (300), Miri (180), Kenpingau (300) and Sandakan (150). The lower ranks were open to all citizens of Borneo, except the Chinese. Apart from basic military skills, literacy in Japanese and propaganda, the two-year courses also provided training in farming, construction and hygiene. However, as Japanese soldiers were deployed to the Pacific and Burma, the companies were used as drivers, farmers and maintenance workers. But, according to Captain Ikeno Ryuli, the Miri Company commander, under interrogation in 1945, the scheme was not a success for several reasons. The Japanese were disliked and some instructors were over zealous. Language difficulties, short periods of training and increasing Allied air raids attacking lines of communication, saw shortages of food and medical supplies. Duties also become arduous leading to demoralization and absence without leave. Relations soured further when Japanese attempts to conscript locals from riverside longhouses were resisted by headmen arguing that taking young men away would mean that the communities would be unable to provide food. The Japanese retaliated by confiscating guns and ammunition, which led to food shortages.

Against Captain Chester's advice to wait until the Allies were closer, on 10 October, the Chinese Double Tenth, Kwok used the announcement of the formation of the Borneo Defence Force to launch a rebellion in North Borneo. His force of 324 guerrillas overran the police stations at Tuara and Menggatal. The Suluk islanders attacked the barracks and set fire to the Customs sheds in Jesselton. But when the promised support from the Philippines was prevented from arriving, on the 19th Kwok surrendered. He and the surviving guerrillas were marched to Batu Tiga Prison where most suffered terribly before a mass execution near Petagas railway bridge. Kempei Tai also made arrests on several islands. On Sulug Island, Panglima Ali was arrested and imprisoned in Batu Tiga. About a fortnight later, a Japanese platoon and several Malay police landed, machine-gunned the islanders and set fire to all the houses, killing fifty-five people. Of the sixty survivors, thirty women and children were detained in Bangawan, where all but five died from ill-treatment. When the Allies liberated the island, an eleven-year-old boy was the headman. Without men, the island achieved a reputation of being a Garden of Eden.

Python 2 landed in January 1944 and, although the Double Tenth rebellion had shown there was anti-Japanese sentiment among the coastal Malay and Chinese, the reprisals had induced fear, which was understandable, given the Japanese response.

When, on 20 October, US forces landed on Leyte, the first of the occupied Philippine Islands to be invaded, the Japanese Navy activated the Operation Sho-Go in which warships and aircraft in three fleets converged on the Philippines. The battleship Yamato, which was part of Vice Admiral Takeo Kurita's Centre Force, had taken on fuel in Brunei Bay. But three days later the Force suffered badly at the hands of two submarines and US naval aircraft in engagements that marked the end of the Japanese naval superiority in the Western Pacific and Kurita transferred his flag to the battleship. US attacks were relentless and when the Yamato fired her main guns, it was for the only time in action. Kurita soon lost his nerve and returned to Brunei Bay with the remnants of his task force. By 1945 Allied warships virtually controlled Japanese maritime lines of communication between Japan and the Southern Area. On 21 April 1945, B-24s and P-38s attacked Miri Airfield for the first of three raids that eventually denied the Japanese from using oil from Borneo. Operation Montclair was the codename given to the invasion of British North Borneo, Dutch East Indies and the Philippines. In the invasion of Borneo, codenamed Operation Oboe, the 1st Australian Corps would land at six beaches supported by the Royal Australian Navy, 7th US Fleet and 1st Tactical Air RAAF and 13th US Air Force. One task given to the 9th Australian Division, commanded by Major General George Wootten, was to land in Brunei Bay and secure a naval base and access to the oil and rubber resources of British North Borneo. Although Signals and Photographic Intelligence were providing information of enemy dispositions, troop movements, evacuation/escape routes and the locations of prisoner of war camps from small amounts gleaned during the two Python operations, detail on tides, beach composition, currents and exits from beaches were lacking. Operation Stallion was an intelligence plan launched to:

- Collect information about British North Borneo
- Interrogate natives extracted from Brunei Bay/Kimanis Bay for information
- Create deception by encouraging the enemy to focus on the Kota Belud area
- Conduct close reconnaissance of Kimanis Bay

It was divided into two with *Agas* (translated as 'sandflies') missions inserted into North Borneo and *Semut* ('ants') missions dropped into Brunei and Sarawak.

With D-Day planned for early June, in March three Agas missions contacted the Dutch wireless station at Batchelor and also established a field HQ, a guerrilla training camp and a hospital on Jambongan Island. An intelligence network was developed with agents recruited in most towns and kampongs in north-east North Borneo. Agas 1 provided intelligence of the Sandakan area for bombing raids and discovered that parties of Allied prisoners, mainly British and Australians, were being marched in groups from an airfield construction camp near the town 164 miles to Ranau. When Allied aircraft bombed the airfield and the Japanese asked two anti-Japanese North Borneans to recommend a route to Ranau, the two believed it was a military withdrawal route and selected the most demanding track. In fact, it was required for a series of deliberate 'elimination' marches. A plan to use Australian parachute forces to rescue the prisoners in Operation Kingfisher was cancelled under controversial circumstances, and mistreatment, starvation and murder saw all but six of the 2,434 prisoners die. The six had escaped from a column. Large numbers of Malays, Chinese and Indians who assisted them were murdered. The finding of a radio at Sandakan seems to have induced the Japanese to react with such brutality

Under the overall command of Major Toby Carter, the original six Semut missions were reduced from six to three:

> Semut 1, commanded by Captain Harrisson, parachuted into the Kelabit Highlands and established a base at Bario. In late May it moved to Belawit in the Bawang valley inside the former Dutch Borneo after a light aircraft airstrip had been hacked out of the jungle.
>
> Semut 2, commanded by Carter, parachuted to Bario in mid-April and, after gaining support from the Kelabit, moved to Baram valley where it was established at Long Akah, the heartland of the Kenyahs.
>
> Semut 3, headed by Captain Bill Sochon, covered the entire Upper Rejang and was supported by the nomadic Punan.

By May about 600 people were supplying intelligence about Tutong, Brunei Town and the Brunei Bay area. Attempts to encourage the Chinese to help were not entirely successful, although some provided intelligence on Japanese troop movements and concentrations. They still feared the Japanese after the Double Tenth rebellion. Ambushing patrols sent to protect supply lines into the interior convinced the Japanese not to stray from the coastal strip. The road under construction from Weston to Brunei was attacked several times. Major Harrisson's thinly spread guerrillas operated along the Lawas, Trusan and Limbang Rivers. When longhouses refused to supply food and labour and patrols sent to re-establish lines of communication were ambushed, the Japanese were prevented from deploying northwards via Malinau. An airstrip at Belawit facilitated landings by Auster aircraft bringing in supplies and flying out casualties. Japanese engineers building the road from Weston to Lawas to Brunei were harassed and effectively prevented from sending reinforcements to Brunei. Harrisson created extensive intelligence networks throughout his operational area and supplied information on Japanese activity in Tutong, Brunei Town, Brunei Bay and the sector from Brunei to Weston, and the Pensiangan-Keningau area, as well as information on the economic situation and local opinion. He had also recommended targets for bombing, such as Japanese evacuation routes from the Tarakan and Malinau areas on the eastern coast towards North Borneo, and from Brunei Bay up the Limbang and Trusan Rivers.

Phase Two of Operation Stallion was divided into three. Phase 2A, from 30 April to 19 May, set out to extract people likely to possess reliable knowledge of navigation in Brunei Bay as well as information on possible assault beaches. In terms of priority, sources were to be 'members of the Brunei tribe' (in other words, Malays), Chinese, *prahu* skippers and crew and, finally, anyone else. The cover for the presence of aircraft was Photographic Intelligence. On 1 May a RAAF Catalina flying boat searching Brunei Bay and Labuan Island intercepted two *prahus* north of Kampong Kuala Lawas and debriefed eight Malays. Two brothers, Latif and Gapar bin Jalil, agreed to be extracted. Tanjong Nosong and Pulau Tiga were overthrown – there was no evidence of the enemy and no interference from radar units and anti-aircraft guns. Two airstrips at Keningau appeared serviceable and the Keningau to Tambunan road seemed in good condition. The brothers gave valuable intelligence on the dispositions, strengths, communications and transport of Japanese forces in Brunei Bay; offshore conditions at Kuala Mengalong, Kuala Lawas and the state of some rivers; and the socio-economic and political situation around the Bay. 'Kuala' means 'at the mouth of the river'. While they could not help with assault beaches, they recommended three sea captains from Kampong Mengalong.

Phase 2B, launched on 19 May, extracted seven seamen from a sea-going *prahu* in Kimanis Bay en route from Brunei Town to Labuan. One, the headman from Mengalong, was a known Japanese sympathizer. On the return journey, the Catalina photographed the town of Tawau on the south-east coast of North Borneo. At dusk on 15 May Phase 2C commenced when three Allied officers and the Latif brothers landed two miles north of Mengalong. The officers were picked up by Catalina the next day while the brothers headed for Labuan in a *prahu* to organize the exfiltration of two of three captains at dawn on 19 May. An aerial reconnaissance revealed that there were good roads from Mempakul to Menumbok and there were no telephone lines, rolling stock or activity in the Mempakul area. The ground between Mempakul and Tanjong Sakat appeared firm and level.

Phase Four of Operation Stallion focused on reconnoitring the Kimanis Bay area, specifically enemy dispositions in the headlands in Nosong-Papar area, volume of traffic and the Beaufort-Papar railway. Train derailment and destruction of the Papar Bridge were on the agenda, as well as severing telephone lines, to be executed on the eve of D-Day. Construction of the railway had started in 1896 to take tobacco from Beaufort through rubber plantations at Bukau to Lingkungan and then to the port at Weston. By 1903 it had been extended to Tenon, Melalap and finally to Jesselton but, in 1945, it had largely been destroyed by Allied bombing.

Agas 3, inserted on 29 May by Catalina south of the Bongawan River, contacted an influential 'Captain China', a Chinese village chief, and, while he refused to supply guerrillas or long-term intelligence agents, he agreed to provide on-the-spot information of Japanese troop movements, concentrations, and other related matters. The mission then reconnoitred the Beaufort railway by analyzing troop, cargo and timber trains. Exfiltration on 5 June was prevented by the number of Japanese troops in the area, and the fear that they may hear the wireless generator meant that the mission had to wait two days.

With the decision to land 20 and 24 Brigades on beaches in Brunei Bay, Stallion Phase III set out to deceive the Japanese into focusing their attention on the area between Kota Belud and Langkong. Leaflet drops advised coastal villagers to leave the area. Five adults and a child were extracted from Kuala Tambal at the mouth of the Tuaran River on 27 May, six more three days later and thirteen from north of Jesselton area. On 4 June, Semut 2 captured the important Japanese wireless station at Long Lama. The next day Agas patrols spread rumours of an invasion and advised natives to evacuate the coastal area. Guerrillas sabotaged telephone lines, and leaflet drops and the bombing of Jesselton-Kota Belud-Langkong sector added credence to the spreading rumours of a landing north of Jesselton.

Two additional phases of Operation Stallion were launched when HQ 9th Division planned to use the Divisional reserve, 32/2 Battalion, to block the Japanese from moving from Jesselton to Brunei Bay by seizing Mempakul and Weston and to use Kimanis Harbour and Beaufort. On 8 June a Catalina landed near an uninhabited island at the mouth of the Lakatan River and intercepted a woman and child on the Padas Damit River; the woman introduced them to her husband. The headman of Melatup, a fellow villager and two people from Weston provided reliable information on the Japanese, local inhabitants and landing beaches. Operation Mare, launched simultaneously, plotted detailed intelligence on Japanese strengths, deployment and defended positions, obstacles, and bivouac areas in the Mempakul-Menumbok and Weston-Sipitang-Beaufort sectors. Next day, Semut 1 attacked several small Japanese garrisons in Brunei Bay.

By the time that Division crossed to their lines of departure in their landing craft, SRD operations in British North Borneo meant that it collected considerably more intelligence on the Japanese order of battle and dispositions than was available three months before. Defending Labuan was 56 Independent Mixed Brigade and 371st Independent Infantry Battalion, commanded by Major General Akaashi Taijiro. Its six infantry battalions, combat support and logistic troops had arrived in October 1944 and had deployed to Tawau. In early March, Brigade HQ and 366th and 367th Battalions had marched to the Brunei area to reinforce HQ No. 62 Anchorage and a small base and a field hospital commanded by Colonel Tohara Kanji, but 367th Battalion lost more than half its soldiers to harassing Allied aircraft. The estimate of 31,000 was 4,000 short of the actual figure. Enemy concentrations in the area of Jesselton-Keningau-Beaufort were assessed to number 6,000 troops. Elsewhere in the Pacific the Japanese tactic tended not to contest the landing but to take up strong defensive positions inland. Enemy withdrawal reports were continuously interdicted by Allied aircraft. Areas free of enemy occupation were patrolled. Towns and villages throughout British North Borneo were connected by a wireless network. Safe landing sites had been cleared for the Catalinas and supply drop zones plotted.

Phase One of Oboe 6 had begun on 1 May when 26 Brigade landed near Tawau and advanced north-west toward Beaufort. The second phase of simultaneous landings on Labuan and Brunei Bay was delayed until 10 June due to insufficient landing craft. To co-ordinate the Semut and Agas missions, SRD liaison detachments were attached to 20 and 24 Brigades with a wireless link connecting the two missions, HQ 9th Division and Advanced SRD HQ at Morotai.

Following fierce naval bombardments and air attacks, 2/28 and 2/43 Battalions, of 24 Brigade, supported by a Matilda squadron from 2/9 Armoured Regiment, landed largely unopposed on Brown Beach near the town of Victoria on Labuan island and encountered unexpectedly grim fighting at The Pocket, a strong defensive position in swampy jungle some distance from the beach. It was eventually overrun by 2/28 Battalion after being bombarded, shelled and bombed for five days. Just six of the 200 defenders were captured. The fighting on Labuan continued for another two months.

Also supported by a Matilda squadron, 2/15 Battalion from 20 Brigade landed across White Beach at the south-east tip of Muara island without opposition, while a mile and a half away 2/17 Battalion landed at Green Beach, north of Brooketon, Brunei. The defunct colliery was connected to the deep sea anchorage by a wooden railway.

Three days later, after Brunei Town had been flattened, the Australians entered the town. The only building standing was the Chinese Temple on the river-front wharf. Meanwhile, Major Chester organized an intelligence network covering the area between Ranau-Keningau Road and Jesselton-Beaufort Railway, to provide early warning of major enemy movement south from Ranau or Jesselton, and created a screen to protect the Brunei perimeter. Three more Filly intelligence-gathering missions landing between 13 and 14 June ascertained enemy troop disposition in the Brunei Bay area and on Daat Island, situated midway between Labuan and Mempakul. On 16 June, the Divisional reserve, 32/2 Battalion, landed at Padas Bay in North Borneo and occupied Weston but the lack of roads and the indefensible nature of the railway led to patrols using the Klias River. Operation Colt landed between 16 and 18 June and seized a Japanese administrator at Sipitang. On 20 June 2/13 Battalion landed at Lutong and recaptured the oilfields. Engineers began plugging thirty-seven oil wells sabotaged by the Japanese. Between 23 and 25 June Operation Foal contacted an Indian manager at the Membakut Estate and captured a Japanese soldier for interrogation. Meanwhile, 20 Brigade used landing craft to move quickly along rivers and streams.

Further minor landings were made at Mempakul on 19 June and Sabang on 23 June by 2/43rd Battalion, from 24 Brigade, and 2/11 Commando Squadron to secure Beaufort. Although hindered by torrential downpours and unforgiving terrain, the Australians secured their objectives but faced largely uncoordinated night counter-attacks. When one company was isolated by the Japanese, for his actions during fierce fighting to relieve it, Private Leslie Starcevich was awarded the Victoria Cross. By 29 June the Japanese had withdrawn. On 6 July, the Australians advanced cautiously, frequently using mortars to beat their axis and thereby limit casualties. The occupation of Papar six days later heralded the ending of operations.

The fighting in British North Borneo, that cost the Australians 114 killed or dying of wounds and 221 wounded, was controversial because the Australian public believed that Borneo had little strategic value and the Japanese were already isolated. Japanese losses were 1,234 and 130 taken prisoner. A further 1,800 Japanese were killed in SRD ambushes, raids and attacks with SRD estimating in 1959 that Semut 1 had killed more than 1,000 Japanese, out of the total of 1,700, at the cost of 112 guerillas. None were lost in Semut 1. Harrisson attributes the success to 'the remarkable response of the native peoples of Sarawak and all within Borneo'.

It was inevitable that questions were raised in 9th Australian Division about the quality of intelligence. HQ SRD advised Major General Wootten that the Brigades had collected misleading information from local sources during the advance but collation had been weak and interrogators had failed to analyze its reliability and seemed unable to differentiate between reliable information and rumour and gossip passed on to please. Generally, intelligence should never be seen in isolation and requires supporting information to add credibility. One example was that captured Japanese documents confirmed that an Independent Mixed Brigade had reinforced the Beaufort area and that its full establishment was 5,500 all ranks. But according to the same documents, sixty per cent of these failed to arrive through sickness, death or straggling, and of these forty per cent were not in a position to fight due to sickness or loss of weapons. Additional factors were the lack of Malay speakers in the Division and the effect of counter-intelligence operations by the Kempei Tai.

CHAPTER THREE

Brunei After 1945

After General Masao Baba, commander of the 37th Army, had surrendered to Major General Wooten at Layang-layang beach on Labuan, the Australian British Borneo Civil Affairs Unit, which was mainly Australian, moved in to provide supplies and an administrative function to a population suffering from the deprivation of occupation and the trauma of the fighting.

Many of the places where 9th Division had landed and then fought were flattened by bombing, naval bombardment and shelling. Roads were damaged by tanks and heavy vehicles during and after the war. The British Brigadier Charles Macaskie described the devastation as ‘appalling’, particularly the damaged oilfields. He was a highly respected colonial administrator who before the war had been Chief Justice and then Deputy Governor of North Borneo. During the war he had escaped to Australia and been sent back to England to form and train the Borneo Planning Department at the War Office. However, the Australian Colonel A.A. Conlon, who was Director of the Land Forces HQ Directorate of Research and Civil Affairs, assumed responsibility for civil affairs and refused to delegate matters to Macaskie, even though it was known that the British would take over responsibility. Conlon reported directly to General Blamey, who commanded 1st Australian Corps. In 1943, Conlon had established the Military Government and Civil Affairs School, whose officers had followed the Australians in New Guinea.

In spite of the disagreements, 21,000 Japanese and several thousand Allied civilian internees and prisoners of war were repatriated. Since martial law was in force, the three British North Borneo territories shared the Military Government authorities. The Legal Department was kept busy drafting proclamations. As Australian demobilization gathered pace, South East Asia Command, then based in Ceylon, assumed responsibility for British North Borneo on 1 January 1946. Before they left, the Australians built a new wharf for Labuan, known as Liberty Wharf. Such was the relationship between the Australians and North Borneo that the Divisional colour patch was incorporated into the colony's coat of arms until 1963, when it achieved independence as Sabah. When 9th Division was disbanded, several soldiers were transferred to 67/2 Battalion as part of the Allied occupation of Japan. When 32 Infantry Brigade arrived, it was accompanied by the British Military Administration in the form of 50 Civil Affairs Unit. The Commonwealth War Commission selected ground about two miles from Port Victoria to bury and commemorate 3,908 men and women who had died in the war. The majority were prisoners of war. Investigations saw Japanese prosecuted for war crimes in military courts held at Labuan, including the Sandakan prison camp commandant, Captain Hoshijima Susuma, and the lieutenant and his sergeant who led the raid on Suluk Islands after the Double Tenth insurrection. All three were executed. Brigadier Macaskie moved to Jesselton to head the War Damages Commision.

Although victorious, Britain's priorities had changed markedly, not only in terms of the economy shattered by the war but also socially, as the country recovered from its second major war in twenty years. Internationally, decolonization saw Pakistan emerge from India and Burma, achieving self-government. While the onset of the Cold War in Europe and the formation of NATO meant that the national focus changed, and the Armed Forces were demobilizing, there was still a requirement to occupy Germany, Austria and Japan. In addition, there were crises in Palestine and Indonesia, the latter generated by the nationalist Ahmed Sukarno struggling to eject the Dutch. In the middle were British and Indian forces repatriating Allied prisoners and civilian detainees and the surrendered Japanese. By 1948, to relieve Great Britain's increasing military pressure, National Service had been introduced.

Sarawak also emerged from the war damaged but not ruined. In May 1946 on Cessation Day, Sir Vyner Brooke ceded the territory to Great Britain and it became a Crown Colony ruled by a Governor, who was also commander-in-chief; in 1962, this was Sir Alexander Waddell.

Politically, the British were content to transfer administrative authority and political power to local communities. In a concept developed in Africa, the colony was divided into five administrative Divisions numbered west to east First to Fifth, each governed by a Resident. They were sub-divided into Districts, each administered by a District Officer, usually assisted by a Native Officer from the Native Officer Service. The Districts were further broken down into Sub-Districts administered by either an Assistant District Officer or a Native Officer. At community levels, the *Penghulu* (translated as 'Iban leader') had day-to-day responsibility for longhouse communities, the *Tua Kampung* looked after the Malay villages, and *Kapitans China* represented local Chinese communities. The colonies had Constabularies but no armed forces.

The Fourth Division Districts of Bintulu, Miri and Baram were emerging from years of isolation. In 1962, its Resident was John Fisher. Highly experienced in local affairs and politically astute, he had joined Sarawak's administrative services as a 19-year-old and was now in his fifties. His wife Ruth was one of two sisters and four brothers to Major-General Walter Walker, then commanding 17th Gurkha Division in Singapore, who would play a pivotal role in the Brunei Revolt and Confrontation with Indonesia.

Parts of the Division were suffering from destructive missionary rivalry as Roman Catholic and Evangelical Missions clashed in the middle reaches of the River Baram. Miri covered the long coastal strip from Bintulu west to the Brunei border. By 1962, the oilfield had been bled almost dry. Fifth Division was the smallest administration and bordered Brunei and North Borneo to the east, with the River Limbang splitting Brunei from its Temburong District. Divisional Headquarters was at Limbang, a prosperous agricultural centre. Limbang District sat astride the river's valley, which was one of the finest in Sarawak, possessing considerable agricultural potential in palm oil. Temburong was under-populated and had suffered from Brunei misrule in the mid-1800s. Connecting the two sectors meant either a long and difficult walk along jungle tracks or forty-five minutes spent covering the twelve-mile voyage to Brunei town by fast outboard along the river. The hinterland is mountainous with Batu Lawas a few metres lower than Kota Kinabalu in North Borneo. On the lower levels, Malays, Kedayans, Bisayas and Dayaks populated the middle reaches, with the Kelabits on the upper slopes. Lawas District contained the Trusan and Lawas valleys. The

Trusan was navigable by any craft beyond Long Tenpoa while the Lawas was much more accessible. Travel beyond the riverheads at Lawas and Long Tenpoa was only by foot. It took about seven to ten days to reach the Indonesian border.

The Muruts in Lawes District had clashed with the Rajah's administration and they were driven to the upper reaches of the rivers, where they suffered badly from smallpox. Resorting to the bottle, they were drinking themselves to extinction until missionaries converted them to Christianity in the 1930s. By the 1960s, the Trusan valley was virtually alcohol free. However, by 1962 an Australian evangelical mission in Lawas, sending out its version of Christian missionaries, upset the community equilibrium in most longhouses.

The Fifth Division Resident, Richard Morris, was born on 7 February 1915 in Boulder, Western Australia to William, a Welsh pharmacist/metal assayer turned gold prospector who travelled the outback on camel, and Mildred. The family settled briefly in Perth, had a short spell in Maitland, New South Wales, moved to England and then returned to Australia, where Morris boarded at Shore School. However, with his father constantly on the move seeking employment during the Depression, his education was continually interrupted, but anything that he may have missed out on at school, he made up for by prodigious reading.

In 1934, Morris joined Vacuum Oil and when war broke out five years later, he enlisted in the 1/2nd Anti-Aircraft Regiment as a gunner and saw service in the Middle East and New Guinea. He relished military life for its sense of belonging. Finishing the war as a captain with the Australian/British Borneo Civil Affairs Unit he investigated Japanese war crimes and dealt with the repatriation of Japanese families who had settled in Sarawak some several decades previously. On demobilization, and knowing that the Rajah Brooke sought his services, Morris returned to Australia to find a wife and met Dorothy Helm in Princes nightclub in Sydney. Dorothy Joan Helm was the third of five children born in Edgecliff, New South Wales to Harry, the town bank manager, and Madeline Helm. In 1932, she matriculated and trained as a secretary, working for Oxford University Press, as a supply clerk for the Army and, finally, with the Red Cross Library Service. Although Morris proposed within the week, Dorothy kept him waiting for three weeks. He returned to Sarawak and was followed by Dorothy travelling on the SS *Merella*, with a borrowed wedding dress and the wedding cake sharing her bunk. When they were married in St Thomas Cathedral, Kuching in November 1946, Dorothy had been warned that the police band had a limited programme and instead of gliding up the isle to the *Wedding March*, they played '*D'y ken John Peel*'. It was a strong marriage and within the year Geraldine was born in Sarawak and was followed eighteen months later by Adrian in Australia. With her husband throwing himself into administrative affairs, Dorothy hosted delegations, experts and academics, undertook responsibilities to the Guides, Salvation Army, and Red Cross, opened shops and handed out prizes at school functions. Although Morris spoke several languages, including Malay and Arabic, his love of English dominated.

The North Borneo Company transferred its territory to the sovereignty of the Crown Colony on 26 June 1946. As in Sarawak, the territory was divided into the Residencies of East Coast, West Coast, Labuan and the Interior. On Labuan, fishing was developed as an industry but, although the airport was an international and domestic hub, it could not compete with Singapore and in 1956 Labuan again became a free port, having lost the status in 1946.

By 1950, infrastructure recovery in Brunei was well under way, although reconstruction was slower than in Malaya because of the relative isolation of British North Borneo. Nevertheless, increasing oil revenues allowed the Sultan to finance most proposals. In June, Sultan Ahmad Tajuddin II died in London under controversial circumstances and was succeeded by his brother, Omar Ali Saifuddin III, who inherited a state numbering about 200,000, compared to 850,000 in Sarawak, most living along the coastal strip. Europeans formed the smallest group – about 0.3 per cent of the population, most employed in the oil fields and civil administration.

Unlike Malaya, which was suffering from the Chin Peng pitching for a communist state, British North Borneo had not been markedly affected by nationalism and subversives. In 1946 some young people in Brunei associated with the North Borneo Youth League generated a little unrest. Although outwardly a nationalist organisation that displayed the Indonesian flag, it was agitating for greater white-collar representation for Malays at the expense of the Chinese. Several members of the Chinese Youth Movement had raised a Red Chinese flag on the Shell Oil Company head offices in Seria. In response, Far East Command in Singapore drew up the four page

Operation Ale contingency plan to provide Military Aid to the Civil Power but it was based less on an operational requirement than on the availability of units, and to that extent was flawed. But as the people of Brunei looked towards the political and economic development of Sarawak and North Borneo by their colonial administrations, there was silent resentment over inefficient health, education and housing policies and political exclusion.

In 1952 into the political vacuum stepped A.M. Azahari, aged 24 years. During the occupation he had been sent by the Japanese to train as a veterinary surgeon in Java and had then fought with Sukarno during the war of independence against the Dutch East Indies government. His grandfather, Sheikh Abdul Hamid, had been entrusted with the mission to seek economic and protective support from US officials in the Philippines when oil was first discovered in 1903. With his practical experience in fighting for independence and his views on the future of Brunei, Azahari attracted a large following and he soon found himself serving six months in prison for dissent.

In 1953, the North Borneo Youth League, all wearing green shirts, attempted to seize power, but were easily rounded up and received short prison sentences for sedition. Nevertheless, in between several failed business ventures, Azahari assembled sufficient following by 1956 to form the nationalist Brunei People's Party (*Partai Ra'ayat Brunei*). The party took as its emblem a water buffalo's horned head on a red and white flag superimposed on the nations of Indonesia, the Philippines and Malaya. As early as 1951, British Intelligence had predicted Azahari to be a potential nationalist leader in Brunei.

In January 1957, following the political debacle over the Suez Canal the previous year, Prime Minister Harold MacMillan's Conservative Government acknowledged that Great Britain's imperial aspirations were no longer viable and that the country should disengage from its colonial responsibilities. This was three years after his 'winds of change' speech in Cape Town. Over the next four years, Great Britain handed independence to those colonies seeking it, mainly in Africa. However, several smaller territories, such as the Falklands and Gibraltar, preferred to remain under British governance and protection. In the Far East, Great Britain's interests lay in four territories. Although the Crown Colony of Hong Kong was under continuous threat, China was abiding by the 99-year lease agreement. Singapore remained a major British naval and military base. Malaya had achieved independence during the year and was stabilizing after the Malayan Emergency. But the Crown Colonies of Sarawak and North Borneo and the Protectorate of Brunei were pawns in Indonesian proposals to form a federation encompassing Indonesia, Philippines, Malaya, Singapore and British North Borneo. Malaya was suggesting that the three territories should ally themselves with Malaya and Singapore. The announcement in April by Secretary of State for Defence Duncan Sandys that National Service was to discontinue in 1960, and that the Armed Forces would concentrate on meeting their primary commitment to NATO, saw the introduction of the Regular Armed Forces.

During a visit to Singapore in April, Azahari proposed that the three North Borneo states should form an independent federation. The British were anxious that independence would risk hostile access to the oil fields; indeed, London felt that Brunei would be more secure allied to Malaya. Protracted negotiations included Azahari meeting Colonial Office officials in London, but his association with the Indonesian Foreign Minister, Dr Subandrio, a known communist sympathizer, led him to being suspected of being one. The anxiety needs to be set in context. Malaya had emerged from the Malayan Emergency, the Korean War had been concluded in 1953 and the French had been ejected from Indo-China (now Vietnam), and the Korean War had just been concluded. The possibility of a communist state in the region promoted considerable concerns and a decision was taken to undermine Azahari politically. He had never professed to be a communist, he was more a nationalist who exploited communism as the natural enemy of imperialism and colonialism.

Using Special Branch and British Malayan Petroleum as a front, British Intelligence penetrated the Brunei People's Party and hatched a scheme to induce an Indonesian response to a crisis in British North Borneo and then persuade British North Borneo of the advantages of merging with Malaya. Using the same tactic with the Pemerintah Revolusioner Republik Indonesia (PRRI) rebels in 1958, when a scheme failed to stir up disaffection among Sarawak Chinese, the US and British covertly supplied underground groups with weapons and encouraged subversion and then double-crossed them.

In 1959 the Sultan visited London to finalize protracted negotiations to replace the 1905–06 Protectorate with a Constitution but the final document reflected his views of the Sultanate retaining strong personal sovereignty supported by provisions to protect his powers, including making amendments of his choice and the Sultan to be head of state and prime minister, but the lack of any parliamentary institutions and the guarantees of independent courts meant that the Sultanate remained an absolute monarchy. The Constitution failed to address the principles of self-determination, any form of democratic process and political governance, and lacked statements on human rights and individual liberty. Nevertheless, the State Council, which was largely made up of privileged people/classes, was to be replaced by the new Executive, Legislative and Privy Councils as advisory bodies. It was intended that the Legislative Council should hold elections within two years. Nevertheless, that the Constitution was written marked a small step in the democratic progress of Brunei but it failed to convince Azahari and he denounced it as a move towards legitimizing absolute monarchy.

Intelligence on Brunei was generally lacking and largely confined to HQ Far East access to political, diplomatic and economic information shared by the Office of the Commissioner-General of the Far East in Kuala Lumpur. During 1959, HQ Far East Land Forces Defence Co-ordination Committee discussed exercising Plan Ale but this was rejected by the Commander-in-Chief, General Sir Richard Hull. However, he acknowledged the necessity of discreet reconnaissance and said that it should be in the form of visiting sports teams. The 1st Battalion, Queens Own Highlanders (1 Queens Own Highlanders) cricket team had visited Brunei in July. Captain Tony Lea, who commanded C Company, 1/2 Gurkha Rifles, and his wife had also toured Brunei in 1962.

The debate on federation escalated when, in a speech to the Foreign Correspondents Association of South-East Asia on 27 May 1961, Tunku Abdul Rahman of independent Malaya said:

> Malaya today as a nation realizes that she cannot stand alone. Sooner or later, Malaya must have an understanding with Britain and the peoples of the territories of Singapore, North Borneo, Brunei and Sarawak... whereby these territories can be brought closer together in political and economic co-operation.

He suggested that the federation should be known as 'Malaysia'. The idea was not new. In 1892 British colonial officials had similar ideas and in

1945–46 British attempts to impose the 'Malayan Union' was rejected outright by the Malays because it envisaged equal rights and democratic self-government and the possibility of a future Chinese, that is communist, majority in government. In 1948, a Federation Agreement replaced the concept by allowing Sarawak and North Borneo to accept some loss in sovereignty, in particular defence and foreign affairs, in exchange for federal government from Kuala Lumpur. Chin Peng denounced the ideas and embarked on the Malayan Emergency from 1947–1960. Although federation was largely rejected by the Sultan, mainly on the basis that Brunei was not a colony and that the country would have to share its considerable oil wealth with its poorer neighbours, this is not to suggest that the Sultan rejected closer ties with Malaya. When Tunku Abdul Rahman said that Brunei was too small to survive outside the Commonwealth, A.M. Azahari was infuriated. Indonesia, through Foreign Minister Dr Subandrio, welcomed the initiative by:

> Disclaiming any territories outside the former Netherlands East Indies, though they are part of the same island [of Borneo], but more than that, when Malaya told us of its intentions to merge the British Crown Colonies... as one federation, we told them we had no objections and that we wished them success with the merger so that everyone might live in peace and freedom.

To some extent the statement was a blind because if Sukarno was to achieve the greater Indonesia, *Malaysia* was essential because negotiating with five governments was more complicated than with a single entity. Nevertheless, relations deteriorated when President Sukarno accused the Tunku of wanting to remain part of the British Commonwealth. The Tunku made efforts to maintain friendly relations with Sukarno to the extent, in 1962, of allowing Indonesia to recruit Malays for the war of liberation against the Dutch in their last Far East territory, West Irian or Dutch New Guinea. About fifty were inducted but, when they arrived in Jakarta, they were later formed into a clandestine organization designed to overthrow the Malayan Government by inciting civil disturbances, particularly amongst the Chinese.

Sarawak and North Borneo were well known to Headquarters Far East. Since units were expected to be capable of deploying at very short notice anywhere in the Far East, both were ideal for jungle warfare and also as adventure training arenas, where leadership and organizational skills could be developed outside the military environment. For 99 Gurkha Infantry Brigade Group, trained and equipped to ensure stability in Singapore and Malaya and defuse threats from the Chinese, exercising in Sarawak was a welcome relief, even if some longhouses thought that the Japanese had not gone away when the Gurkhas appeared.

The police were familiar with exercising with British and Commonwealth forces. Indeed in 1962 they exercised with 40 Commando in Third Division in July; with the Queens Own Highlanders on an internal exercise in Kuching in August; and with the Gurkhas in Second and Third Divisions in September, during which several Sarawak Rangers parachuted. This made the Sarawak Police Field Force keen to learn parachuting. Also, L Company 42 Commando had exercised near Kota Belud in North Borneo in the autumn. Since August the 1st Battalion, The Queens Own Highlanders (1 Queens Own Highlanders) had been supplying Chisel Force of a four platoon company group on six week rotations to reinforce North Borneo Mobile Police Force operations against Philippine pirates. The Force was supported by Twin Pioneers of 209 Light Transport Squadron operating from the forward RAF base on Labuan and Ton class Coastal Minesweepers from 6th Minesweeping Squadron. The Scottish Aviation Single and Twin Pioneer was an ideal communication platform and had the versatility for supply and troop delivery and casualty evacuation. With a short take-off and landing capability, the aircraft could transport some sixteen troops about 400 miles at 20,000ft. They were equipped with two forward-mounted .30in Browning machine guns, with a receptacle for a Bren at the rear, and had external cradles for two 1,000lb or four 500lb bombs. The Squadron forward operating base was at Labuan where the commanding officer was Wing Commander John Graves.

For several years after Cessation Day, when the Brookes family transferred Sarawak to a Governor, there was little increase in Constabulary operational efficiency, wages, equipment, education and leadership of the Sarawak Police. Following the murders of Police Lance-Corporal Matu and two colleagues by communists in 1952, the *Sarawak Tribune* demanded that the police tackle the threat; however, when a state of emergency was declared, North Borneo sent sixty-eight men organized into two companies to help. By 1954 improvements were evident although few Chinese signed up. The pre-war Force A had been renamed the Sarawak Police. Force B had been converted into the paramilitary Sarawak Police Field Force and originally consisted of five forty-two-strong platoons, whose prime role was to support the hinterland communities. It also provided a Public Order Company in Kuching. Miri was allocated a platoon until 1961. By 1962, the Constabulary stood at about 1,400 all ranks. Accidental discharges of weapons stood at an average of 154 annually since 1945. The Auxiliary Police consisted of the Field Force Reserve based at communities, the forty-strong Oilfields Reserve at Miri, and the Reserve of 232 men formed into six platoons. Special Branch dealt with political intelligence and subversion but lacked the resources and the experience to address the Chinese Communist Organisation threat. The police in North Borneo had a very similar structure except that the para-military police were known as the Police Mobile Force. Both Constabularies were commanded by Commissioners of Police. They and senior officers were Colonial Police, most with experience in Palestine and with the British South African Police.

In 1950 Brunei Police Headquarters moved to Kuala Belait with the Chief Police Officer reporting to the Commissioner of Police in Kuching. The training centre was at Seria. The 1959 Constitution required that Brunei have its own Commissioner of Police. In 1960, the remit of the Brunei Police established in 1923 was partly devolved, with Customs, Immigration and Marine Departments being formed. Prisons and commercial licensing permits remained with the police. The Transport Department and Reserve Unit were established, the latter replacing the Sarawak Field Force Platoon that had provided support for several years. Most of the officers were British or Rhodesians serving in the Colonial Police Service with experience of the Palestine and the Malayan Emergencies and therefore had significant experience in counter-insurgency, but the indigenous police were inexperienced with the constables generally recruited from kampongs, not infrequently on personal recommendation. All had been trained on the Lee Enfield .303in rifle and a few on the Bren gun. The seven police stations in Brunei were self-contained barracks surrounded by a perimeter fence and included offices, the Charge Room, cells, an armoury and a small accommodation block.

By 1960 the deteriorating strategic situation in South-East Asia, the uncertainty of how long Great Britain would remain in the Far East, and the inability of Brunei to defend herself led to the Sultan asking the Malayans to help establish a defence force. When he was advised to approach the British, he persisted with his first choice, and in April a small Malayan recruiting team arrived in Brunei and selected sixty recruits from the 102 that had answered an advertisement in the *Borneo Bulletin* to enlist in the new Brunei Malay Regiment. The intake was flown to Port Dickson by a Royal Air Force Hastings and a Royal New Zealand Air Force Bristol Freighter where they were trained at the Royal Malay Regiment Depot. They passed out in November and, after a brief visit to Brunei to show the flag, they returned to Malaya for further experience and specialist trade training with the Royal Malay Regiment. Five Brunei officer cadets had attended the Malay Military College and by 1962 the newly titled Royal Brunei Malay Regiment numbered nearly 600 men.

CHAPTER FOUR

The National Army of North Kalimantan

Malaya's proposals of a federation provided A.M. Azahari with a tool to recruit support for his proposal for an autonomous federation of North Borneo. He succeeded in recruiting members for a pan-Borneo congress and was becoming as well known in the region for his nationalist views as Donald Stephens, the vocal North Borneo politician, and Ong Kee Hui of the left-wing Sarawak People's Party. By April 1962 he had been appointed to the Brunei Executive, where he continued to press for the merger of three North Borneo territories for the benefit of the people, as he saw it, as opposed to a federation with Malaya encouraged by Great Britain for her benefit. Reports of an Indonesian-led 'Liberation Army' hiding in the jungle close to the border with Sarawak was mentioned in the *Borneo Bulletin* in May but little appeared to have been made of the information by the Brunei authorities. One reason might have been the inexperience of Special Branch to analyze the information. In June the Cobbold Commission examining public opinion about Sarawak and North Borneo joining the Federation of Malaysia generally found in favour. Inevitably, the People's Party of Brunei concluded that the inquiry was a foregone conclusion and a fraud; nevertheless, in August, the Commonwealth Relations Secretary in London announced that on 31 August 1963, the sovereignty of Sarawak and North Borneo, along with Singapore, would be transferred to the Federation of Malaysia.

With political destabilization evident in Brunei, Sukarno used the opportunity to undermine the idea of a Malaysian Federation by subversion and mounting intelligence operations in British North Borneo. From dissidents within the Brunei People's Party and the Sarawak Youth Movement (*Barisan Pemuda Sarawak*) spawned the left-wing nationalist North Kalimantan People's Party. This Party allied itself with political groups in North Borneo and Sarawak favouring a federation of North Borneo and from it emerged, in late 1961, the underground National Army of North Kalimantan (*Tentera Nasional Kalimantan Utara* or TNKU).

Haji Muhammad Yassin bin Abdul Affendi Rahman was its commander and the Brunei Military Commander was Jais bin Haji Karim. Its flag was a green triangle superimposed on the red and white rectangular symbol of the Brunei People's Party. All that was needed were recruits and an obvious source was the Kedayan who, seen as second-class citizens, were ripe for propaganda and subversion. The Lawas TNKU was formed in mid-1961 when three brothers of Indonesian origin, posing as crocodile hunters, arrived to observe the activities of the Sarawak Youth Front. A proposal to its branch secretary and chairman to front the TNKU with their organization was agreed.

Members of the TNKU underwent a loyalty ceremony conducted by Oath Administrators in high degrees of secrecy. In Sarawak and Brunei the ceremony involved holding the Koran to the head and reciting in Malay 'In accordance with the organization, if I fail to honour my promise or if I am reported to the authorities, I will be punished by the organization'. The oath was underpinned by 'military police' commanded by a Provost Marshal, ensuring that the existence, organisation and intentions of the TNKU were secret almost until the last moment. Some guerrillas adopted *nom de guerre* with several styling themselves as 'Che Guevara' to emulate the Argentinian Ernesto Guevara de la Serna, the darling of the Cuban Revolution and not much else and gives a clue to the romantic nature some rebels had in the TNKU.

The operational unit consisted of a company theoretically structured to be a headquarters and five officers and five platoons, each numbering about thirty men, and a reserve of eight, giving a total of 163 all ranks. The establishment differed from area to area so that by the time the rebellion broke, an estimated fifteen companies totalling about 2,440 men had been organized. Military Intelligence later suggested that about 8,000 trained TNKU were organized into an order of battle with a further 7,000 awaiting induction and training. The principal firearms were privately owned hunting shotguns and a mix of axes, *parangs* and spears. These would be supplemented by weapons captured from the police. Training and indoctrination by Drill Instructors were rudimentary and discreetly carried out in jungle clearings some distance from roads and inhabited areas. In April 1962, sixteen members from Lawas and eighty from Brunei made their way to North Borneo and crossed the border for three months of military training under the auspices of the Indonesian Combat Command Kalimantan commander, Colonel BS Supardjo. His anti-imperialist and left-wing subversive views led Tunku Abdul Rahman to claim communist interference in Malay regional affairs. At least one small group intercepted by the North Borneo Police were Brunei and Sarawak citizens. And some sixty or more TNKU were trained in the Malinau area of Indonesia. The training itself was badly organized. Weapon skills were taught with wooden rifles and the recruits complained of being made unwelcome by the Indonesian military after such a long march from the border.

Activity by the TNKU in First, Second and Third Divisions was almost non-existent. In Fourth Division, it was estimated to be 440-strong and was centred on Luak, Kelelit, Satap, Bungai, Tiris and Niah along the coastal strip. In Fifth Division, the approximately 450-strong TNKU was divided into six companies, three at Limbang and three at Lawas, supported by the Sarawak Youth Front (*Barisan Pemuda Sarawak*), a strongly anti-British Malay nationalist party being used as its subversive element. One commander was Salleh bin Sambas, aged 42 in 1962 and born in Bakuak village near Limbang. He wrote:

> My father was farmer. As a boy, I experienced the Japanese occupation. It was a very difficult time and food was scarce. Soon after war ended, I joined the Sarawak Constabulary and after training at Kuching, I was posted to Miri. I was then assigned to the Police Field Force. Our platoon commander was an Army officer called Captain Lewis. He taught us weapon training with the Lee Enfield rifle, Bren gun, pistol and Sterling sub machine gun. I leant a lot from Captain Lewis and it was he who nicknamed me 'Father Bren' because I was good with the weapon. In 1954, I was posted to Limbang, where I was married. After serving in the Constabulary for eight years, in 1958 I resigned and worked as a farmer and also rubber tapper. I then joined the

TNKU and was appointed deputy commander to Khairul Salleh Kerudin. However he was arrested, as was Haji Pilok and Gantang bin Lubin.

Sambas was distinctive because he had a beard and was known as 'Salleh Jangut' or Salleh the Bearded One to differentiate him from other Kedayans with the same name. He styled himself 'Lieutenant Muda' and was fourth in the chain of command. There is no doubt that his experience, training and knowledge of Security Forces' standard operating procedures gave him the skills to lead an effective guerilla force. The Limbang District TNKU emerged as tough and ruthless, and developed into the core of the rebellion. Its Pandaruan Company was based around houses and hamlets along the Limbang to Panduran Road and was commanded by Sambas.

North Borneo was on the labour migratory route to Indonesia, which was used to infiltrate TNKU destined for training in Indonesia, although no members in North Borneo were thought to have received military training in Indonesia. There were about 14,000 Indonesian labourers working in timber estates, such as the Wallace Bay Company and Borneo Abacus Limited in Tawau District. They were a vital component of the economy of British North Borneo and of North Borneo in particular. Many were in their twenties and had served in the Indonesian National Army, either as regulars or in the home guard militia. Apart from occasional industrial dispute, these Indonesians were law abiding; nevertheless, they presented a threat to the stability of British North Borneo.

The three companies of the TNKU in North Borneo were centred on the Interior Residency bordering Fifth Division. Its administrative centre was Beaufort. The organization was strikingly different from Sarawak and Brunei for two reasons – there were no leaders of note and the rank and file were later assessed to be illiterate and incapable of thinking for themselves. Most were promised that land previously annexed by Sarawak would be returned after the success of the revolt. The rebels were broken down into three companies, the largest company of 185, commanded by Jaya bin Hassan, being centred on Masapol, Ulu Sipitang, Sipitang town, Lubok and Pantai, which were strung along the road from the border with Sarawak. Translated from the Malay into English, *ulu* is the interior. The equivalent in Africa is 'the bush'. Forty TNKU were in

Gadong, a kampong on the low-lying peninsula to the north-west of Beaufort. About a third in each group had received some form of military training. The oath differed and involved the aspirant cutting a finger and allowing the blood to drop on to a piece of cloth on which his name had been written.

The TNKU rank and file in Brunei believed the propaganda broadcast by their leaders that the only method of achieving independence outside the influence of Malaya and Great Britain was by seizing power and forming a federation of North Borneo into a single country. They were assured assistance would arrive from the Philippines and Indonesia immediately after the success of the rising and, more critically, they believed that Sultan Omar had blessed the revolt and agreed to be become head of state with Azahari as his prime minister. D-Day was set for 24 December, Christmas Eve.

After several delays blamed on technical reasons, the long-awaited elections in Brunei were held between 30 and 31 August, with the Brunei People's Party demanding responsible government, immediate independence on the basis of the federation of North Borneo, and the transformation of the Protectorate into a republic with a socialist economy. With more than 90 per cent of the total electorate voting, the People's Party won a stunning victory over its conservative rival, the Brunei National Organisation, by winning fifty-four of the fifty-five district council seats and securing sixteen seats in the thirty-three seat Legislative Council. The result was a disaster for Sultan Omar and it seemed that he would be relegated to puppet monarch status, but the Constitution made no provisions to allow a political party to form a government. When the Sultan nominated seventeen members, the People's Party was in the minority by one. The Legislative Council then agreed that Brunei should negotiate to join the Federation of Malaya. When the People's Party then demanded a debate on the appointments of the unelected Councillors, claiming that the electorate had been denied their rights, the Council procrastinated, first in early September and then in October and November.

In early November, Sarawak Special Branch had detected that something was up. Its commander, Superintendent Paddy Prince, arrived in Lawas from Kuching and stayed in the government Rest House. Prince was aged about fifty and, although a 'good fun guy' according to Peace Corps worker Andy Power, he was tough and had the support of the local constabulary. Power was on a two year US Peace Corps assignment with the Sarawak Public Works Department building roads and was also staying in the Rest House. When the police requisitioned a 40bhp outboard engine, leaving him with an 18bhp engine, Mervyn Swyny, a senior Eurasian Public Works Department manager, told him something was on.

On 2 November 1961 President John Kennedy had appealed for 'talented men and women ready, willing and able to fight poverty, disease, affray and ignorance' to join the Peace Corps and leave US shores to work in a Third World nation. Within the year the take-up had been massive and, in 1961, the first training courses began at Rutgers University. Most who joined the Peace Corps were middle class Americans with little experience of the dramas that had affected Europe and other parts of the world for centuries. Virtually all were pacifists and others deeply religious and all firmly believed that they could help the less well off. Governments, such as Sarawak, were only too pleased to see the Peace Corps as a means of educating their farmers in modern methods.

Three weeks later, Prince held a high-level meeting in Lawas. At about the same time, an elderly woman arrived at the Police Station and asked for help to release her grandson from 'the army' so that he could help her till the fields. 'And which army might that be?' she was asked. 'The local one. Look, I have been making his uniform.' When she produced a green military-style shirt complete with TNKU buffalo insignia sleeve patch, it was the first hard intelligence of the existence of the TNKU. Police officers sent to markets and local tailors discovered there had been a run on green cotton cloth to the extent that additional supplies had been sent from Singapore. The shortage of the green cloth was also noted by Alastair Ker-Lindsay, a 22-year-old Scottish chemical engineer managing the offshore construction division of the family business. Educated at Geelong Grammar School in Australia, he had joined his father in Brunei in 1958 and lived in Kuala Belait. Most of the construction work was on contract for Brunei Shell Petroleum Co. Ltd in Seria.

In Limbang on 23 November, Richard Morris received a warning from a Brunei friend that the Brunei People's Party was planning something for 19 December. Remembering that during the 1953 rebellion the rebels had worn olive green military-style shirts, Morris and Abang Zainddin, the newly arrived Limbang District Officer, used one of the latter's regular tours of the bazaar to check. Dropping in on a Chinese tailor, they noted an unusual number of bolts of green cloth, even though the owner said that business was slack. They visited another shop, not a tailor's, and noted bolts of green cloth on a shelf. But the locals rarely wore green cloth and since very few people were wearing green shirts, this led Morris and Zainddin to conclude that some sort of military action was imminent.

On 1 December, Prince and about twenty Sarawak Police Field Force re-appeared at Lawas in the police launch *Lefee.* Prince moved out of the Rest House on to the launch to improve communications with Police Headquarters at Kuching. Five days later, Prince told Power not to stray from Lawas because it was 'a little hot'. Morris also expressed concerns at the disquiet among the Kedayans. On 3 December Mr W.J. Parks, the Acting High Commissioner for Brunei, wrote a letter to High Commissioner Dennis White in Kuala Lumpur, briefing him on the activities of the TNKU as militants within the People's Party of Brunei. The following day the Sarawak Police conducted a major sweep through the Lawas area and arrested ten suspected TNKU, after they had attended a Sarawak Youth Movement meeting in Bangar. Two were senior commanders and one was the Oath Administrator. All were from the Limbang Company. Since Sambas was fourth in the chain of command, he took command of operations in Limbang. This activity was reported to the Colonial Office by the North Borneo authorities.

When the People's Party had demanded a debate on the outnumbering of the elected Councillors, claiming that the electorate had been denied their rights, the Council procrastinated in September, October and November and then for a fourth time in December. The denial was the catalyst for rebellion and TNKU couriers spread word from Brunei that the outbreak was to coincide with the visit of Tunku Abdul Rahman to Jesselton in North Borneo, but this was rescinded when a split developed between the politicians in the Brunei People's Party and the TNKU about when military action should take place, with one branch resigning en masse in protest at the inaction. They had a point. It is inevitable with such a momentous act as rebellion that the word would seep out. The longer that Azahari and Affendi, the TNKU commander, procrastinated, the more likely Special Branch would discover the insurrection. But there had been other intelligence indicators that there was something brewing in Brunei.

On 6 December, when Richard Morris alerted Governor Waddell that he had heard the rebellion was to begin on 8 December, Waddell advised the North Borneo Governor Goode and Alan Outram and Donald Mathieson, Commissioners of Police for Brunei and North Borneo respectively, and the police across British North Borneo were put on full alert. The next day Pat Linton, the Shell Managing Director at Seria, telephoned W.P. Parks to say that he had received reliable information that a revolt was planned for the early hours of 8 December. Shell was always very well informed. On the same day, John Fisher, the Fourth Division Resident, also reported that something was up.

On 2 December, Tunku Abdul Rahman had expressed his concerns to Lord Selkirk, the Commissioner-General of the Far East, who decided to visit Brunei and North Borneo and had met with Sultan Omar. Selkirk found the air was one of complacency. The Sultan was reluctant to recall the Malay Brunei Regiment from Malaya because it was inexperienced and he had little faith in the reliability of the police. Selkirk assured Omar that British military support was available under existing treaty obligations. Returning to Malaya, Selkirk penned an account of his meeting to the Colonial and added that, as he left Brunei, reports were emerging of 'an armed attack on the oil installations in Miri planned for 2.00am on Saturday, 8 December'. Selkirk despatched the telegram on 7 December.

Another visitor had been Sir Claude Fenner, the Inspector-General of the Malayan Police. Although he found no clear indications of insurrection, he was sufficiently concerned after meetings with police commanders to warn Admiral Sir David Luce, Commander-in-Chief Far East, that unrest seemed to be simmering in Brunei but nothing more was known, in particular the date. Luce instructed his Chief-of-Staff, Major-General Sir Brian Wyldbore-Smith CB DSO CBE, to dust off and review Plan Ale, the 1953 contingency plan to despatch an Initial Force of two companies of the British battalion in 99 Gurkha Infantry Brigade Group, small detachments of Royal Engineers and Royal Signals, and a Military Intelligence Officer to support the civil authorities in Brunei. Mention was made of a third infantry company as a reinforcement. A naval contribution was not considered because, apart from occasional visits to ports, the Royal Navy was unfamiliar with local navigational hazards. The RAF was only required for the initial fly-in. Since flying operations would use Labuan, there was no need to use Brunei airport and consequently aircrew knowledge of Brunei airstrips was minimal.

Even as the intelligence picture developed, while Great Britain had a defence agreement with Brunei, it was not responsible for its internal security and therefore HQ Far East saw no need to warn other Service HQs, HQ 17th Gurkha Division and 99 Gurkha Infantry Brigade Group. A few weeks before, Far East Command had re-organized from three Service HQs into a joint HQ with three Services taking it in turns to appoint a commander-in-chief.

During March 1962, Major Patrick Webb, who commanded 249 Gurkha Signal Squadron, formally visited Brunei and identified potential headquarters and communication positions. The Squadron, formed in 1958, consisted of Radio Relay, High Frequency Radio, Communications Troops and a Light Aircraft Troop of three Sioux helicopters to support HQ Far East Land Forces. Webb was greeted 'with incredulity as if to say how anyone could be so stupid as to imagine an internal security threat arising in Brunei'. On his return to Singapore, he was directed by HQ Land Forces to assign a Land Rover fitted with a 53 High Frequency radio set and four men to provide rear link support for Plan Ale. Otherwise, the British Forces in Singapore were looking forward to yet another relaxing weekend in an idyllic posting. Christmas was only a fortnight away and already the traditional celebrations in the various messes were underway.

Lawas Jail was too small and when the majority of the ten men arrested on 4 December were transferred to Limbang, Affendi re-evaluated his timings and decided that if operational security was to be preserved, the armed struggle should begin as soon as possible and the arrested men released before they divulged too much under Special Branch interrogation. However, he was concerned that the TNKU lacked weapons and therefore the police stations would have to be attacked first. During 7 December, couriers discreetly left his War Committee headquarters at Padang *kampong* with instructions for his TNKU commanders that H-Hour was 2.00am on Saturday, 8 December. The plan was:

> Sultan Omar to be proclaimed head of state of the Borneo Federation in order to retain popular support and give credibility to the uprising. In the event that the Sultan refused to co-operate, his palaces in Brunei and Panaga were to be seized.

> Radio Brunei and several transmitter stations were to be captured and the shadow 'Deputy Prime Minister', A.M. Azahari, was to announce the rebellion with the aim of soliciting international support.
>
> Public Works Department depots and utilities were to be captured so that public services could be continued with minimum interruption.
>
> Brunei and Anduki Airports to be seized to facilitate the fly-in of arms, ammunition and equipment from Indonesia.
>
> Police Headquarters in Brunei town was to be captured.
>
> District police stations in Limbang, Tutong, Seria, Panaga, Kuala Belait, Miri and Bekanu were to be seized and occupied. From these Bren guns, rifles and ammunition could be captured. Panaga was particularly important as it had the largest armoury in Brunei.
>
> Production at the Miri and Seria oil fields was to be kept open.
>
> Hostages were to be taken as bargaining counters.

Orders were sent to a *prahu* skipper, known as 'Che Ariff', to deliver arms and ammunition to a TNKU party waiting near a beach not far from the port of Weston in North Borneo. It was intended to control the rebellion by a system of couriers, in much the same way as Colonel George Grivas had successfully done in Cyprus during the EOKA crisis. Indonesian active complicity in the rebellion is unclear, even today.

Azahari had passed through Limbang on his way to Manila via Singapore. It is inconceivable that he was not aware, as is sometimes claimed, that rebellion was imminent. He left his wife behind in Brunei.

Sambas was instructed to report to Sedang and wait in an empty house. This he did with another TNKU commander and spent an anxious few hours until, at about 4.00pm, a courier arrived with written orders that Limbang was to be attacked at 2.00am. Sambas recalled

:

> The order to attack came from my superior. I estimated the number of my followers to be 1,000 people from various races, namely Malays, Kedayan, Chinese, Muruts, Iban and others. Because time was short, we could not gather more people.

Returning by boat to Rangau, Sambas and his colleagues slipped into their villages at about 10.30pm and assembled their men. Sambas led the Pandaruan Road Company, about 200-strong. His job was to capture the Limbang Police Barracks and senior government officials in their houses, hopefully by talking them into surrendering. As a former policeman, he knew most of them.

To reinforce the Brunei Police, Wing Commander John Graves, the commanding officer of 209 Squadron that was supporting military operations against piracy in North Borneo, flew a North Borneo Police Field Force platoon from Jesselton to join Commissioner Outram at Police Headquarters at about 10.30am. Flight Lieutenant Morris, the forward air controller, decided to deliver the police to Brunei Airport in two aircraft and instructed that they returned to Labuan. During the afternoon, Graves left for a scheduled meeting in Singapore.

After lunch, Richard Morris discretely reconnoitred Limbang for places that could be converted into strongholds for loyalist families and held by the civilian authorities until the arrival of military forces. To avoid spreading alarm and confusion, he decided against issuing any warnings because it was still by no means certain that an attack was imminent. However, when he gained permission from Commissioner Outram to place the Sarawak Constabulary on a higher state of alert, he alerted the Limbang Police District Commander, Inspector Haji Abdul Latip bin Basah, that a rebel attack was imminent but targets and times were not known. He instructed that nine police officers living in the town should be issued with their personal weapons and twenty-five rounds of ammunition, which they could retain at their quarters. This left nine police officers in the Police Barracks. At midnight, a police Land Rover commanded by Sergeant Suhaili Nasir returned from a patrol along the Pandaruan Road and reported that several small branches of trees had been found on the road, possibly as obstacles, otherwise all was quiet.

In North Borneo, Lieutenant Jaya bin Hassan and sixty rebels from Ulu Sipitang were hiding at Milestone 1, the junction of the main road a mile north of Sipitang and about 500yds from the beach. They were collecting arms and ammunition from 'Che Ariff' who was bringing a *prahu* from Brunei.

John Parry, who was the Acting District Officer at Sipitang in the

Interior Residency of North Borneo, first heard about possible civil unrest on 7 December when he received a confused verbal message, based on information received from Kuching, that an internal security problem was expected on 8 and 9 December. His superior was Mr Paul Dillamore, who was District Officer for Beaufort District. In the absence of further information, he instructed the Duty Corporal at Sipitang Police Station to double the shift and asked several reliable people in the area to keep watch at two strategic points, one south of the Sipitang Road in Ulu Sipitang and the other one on the coast.

In Singapore, the HQ 99 Gurkha Infantry Brigade Group Officers' Mess had sat down to a formal Guest Night. After a busy week Lieutenant Colonel Gordon Shakespear MC, the Commanding Officer, 1/2 Gurkha Rifles at Slim Barracks, was looking forward to a round of golf on Saturday. Lieutenant Colonel Charles McHardy MBE MC, commanding 1 Queens Own Highlanders, was having dinner at a restaurant and was expecting to meet his in-laws flying in to RAF Changi. In Seria, a Tombola Night was in full swing in the Shell Club with several guests having driven from Brunei. There had been rumours of strikes in the oilfields and several expatriate engineers remained at home ready to respond to trouble.

CHAPTER FIVE

Brunei Revolt 8–11 December

On time, at 2.00 am on 8 December 1962, the TNKU swarmed across Brunei and Fourth and Fifth Divisions and met varying success.

In Brunei town, the TNKU captured the power station, cutting power, but failed to seize the radio station and telegraph office. Police Headquarters was then attacked. The response was hesitant until the TNKU started to climb its perimeter wall. An attack on Chief Minister Dato Setia Awang in Kambang Pasang Road was repulsed when six constables, led by an inspector, arrived from the Headquarters and, after a brief stand-off, made several arrests. A TNKU delegation that went with a petition to the Istana Kota Menggalela, the Sultan's Palace, failed to see Sultan Omar and were advised to present their concerns to the Chief Minister, who was then sheltering at Police Headquarters. When the Minister also refused to accept the petition and the delegation attempted to leave, they were arrested.

Sultan Omar then sent a telegram to Lord Selkirk, the Commissioner-General for South East Asia, invoking the 1959 Treaty and asking for military assistance. Although he had raised the Royal Brunei Malay Regiment, they were insufficiently experienced to deal with the crisis and the Brunei Police could not be trusted. Selkirk forwarded the request to the Colonial Office for advice. Meanwhile, at about 3.15am, Mr Parks had sent a cable to Headquarters Far East Command, also seeking help. Shortly afterwards, he was attacked in his house by TNKU and tied up.

Shortly after 6.00 am, the Sultan broadcast that several people had been killed in the fighting and that he knew who was responsible and that the strongest measures would be taken against those found to be guilty, including the death penalty. Imposing a state of emergency under the Public Security Ordinance, he announced a 6.00pm to 6.00am curfew to be enforced until Tuesday 11 December. The Brunei People's Party was banned and warrants issued for the arrest of hundreds of its members, including Azahari. He then declared that the rebels had coerced others to say that he supported the rebellion, which he did not. At about 8.00am, Commissioner of Police Alan Outram and an officer of Her Majesty's Overseas Service released Parks. Outside Brunei Town, Seria and Tutong Police Barracks were overrun and the loyal police officers locked up in the cells. Police in Panaga and Kuala Belait were resisting. The Sultan's Country Palace and Brunei Police Mobile Unit Barracks outside Panaga were overrun.

Meanwhile, Graves, who had spent the night in Kuching en route to Singapore, returned to Labuan and instructed his squadron to assemble at the airfield. At about the same time as the platoon arrived, 200 armed TNKU advancing along Residency Road with a hostage, Mr Clark, in front, were confronted by police commanded by Commissioner Outram at the junction with Sultan Road. He demanded that they release Clark and surrender, which they did after several shots were fired. The TNKU were then detained in the tennis courts at the corner of the Padang where they were processed, with some being interrogated at the Teacher Training College at Barakas. Identified hardliners were sent to Jerudong Prison.

Sultan Omar had shown considerable courage in the face of armed insurrection. He had refused to accept the TNKU petition, had faced down an armed group at the *Istana* and had refused the use of a Shell Oil Company launch, and had no intention of surrendering Brunei to the People's Party of Brunei. Shell Oil probably had the best intelligence organization in Sarawak and Brunei and, apparently having prior knowledge of the revolt, had sent a launch to lurk off the *Istana* should Sultan Omar need to escape. Although he appears to have believed that he was in no personal danger, Commissioner Outram insisted that he and his family move to Police Headquarters, where the cells were used to accommodate him.

A vigorous attempt to seize Brunei Airport was beaten off by Mr Glass, the Brunei Controller of Civil Aviation, assisted by several loyal members of his staff and the civilian fire brigade. Built during the Second World

War, it handled two regional airlines using aircraft no bigger than DC-3 Dakotas and a few private aircraft. It is of interest that the day before the rebellion, several wealthy Chinese families had flown to Labuan. The runway had been resurfaced in 1959.

Azahari, on his way to Manila, was surprised by the rebellion. However, during the afternoon, claiming to be the 'Prime Minister, Foreign Affairs Minister and Defence Minister' of the new 'Unitary State of North Borneo', he broadcast that the three British North Borneo territories had broken from their shackles of colonialism and were unified under the Sultan. He also criticized the British:

> because of their refusal to give the Borneo people the right of self determination and their attempts to push Brunei into the Federation of Malaysia.

In common with independence and liberation movements, the People's Party of Brunei published a fifteen clause Proclamation of Independence giving their rationale for the outbreak. In brief, this demanded the restoration of inalienable rights so long denied them by the Colonial powers. In fact, Brunei had been always been governed by a Sultan. The aim of the revolt was to unify all the peoples of Brunei and extend the Sultanate's influence in Sarawak and Borneo, in effect a return to the days when Brunei was a major power in the region. The Proclamation also demanded political reform and criticized the election, which had seen the People's Party of Brunei denied its electoral victory, as well as rejecting the concept of the Federation of Malaysia in favour of the Federation of North Borneo. And, therefore, it stated that:

> The acknowledged leaders of Sarawak, Brunei and North Borneo, meeting in the name of Liberty, Justice and Humanity, have this day, December 8, 1962, solemnly proclaimed the absolute and complete Independence of Negara Kesatuan Kalimantan Utara, with Sultan Omar Ali Saifuddin as the constitutional and Parliamentary Head of State.

Announcing that twenty TNKU divisions had captured twenty towns, Azahari threatened that if the British attacked, the Seria oil fields would be set on fire. He added that he would be flying to New York to present the nationalist case to the UN and, responding to appeals for British military assistance by Sultan Omar, he appealed to UN Secretary-General U Thant to intervene in order to 'prevent further bloodshed'. Azahari claimed that the Sultan's disowning of the rebellion was British propaganda broadcast from Singapore and gave assurances that he would return to Brunei to lead the nationalist intervention and then, 'the British will have a taste of our strength when our forces attack Kuching'. But he was soon himself at risk of being isolated when the Philippines government disclaimed any official dealings with Azahari. His appeals for weapons were met with no response and, when it later became clear that he was unable to offer practical support to the rebels and had been unable to raise support from several African and Asian heads of state, Azahari later quietly left Manila and flew to Jakarta. This announcement was the first formal confirmation of insurrection in Brunei.

In Kuala Lumpur, Tunku Abdul Rahman met his Cabinet, Service Chiefs and the British High Commissioner and announced plans to evacuate Malay officials working with the Brunei Government, but they sent a telegram declaring that with British military forces on the way, they wished to remain in the Protectorate and help resolve the situation although it would be valuable if their wives and children could be flown out. The Tunku thanked them for their commitment and offered to send 150 police officers to reinforce the Brunei Police plus the services of the Malayan Armed Forces, offers that were rejected by Sultan Omar.

In Fourth Division, sheer ineptness prevailed. The TNKU intended to attack Miri at 2.00am but thirty TNKU reinforcements expected from Bekunu did not arrive until 5.00am and the two leaders, both from Luak, postponed the venture. An hour after most had returned home, police reinforcements made several arrests.

In Fifth Division, Sunday, 9 December was tense. Resistance in Lawas had developed quickly. On 7 December, Andy Power and two local colleagues had been taking soundings prior to building a bridge upstream and had returned to the town at about 1.00am to find the normally thriving town silent and deserted. Power later heard voices from inside a closed Indian café and, bashing on the shutters, learnt from several civil servants and police officers that the regular 2.00am radio check with Limbang Police had been lost. Communications had also been lost with the Fourth Division Police Headquarters at Miri and there were reports of fighting in

Brunei Town, Kuala Belait and Seria. Mervyn Swyny, who managed the Public Works Department in the town, then rallied his men and loyalists in Lawas to defend their town. The District Officer's bungalow was made into a stronghold surrounded by barbed wire, trenches and sandbagged sangars, manned by Murat volunteers with blowpipes, a Sarawak Rangers detachment and police officers. Swyny personally directed the clearance of jungle and undergrowth and selected fields of fire. Lights erected to illuminate these approaches were connected to a generator in the bungalow. Strips of corrugated iron fitted to the lights were angled so that the beams shone across the ground and would blind attackers. Power declined the offer of a carbine, citing that he was better employed in negotiations; nevertheless, he contributed to the defences by building a vehicle and pedestrian barrier gate for his compound. The greatest threat to Lawas from Limbang was the bridge over the River Trusan, downstream of the town. Power used a pair of his binoculars to observe approaches. Fortunately it was a moonlit night. Superintendent Prince later told Power that a revolt had broken out and the Sultan was still in authority. Great Britain had been asked for help.

Reports then began to circulate that 2,000 TNKU, some in canoes and boats, were making their way to the town. The defences were improved when a bulldozer cleared the jungle almost to the back door of the District Officer's bungalow. The tension increased when a motor boat was heard from downstream until slowly around the bend came the police launch *Lefee*, its two .30-calibre Browning machine guns manned. Standing on the bow was Superintendent Millington sweeping the town with his binoculars. Not knowing what to expect, he guided the launch to the bank, landed a couple of police officers and took a position mid-stream so that the boat's Brownings covered them. To the relief of both sides, the defenders in the District Officer's bungalow met the police officers and confirmed Lawas remained in loyalist hands.

During the night, the 200 men of the Limbang Company, armed with shotguns, spears, parangs, and even catapults – anything they could find – moved into position with Sambas and the Pandaruan Company deploying them around the power supply shed, the Police Barracks, the Jail, the Residency, the Government office and Inspector Latip's house. A small force was sent to detain the Resident and other Government officials. The companies from Batang Limbang/Sungei Lubai and Bakul and Bukit Loba moved into positions upriver of the Police Barracks. At 2.00am, the TNKU seized their objectives with reasonable ease, except for the Barracks, the Jail and District Office. Sambas led the attack on the Barracks:

> When we attacked the police station, all we wanted to do was release our friends and end colonial rule in Sarawak. Only after we captured Limbang did more people join. I ordered my men to surround the Police Station. When the time came, they were to shout at the top of their voices. By doing this, I hoped that the police would see the size of force and surrender. However, things did not turn out as I had hoped. As we moved toward the Police Station, a drunken Chinese man alerted the police of our attack so they were ready for us and opened fire from inside the Police Station.

Although the Barracks were not designed to be defended against a military assault, the eight police officers inside defended it aggressively as several TNKU began scaling the fence. Corporal Kim Huat, in command, made his way to the recreation room to meet the assault from the south. Constable Wan Jamaluddin bin Tuanku Alek dashed into the accommodation block at the back to warn his colleagues but encountered a rebel at the corner of the compound and was killed during a short exchange of fire, as was the rebel. Constable Essa bin Meratim, who was in the accommodation block, killed a rebel who tried to enter the covered way linking the accommodation with the offices. Constable Bishop anak Kunjan and Constable Sanggah anak Jampang took up positions in the Charge Room where Bishop manned the Bren while Sanggah picked off TNKU with his .303in rifle. Constable Insoll anak Chundang was killed while collecting more ammunition from the arms cote. Constable Bujang bin Mohammed was seriously wounded manning a position in the Sergeant's Office, as was Corporal Huat, and died during the night.

At the dilapidated Government offices, Constable Zaini bin Titun, a radio operator with the Wireless Division of the Sarawak Police Communication Department, heard the firing around the Police Barracks. Then, seeing rebels, he telephoned Constable Sanggah in the Barracks to tell him that he was exchanging fire, but he was quickly overwhelmed.

Constable Muling anak Kusan on duty at the Jail heard the attack on the Government offices and counter-attacked but he soon ran out of ammunition and hid as the prisoners were released. This included the five TNKU leaders arrested in Lawas. Half a mile from the Police Barrack, Inspector Latip was asleep in his married quarter near the Jail when he was woken by the firing. Collecting his Sterling sub machine gun and running to the road, he was ambushed from several directions and was wounded in the arm by a shotgun. Crawling across the road, he hid in riverbank foliage. He would have been a valuable captive had he been taken early in the insurrection.

Mr and Mrs Morris were woken by the shooting and, seeing armed men approaching the front of the Residency, they escaped by the back door but were captured and led into dense jungle above a small stream with very steep banks behind the Residency. Dorothy Morris wrote afterwards:

> We sat there with every form of biting nightlife assailing us, Dick was clad only in underpants, jockey type without much seat in them and the inevitable perished elastic band at the top and no safety pins. Having had certain security measures to take before quitting the house, he couldn't spare the time in the dark to locate more dignified clothing. I had had the extra minute or so in which to fumble about and dress more adequately, and to find some heavy shoes. Dick was fairly savagely bound with nylon fishing cord, but my hands were free. Two decidedly hysterical little thugs squatted unpleasantly and unnecessarily close on either side of me, each clutching an arm. The thug on my left was all the time pointing a kris unpleasantly close to the middle of Dick's back.
>
> In an attempt to impress on them how unlikely would be any attempted break for freedom by either Dick or myself, I tried indulging in light drawing-room conversation, telling them how my brother had been among the Australian soldiers who had rescued them and their parents and others from the Japanese in Limbang not so many years ago, enquiring whether they were married, what children they had, stressed the importance of sending them to school regularly, concluding with vehement assertions that I was old enough to be the grand-mother of their children, and capping this with the ghastly truth of my own age. Followed a

> whispered conclave between the two of them and one produced a match, struck it, held it close to my face, and from the pair of them there issued a prolonged groan, expressing a mixture of disappointment, disgust, resignation, and, I like to think, disbelief. It was with some relief an hour or so later that we were ordered to blunder up the slope again to a clearing above the Residency and thence down a very ill defined path with cobblestones and irregular steps. As my hands were still free I was firmly held by a tough on each arm, but threw them off half way down by the simple, if unplanned, expedient of losing my footing on a flight of seven old worn steps and slithering down to the bottom and earning a really worthwhile bruise from hip to shin. After that, they let me walk unaided to the District Office.
>
> Following a charming little scene in which large numbers of rebels, all looking very scruffy and dedicated, despite a hotchpotch of uniforms and weapons, filed past me. Some stopped and stared with no noticeable affection and one, whose aim was fortunately very poor, attempted to spit in my face. Definitely a low point. The 'high' followed when I once again sighted Dick who had been taken off separately and questioned in his own office, at considerable length. After further delays, we were taken, just as dawn was breaking, to the Jail. This is a square wooden building of four cells, divided by a central passage. Built on piles it is not remarkable for lighting or ventilation, nor is the bathroom and toilet block at the back remarkable for sanitation.

One of the two convicted prisoners who had refused to leave the Jail was Asan anak Jimbu, an Iban from River Medamit. He had been sentenced to three months after stealing a canoe, a serious offence in a country that relied upon waterways for travel. Although told to go home by the TNKU, he chose to stay. When the Morrises arrived in his Cell Number 1, he was changing from his prison garb of canvas-like shirt and drawstring pants into his own clothes. The Morrises knew Asan because every morning at about 9.00am, he walked the 150yds up the hill from the Jail to help Mrs Morris in the overgrown Residency garden.

As dawn broke on 9 December, the Police Barracks was still under siege; however, several TNKU were inside the perimeter fence and were crouching underneath the windows. Sambas decided it was time to persuade the police to surrender:

> The fighting lasted from 2.00am until daybreak at 6.00am. I then took my sergeant to the Resident's office and was told that he and his wife had been captured and were tied up with their hands behind their backs. I went to see the Resident and asked him to accompany me to the police station and order the policemen to give up their arms. However, when the Resident shouted for them to surrender, there were more shots from the police and the Resident and I both dived for cover. When the firing stopped, the Resident again ordered the police to give up and it was then that they recognized his voice when he shouted, "I am the Resident, I am the Resident and you are all to surrender".

The fighting had cost the lives of three police officers. Corporal Kim Huat, a mixed Land Dayak/Chinese, aged 37, was married with two children. Constable Wan Jamaludin bin Tuanku Alek was aged 25 and had been in the police since 1955. Constable Insoll Anak Chundang, aged 26 and single, was a Sea Dayak who had been a teacher before joining the Sarawak Constabulary. A fourth police officer, Constable Bujang bin Mohammed, 29, an experienced Malay police officer who had arrived in Limbang in 1961, died from wounds at 8.30am. They are commemorated on the waterfront memorial at Limbang. Constable Essa and Muling were missing. Muling was captured in the morning while hiding in-between the Police Barracks and Residency but managed to escape. The survivors were locked up in the Jail. Five rebels had been killed and seven wounded. Fritz Klattenhof, a Peace Corps member living in Limbang, was at liberty.

Raised on a dairy farm near Vancouver in south-east Washington State in the USA, Klattenhoff had joined the Peace Corps on 30 May 1962, the day after graduating from Battle Ground High School, Hilo, Hawaii. After training, he arrived in Sarawak in August to teach English and physical training; however his experience of dairy farming and his membership of the Future Farmers of America led to him being assigned to develop a Department of Agriculture project in Limbang on agriculture and fish farming. The Peace Corps programme in Sarawak was well advanced with a headquarters in Kuching and a number of individuals spread throughout the country.

While Morris was persuading the police officers to surrender, he identified an Iban, several Malays and about six Muruts siding with the TNKU. When he returned to their cell, Asan was so appalled at the dishevelled and humiliating state of the Resident that he gave him his Government Issue prison shorts to cover his torn underpants. They were a treasured gift and gave Morris much needed respectability. Asan had already given Mrs Morris his sleeping mat and pillow and a cup of coffee. The young lad was in tears and asked the rebels if he could stay to look after the Morrises but this, not surprisingly, was refused and he was practically ordered to return to his longhouse at Ulu Medamit, some two days' walk upriver. Also in the Jail were Mr Withers, of the Public Works Department, and three Roman Catholic priests from the Mission. This included Father Vaneman, a 30-year-old Dutchman. Highly respected in Limbang, he had recently been diagnosed with lung cancer and was due to be repatriated to the Netherlands. Also locked up was Mr King Shih Fan, the Divisional Engineer who, because he was a Hong Kong-born Chinese, was considered by the TNKU to be British. During the morning, District Officer Abang was placed under house arrest in his bungalow and guarded by three TNKU.

The capture of the Police Barracks meant that the TNKU had captured a Bren gun, a Sterling sub machine gun, several .303in rifles and shotguns. Khairul Salleh bin Kerudin, who had expected to lead the rebel attack in Fifth Division until his arrest in Lawas, took command of operations in Limbang. Although he believed that the combination of the hostages and his 300 men was sufficient to deter an assault, he deployed two companies to defend approaches from the river and placed the third in the jungle to the east. Sambas defended the Police Barracks with his Pandaruan Company, which had been reinforced by TNKU from North Borneo. Richard Morris, a former soldier, had noted that they were reasonably well disciplined and had demonstrated an ability to carry out simple infantry tactics of fire and movement.

The town of Limbang was firmly under TNKU control and patrols maintained a degree of tranquillity and prevented looting, although the premises of the Borneo Company Ltd was broken into and a large quantity of cigarettes taken. Morris lost a pair of binoculars, some clothing and linen and, for some unknown reason, an electric razor from the Residency. Some low value items were taken from other government houses but no jewellery or valuables. A systematic sweep of the bazaar enabled the rebels to collect shotguns and ammunition from shops, Government boats and outboards, and transistor radios. Morris later estimated the financial total of looted and stolen property and food amounted to about $40,000. About $60,000 was taken from the Limbang District Council offices, some of which was shared among the rebel rank and file. The rest was believed to have been shared between senior commanders in Limbang and at TNKU Command. However, when rumours later circulated that all was not going well twelve miles to the north in Brunei town, some began to desert.

The TNKU jailers made no attempt to feed or water their captives and left it up to the police officers to share the rations delivered by their wives. Morris did not believe that any brutality was intentional although there were a few individuals who were tougher and more rigorous than others. Later, a Chinese friend of the Morrises arranged for a member of his family to take bread, rice and cigarettes. Clean water was always a problem. Sanitary conditions were appalling, with the hostages being escorted to the toilet and an adjoining bathroom some 20yds behind the Jail. The lavatory was of the local squatter type and, within a short time, the combinations of increased occupancy and the toiletry habits of some TNKU being less meticulous than those of the Europeans soon ensured it became blocked. Privacy, in particular for Mrs Morris, was impossible. The hostages washed from a large jar of rainwater in the bathroom.

In the Seria oilfields, there was much less shooting. At 6.15am, Mrs P.M. Bennett, whose husband, Donald, worked in the Gas Processing Plant, bade him farewell after he said that he ought to go to work half-an-hour earlier, just in case there was trouble. He was one of those who had not gone to the Tombola the previous night because he was expecting a strike. At 7.30am, the driver of a car that took her to work mentioned that during the night the People's Party of Brunei had started a rebellion, intending to seize power. Mrs Bennett noted the absence of police and that the streets were empty of buses, taxis and people and then, at her office, she learnt that her clerk was a hostage in Seria Police Barracks. Her husband then telephoned her telling that he was also a hostage in the Barracks. Shocked and bewildered, she locked important documents in the strongroom and returned home to explain the situation to her amah, Ah Chuen, who undertook to pray to her goddess, Kwan Yin, for Mr Bennett's safe return.

Alastair Ker-Lindsay was on his way to Seria from Mr Linton's house in Panaga for a meeting. Not only was he sub-contracted by British Shell Petroleum on several construction projects, he was courting Linton's daughter, Penny. Ker-Lindsay was on his way to the refineries when he was stopped by a police roadblock where a police officer told him that there had been some trouble in the small hours of that morning and he should proceed to the Roxana Cinema car park, leave the keys in the ignition and report to the Police Barracks. Not suspecting anything, he did precisely what he was told and it was only when he was admitted into the Barracks that he realized that the 'police' were TNKU masquerading as police officers. Ker-Lindsay told them that they were stupid to think they would get away with such a stunt, whereupon he was called a 'white ant' and frogmarched to the 12 by 12ft cell containing fifty men, eight women and three children, and which became known as The Black Hole of Seria. The size meant that virtually everyone had to stand.

The hostages were a mix of Shell employees, contractors from World Wide Helicopters based at Anduki airstrip, a computer technician and a reverend. Ker-Lindsay was lucky that his Malay was good and he was able to keep abreast of what was happening. Later in the day, Mr Bennett persuaded the TNKU to allow him and seventeen oil workers to return to the refinery to keep the Gas Processing Plant machinery working, ensure the running of the oil field and reduce the risk of an explosion. Although he had been given a safe conduct pass, an armed and uniformed TNKU rejected this and the group returned to their cell, except for two who managed to escape. A Chinese shopkeeper, Mr Yick Fat, organized some food and cigarettes for the captives. This was fortunate because the TNKU had thought that the *coup d'état* would be quick and had not made any administrative arrangements for prisoners, let alone for themselves. That evening Mrs Bennett stayed with a friend whose husband had also been seized. Fat again telephoned to tell them that he had seen their husbands and they were not to worry. Other expatriates and Brunei citizens were confined to their houses and offices.

After dark, the women and children looked on helplessly as their jailers assembled forty-three male hostages and, after tying them up, drove them in lorries to a point on Jalan Tegah about 400yds from the besieged Panaga Police Station. They were then pushed into a column three abreast and prodded toward the compound perimeter gates, but the curfew was in force and since the police had orders to open fire at any movement, the first volley whistled over the heads of the column. The second one struck the leading files and instantly killed Clifford Joseph, the Eurasian air traffic controller at Anduki Airfield. Dr Brondijk was shot in the stomach and Tom Rae, in Shell Engineering, had his upper arm broken by a bullet. Mr Fisher, who was employed by an air conditioning company, was wounded in the thigh and Mr Eighme, sub-contracted by World Wide Helicopters, was also wounded, as were Mr Kirby, an aviation engineer, and Mr Knight of the Shell Transport Department. The guards leapt into a 4ft-deep monsoon ditch with 18in of water and mud, closely followed by the hostages, all of whom had wriggled free of their bonds and began to shout at the police officers to cease fire. For the next hour and a half a gun battle developed, with the TNKU firing a Bren gun in short bursts from the rear of the column over the heads of their human shield. Very light flares and flames from a gas line punctured by a bullet illuminated the body of Joseph lying on the road until a guard dragged it into the ditch, where he was declared dead. Dr McLean, a Shell doctor, reached Mr Brondijk and, finding that he had a serious abdominal wound, dragged him into the ditch where, by the light of matches and lighters, he stemmed the blood loss using shirts from other hostages. By 10.00pm the shooting was intermittent and under cover of the darkness fractured by flares, the guards and hostages withdrew along the ditch toward the Fire Station. The death of Joseph and the wounded unnerved several TNKU and Ker-Lindsay was able to convince one to hand over the keys to a Land Rover. Ker-Lindsay then confiscated a red fire engine and asked Mr Williamson, who was employed in Finance, to follow him to the Shell Hospital at Kuala Belait where he asked staff to open up the operating theatre so that hostages shot in the thigh and stomach could be treated. Meanwhile, Dr Brondijk had been dragged in great pain to the Land Rover where Dr McLean persuaded the TNKU to allow him to take the wounded to hospital. Brondijk underwent an operation.

By the time they returned to Seria Police Station four hours later, there were eighteen hostages; the remainder were casualties or had escaped. The hostages were returned to the Black Hole, filthy, cold and wet and unable to clean up because the washing facilities were not functioning.

Herbert Blanche, in the Shell Drilling Department, escaped from the ditch with a friend and, after running into the cover of the jungle, reached a bungalow, where they stayed until the next day. Avoiding rebel patrols, they reached a house near the Shell radio station. Blanche telephoned a work colleague and learnt that British troops were in Brunei Town.

There had also been casualties among the TNKU and when Sister Jean Scott, who was employed by the Brunei Government, was instructed at about 1.00am to treat a senior TNKU officer, she refused to do so and began negotiating the release of the women and children. She had created a makeshift clinic for the wounded hostages. Within the hour Sister Scott had secured the release of the eight women and four children and at about 2.00am, she drove them to their homes and then returned to the Police Station and took the wounded rebel leader to hospital. She returned to the Police Station and negotiated the release of Mr Eighme and Mr Rae and took them to the Government Clinic for stabilization before driving them to the Shell Hospital at Kuala Belait. Early next morning, Dr Sweetman, the Shell Chief Medical Officer, found her treating Rae and Eighme and after he had examined them he went to the Police Station to negotiate the release of two other wounded hostages, Mr Kirby and Mr Knight, but was then taken hostage himself. At about 2.00am Sister Scott took her two patients to Kuala Belait Hospital. For her courage and dedication, Sister Scott was awarded the MBE in May 1963.

Meanwhile, loyal police set about dominating areas not occupied by the TNKU by setting up roadblocks and searching any vehicle moving along the roads. Ker-Lindsay stayed in the hospital for the rest of the night and was joined, the next morning, by a group of loyal Iban workers from his Kuala Belait workforce, all of whom had received basic military training from him in preparation for this type of eventuality. The senior Ibans were selected by their capacity to drink beer; however, Ker-Lindsay's ability to sink three-quarters of a bottle of whisky, needless to say, gave him greater authority.

Evelyn Joseph, aged three years, was waiting for her father to come home to her birthday party. He never arrived. Mrs Bennett and her friend at the Panaga married quarters had heard the firing but had no idea that their husbands were in extreme danger. The anxiety of the night was heightened when a bullet knocked out a transformer near the Police Barracks. It was a long night interrupted by bursts of gunfire.

By dawn it was evident to Affendi that, while the attacks at Limbang and Seria had been successful, all was not going well elsewhere, particularly in Brunei Town. At 3.00am a courier had arrived at his headquarters at Bukit Salileh near Brunei Town to report that the police were resisting at Police Headquarters, and that Kuala Belait and Panaga police were also resisting. This was serious and when no more news arrived, at 4.30am Affendi and bin Karim, the TNKU Brunei Military Commander, decided to find out what was happening. At about 8.30am, they learnt that the Sultan was under police protection and that a general uprising had not happened. It was clear that determined police resistance had undermined the rebellion and so bin Karim paddled home to his *kampong* at Kilanas. He was arrested on 17 December. Affendi prepared to go on the run.

In Seria Sunday, 9 December was tense. Telephone conversations were kept to a minimum because the TNKU had captured the Telecommunications Centre, although a few expatriates racked their brains to recall French or perhaps Latin. Conditions among the hostages crowded in the police cells were very basic. There were very few mats and everyone slept on either the cold concrete or on a plank. The men who had been forced to march as human shields were filthy and cold. Another threat was made to use a human shield of all the hostages, including women and children, to force the surrender of Panaga Police Station and, if this failed, the oil field would then be set on fire and the Shell Company employees and residents murdered.

CHAPTER SIX

North Borneo

The only military force in North Borneo was Chisel Force; however, it was not diverted and consequently the authorities were left to their own devices, which they used with considerable efficiency complemented by good luck. When the North Borneo Special Branch assessed the reports of unrest in Brunei, the two towns nearest the border, Pantai and Sindumin, were showing little signs of agitation although it was becoming clear that Weston and the area around Lubok and Lingkungan were restless.

During the evening of 7 December, a confused message had been received from Kuching that 'widespread trouble was to be expected on the 8th and 9th'. The Assistant District Officer in Sipitang, John Parry, immediately placed his police stations on alert by doubling the duty watch that night. He also asked some reliable people to watch two important features, one on the coast and the other near Ulu Sipitang Road. One person who gave Parry moral support, practical common sense and a steadying influence in a period of considerable uncertainty was Tom Kajer, a member of the Peace Corps of Czech descent. Although Kajer was offered the opportunity to be evacuated to Labuan, he remained at Sipitang, a decision which did not sit well in an age when the United States saw itself on the side of the oppressed against British colonial rule, and which did not fit in with the pacifism expressed by the Peace Corps. He later found himself in trouble and was ordered back to the United States before the New Year.

The previous evening at Sipitang, Parry had collated a list of shotgun owners so that he could ask for their guns to be deposited in the District Office, but Inspector Osman of Special Branch thought this was not a good idea. Parry had no military experience but had spent vacations from university with the Merchant Navy employed by companies such as Union Castle and P&O. His only exposure to the military was when he was signed off a ship in Johore Bahru and travelled on a military train to Malacca towards the end of the Malayan Emergency. He had also read Mao Tse Tung's theories of revolutionary warfare and, over the next few days, applied four useful principles:

> When the enemy seems about to attack in force – withdraw.
> When the enemy encamps – harass him.
> When the enemy seeks to avoid battle – attack him.
> When the enemy retreats – pursue him.

At about 2.30am on 8 December at Sipitang, Parry received two reports, the first suggesting that a large number of people had been seen approaching the coast from Ulu Sipitang and the second one that an outboard motor had been heard in Brunei Bay about a mile out to sea. A police corporal then arrested the boatman entering the River Sipitang in a *prahu*, although there was a possibility he might have been a fisherman. There was also a report that the Weston to Beaufort train was missing. Parry was suspicious enough to patrol the town at 4.00am and then drove his Land Rover along the coast road about a mile-and-a-half to the east but did not encounter anything.

He was not aware that Jaya bin Hassan and sixty ARAS from Ulu Sipitang had been waiting since 2.00am at the junction of the main road at Milestone 1 to collect arms and ammunition being brought in by *prahu* from Brunei. Jaya was a TNKU platoon commander with responsibility for Masapol, Ulu Sipitang, Sipitang and Pantai, all of which were strategically placed on the road to the border. But when the group saw the headlights of the Land Rover they thought that they had been seen and the police were on the way to arrest them. The *prahu* also sheered away when the boatman saw the headlights. Only Jaya was armed with a revolver but in the scramble to leave he lost it. Inadvertently, Parry had prevented weapons being landed and destabilized unrest. Jaya's group was henceforth confined to using a few shotguns, home-made bombs and a few low calibre rifles.

At dawn Corporal Mohammed Ali, who commanded Sipitang Police Station, and Parry planned the defence of Sipitang. Several observation posts were identified and a large distress signal beacon built at Tanjong Marintaman to signal Labuan if communications failed and assistance was required. Meanwhile, Superintendent S.G. Ross, the Interior Residency Police Divisional Commander, was on his way to Lawas via Sipitang when he was met at Beaufort Railway Station by Inspector Makan Singh, who commanded Police District Beaufort, and Paul Dillimore, the Beaufort District Officer, who told him that he could not go on to Sipitang by rail. After being seriously damaged during the war, it had been repaired between 1949 and 1960 as a metre-gauge track carrying passengers, timber and other goods. The main railway ran to Jesselton. When Dallimore told Ross that he was worried about the situation in Weston, Ross agreed that a patrol should be sent from Sipitang to investigate. He then instructed that the ferry connecting Beaufort and Beaufort South be kept on the Beaufort side of the river and that the police ambush the riverbank and the road to Kota Klias.

Parry had returned from a proposed observation post near the beacon at about 10.00am when his chief clerk, Ismail bin Murah, informed him that instructions had been received to send as many police as possible to Weston immediately. Leaving a small number of men to guard the District Office, he sent five in a police Land Rover while he took a party of four men in a hired *prahu* and a Government *prahu*. He had no idea what to expect but thought it likely that Weston was probably to be attacked by the TNKU and that his force was part of a larger force being assembled from Beaufort sent to defend the port. Parry recalled:

> Passing Batu Batu I observed that the place seemed deserted. Lubok too showed no signs of activity and there seemed less boats there than usual. My two boats approached Weston in the normal manner staying a little further out than usual and the Government prahu about 300 yards behind. Until we came opposite to the wharf everything seemed fairly normal. The (missing) train was in the station and there were people in it and also walking out on the platform. On the wharf there were about fifteen armed men in green drill uniforms standing about quite casually and seemed pleased to see us approaching. It seemed obvious that a force of police from Beaufort was in control of the situation and I gave orders for the boatmen to put to shore. It was only then that a gust of wind moved

the flag at the wharf and I saw that it had the green red and white colours of the rebels. It later transpired that while I was convinced that Weston was in the control of the police, the insurgents on their part thought that my party were rebel reinforcements from Brunei! My choice of prahu was very inopportune. It was painted with the red and green of the Party Ra'ayat! The boatmen started to turn the prahu and the men on the wharf scattered and went down on their stomachs and also took up positions behind the buildings by the wharf and opened fire. The boatmen of our hired prahu leapt over the side and the man driving lay down on his face in the bottom of the boat. For at least 2 minutes the prahu was out of control and the position was extremely precarious. My force returned the fire while I got the engine operator to take control again. Our 40 horse power engine had stalled and so he started a small 10 horse power motor which pulled us slowly out of danger. There was a considerable amount of firing from the land and the water all around was being splashed with shot. The boat was struck several times, in one place by what must have been a .303 bullet. I considered that we had a narrow escape. The boatman who had been clinging to the side scrambled in again and the engine operator tried without success to get the 40 horse power engine started again. I called the Government prahu over and this helped to pull the larger boat along. The party had been very taken aback by the surprise engagement and I considered them unready to face the rebels again immediately.

Two boats had left Weston and were following us and the two boatmen in our prahu I can only describe as distraught with fear. I ordered the boats to land on the southern side of the Tanjong at Batu Batu so that everybody could be put into the larger boat and under the control of the Government boatmen who had remained calmer than their counterparts in our boat. The following rebel boats were seen to have landed on the other side of the tanjong so I placed guards on all the approaches to our landing place whilst we prepared the boats. I assessed the position as serious in that I had seen or heard no sign of my land party or of any force from Beaufort and so it seemed that a fairly significant armed uprising had taken place. Knowing that considerable ARAS support existed

> around Sipitang itself I decided that my place was to consolidate Sipitang into a defensive position and find out in due course what was happening to the north. I would have liked to have held Batu Batu but did not consider I could leave an adequate force there without seriously jeopardising the position of Sipitang. I therefore ordered the party to withdraw. This we did in the large prahu, towing the empty Government boat behind.

Parry returned to Sipitang and, contacting Dallimore, mentioned that the land party he had sent via Lingkungan had not returned. With Mobile Force police support, Parry then pinpointed the whereabouts of ARAS members and suspects in the town in case he was ordered to arrest them. Realizing that military support was not forthcoming, he began to prepare for the night and recruited volunteers from the local population for a defence force. Much to Parry's relief, the Transport Company Land Rover vehicle that had taken the land party to Weston had arrived back at about midday, the Chinese driver reporting that the patrol had been ambushed at Lingkungen and the vehicle damaged by a home-made bomb and hit by a bullet. After several anxious hours, the patrol returned in the evening having engaged a numerically superior TNKU force in the village and had then walked back to Sipitang. There were flurries of reports and rumours suggesting an imminent attack from Ulu Sipitang, Lubok and along the border by TNKU in Sarawak using the River Menggalong, which flowed close to the border south of Pantai. Uniformed men were reported assembling in at least five places close to Sipitang. The District Officer Labuan, Richard de-la-Poer Berrisford-Pierce, then sent a launch to collect Parry's wife, Barbara, their baby son, Mark, and the Peace Corps volunteer's wife, Mrs Kajer, which was fortunate because intelligence extracted from captured documents indicated they were to be murdered.

To defend Beaufort, Ross mobilized the Special Constabulary. Volunteers, who included members of the public and four European planters, namely Messrs McGilvray, Lawes, Robertson and Douglas, were enrolled as Specials and were to play an important role as guides for foot and mobile patrols, search teams and police reinforcements. They were active principally between 8 and 17 December and were gradually reduced in strength until 21 December when the force was disbanded. The enthusiasm of the Volunteers boosted loyalist morale and confirmed that the majority of North Borneo did not support rebellion. Sergeant Lai Shong Tai was instructed to keep the Chinese 'on side' by advising them of events. The tension increased at about midday when reports emerged that the two Land Rovers and 300 Bruneis approaching were, in fact, Sipitang Transport Co. Toyotas carrying ordinary passengers from Weston.

Expecting support from Superintendent S.G. Ross at some time during the night, Parry set about defending Sipitang and when he asked for Mobile Force reinforcements from Pantai, five police officers arrived in the late afternoon. With the help of volunteer labour, including boys from Sindumin Secondary School, concrete culverts were rolled from the Public Works Department depot underneath the District Office and then buttressed with telegraph posts. The defenders then had sheltered fire positions and somewhere dry and reasonably warm to shelter. A second position was in a large hole dug for storage tanks at the proposed Shell filling station. Throughout the night police and mobile Land Rovers and a Public Works Department lorry patrolled and although rebels were sighted twice, each time they dispersed before a patrol arrived.

A man arrived from Weston at about 10.00am reporting that the town had been occupied by some sixty TNKU during the early hours and that not only had the telephone line been cut but several Government officials had been captured and the rebels were talking about marching on Beaufort. By this time the Police patrol had been despatched but it was too late to recall them. Contact was then made with a railway employee about five miles north of Lingkungan. He was about to abandon his post but was unable to give much information of value. Ross reported this to Police Headquarters at Jesselton and, since he was confronted with a major problem over a wide area, requested reinforcements. He and Dallimore then established their headquarters in the Telephone Exchange. He had planned to use the radio in the Police Station Charge Room but it was susceptible to power surges and weak transmissions when power was low. Using the Telephone Exchange proved a wise decision because communication between Beaufort and Jesselton was only possible through the efforts of the Posts & Telegraphs Department telephone operator in Beaufort, who Ross later described as 'excellent'. While efforts were made to contact Jesselton, another man, Mr Jappar bin Lamit, arrived and confirmed the information given earlier by Matali that Weston had been occupied by the TNKU.

During the morning Ross had an erratic telephone call with Police Headquarters, in which it was suggested that a patrol should reconnoitre Weston but he preferred to attack with a larger force from Beaufort, and was instructed to wait until Mobile Force reinforcements arrived. News was then received from John Parry that Weston was still in rebel hands. In spite of Ross being instructed not to take any action, Dallimore was under no such authority and, at about 11.00am, set off for Weston until he received a report from Ross that at least 300 TNKU had landed at the port and were advancing on Beaufort, some in two Land Rovers. Ross set about defending Beaufort and instructed Inspector Singh to ensure that the ferry across the River Padas connecting Beaufort and Beaufort South be kept on the northern side of the river, thereby effectively creating a barrier to approaches along the road from the border crossing point with Sarawak. Ross also instructed that all available police were to be deployed in ambushes covering the rivers and the road to Kota Klias and that the northern beaches were also laced with ambushes. Everyone relaxed and at midday Dallimore organized lunch for the European defenders. It was while this was under way that Parry confirmed that Weston was in rebel hands. Police Reservists from Tambunan, Keningau and Tenom areas in the interior had already been mobilized by Police Headquarters, with seventeen reporting for duty at Beaufort. Police Headquarters advised Ross not to expect the arrival of the first Reservist reinforcements before 2.00pm. More Mobile Force would follow under the command of Sergeant Pengiran Salleh, a police officer who originated from Brunei. While waiting, Ross began planning the attack and asked Mr Dallimore to arrange road and rail transport. Sergeant Okala was to take over the defence of Beaufort, which would then release Inspector Singh to take over the Weston area once it had been recaptured. Okala would be reinforced by ten men from the batch commanded by Sergeant Pengiran. At about 2.30pm the first reinforcements of twenty Mobile Force under Inspector Ansibin arrived by train from Jesselton and, after being ferried across the river to Beaufort South station, boarded a train. At about 3.00pm the train left and when it reached Milestone 16, Ross's force transferred to two Public Works Department trucks and a Sarawak Borneo Timber Co. lorry and drove towards Weston. The train returned to

Beaufort to collect the reinforcements. At the Lumadan Estate, Ross telephoned a situation report over to Police Headquarters. The stop allowed the reinforcements from Jesselton to sort themselves out, fill their water bottles and buy some food from the Estate shop. One of the Volunteers, Mr McGilvray, returned to his estate. The convoy then passed through the Tunah Valley and arrived at Bukau Bridge where two Posts & Telegraph staff and a field telephone were collected. Rumours of TNKU activity were rife – the rebels were in the immediate vicinity; Lingkungan had surrendered to the rebels; the 300 TNKU had landed; and boats fitted with outboard engines were on their way up river from the Bay of Brunei.

With Sipitang safely under the control of Weston and confident that the rebels would not harm the inhabitants of Weston, Ross advanced to Milestone 6 at Kongsi, where the road and railway separated, which he made his overnight base. Accepting the risk that the rebels could send a force by river to Beaufort, he divided his men into two ambushes covering Burkau Bridge and the river controlled by Inspector Singh and a third ambush at Kongsi consisting of a police section, Dallimore and three planters. The field telephone was connected to Police Headquarters and Mr Davies, while Mr Roberston, the Tunah Valley Estate manager, organized a meal from the estate shop. Soon it was dark and heavy rain set in which lasted all night. During the night, the fifteen police reinforcements commanded by Sergeant Salleh arrived, as did Mr Davies with ten more police. Now the force numbered forty-five men. A few days previously Davies had handed over the appointment of the Interior Residency Superintendent to Ross.

At 5.00am Ross assembled his men and divided his mixed bag of Regular Mobile Force, Reservists, General Duty and Europeans into the Road and Rail Groups, each of about twenty-five men, with Davies on the train while he took the road. Orders were issued to attack Weston. After the heavy equipment was loaded on the train, he briefly exercised the men in detraining drills and then at 6.00am, as dawn was creeping across the steamy jungle, the advance continued with Mr Dallimore recommending that both groups approach the next objective of Lingkungan on foot. The village was entered. Ross learnt from the villagers that the TNKU had stolen their firearms; otherwise everyone was unharmed. He was also made aware of the damaged Public Works Department lorry and Transport Company that had been ambushed the previous day. The force continued on foot and entered Weston at about 8.00am without further incident. Ross ordered all round defence and that the men should have breakfast before moving on to Kampong Lubok, which was reported to be in rebel hands. The missing train was found intact and the railway serviceable. Shopkeepers said that the rebels had left the previous evening at about 5.00pm taking captured firearms with them.

While Ross was debriefing the Rural Constable, whose police post was on the wharf, there was a commotion and he was informed that a *prahu* had been sighted about 200yds offshore and was acting suspiciously. A Bren gun team in a house some distance from the wharf was about to open fire when Inspector Singh restrained them because, of the twelve men seen on board, two or three wore civilian clothes and the rest were in jungle green and might be Mobile Force reinforcements from Sipitang. When the *prahu* suddenly altered course and disappeared behind a headland, Ross followed police officers rushing towards the Government Primary School where a civilian indicated where the *prahu* had landed its passengers. Ross ordered Superintendent Davies and Inspector Ansibin to deploy their sections in an extended line across a small plateau of high grass and coconut trees. However, the ground was deceptive and the pursuit slowed to a crawl when the extended line plunged into a swamp. Believing it unlikely that those on the *prahu* would have landed in the swamp, Ross told his men to look for a path and asked District Officer Dallimore to return to Weston, warn those manning the defensive positions of the landing and find a guide. While the police were wading through the swamp, a Reserve Policeman slipped and his rifle went off. A shot was then returned from undergrowth a few yards away from the police officers and then a chase developed when three men were seen running into the distance. Shortly before Dallimore returned with a guide, a track through the swamp was found; however, the guide insisted on leading the column along a narrow and rotten catwalk to an old sawmill about a quarter of a mile away. Just before they reached it, an outboard motor was heard in the Bay of Brunei and it was assumed that the three men had escaped. Somewhat dispirited, Ross returned to Weston at about 10.00am to find that Parry had arrived from Sipitang.

Parry had been under the impression that Ross would be going to Sipitang and left the town with two Land Rovers and a lorry to ferry his men there. At Lingkungan he found the vehicles left by Ross across the road about an hour earlier. He arrived at Weston shortly after Ross and Dallimore had returned after their fruitless pursuit through the swamp some twenty minutes earlier. Since Lubok and Batu Batu had yet to be recaptured, Parry was reinforced with a section of ten mixed Mobile Force men and Jesselton Constabulary under Sergeant Salleh, and left for Sipitang at midday.

For the attack on Lubok, Ross requisitioned two *prahus* fitted with outboards and a *kumpit* from Orang Tua Suleiman and Chew Kim Ting, two Weston businessmen. A *kumpit* is a small motorized inshore cargo vessel able to carry 25 tons and, since the owner frequently lived on board, there was usually a cabin aft. Ross and Davies took the two *prahus,* skippered by the boatman-owner and carrying five police officers. The deeper draught of the *kumpit* meant it could not pull alongside the jetty and Ross intended to use the *prahus* to ferry his force ashore, as well as evacuate casualties and prisoners to Weston.

There were an estimated seventy TNKU activists in the kampong. Dallimore again decided to leave Weston but then changed his mind and travelled in the *kumpit.* Leaving Inspector Singh and a small party to police Weston, the assault force left at 11.00am and sailed up river toward Lubok. As the force approached Batu Batu, three men in a *prahu* were recognized as the suspects seen during pursuit that morning. Ross was about to order the police on the *kumpit* to alter course and intercept the *prahu* when he saw it change direction anyway and head toward the jetty. In fact, it was avoiding shallows. Ross then stood off while Mr Davies headed for the jetty where the three men were arrested without trouble. All were in possession of TNKU paraphernalia. When one of the men was identified by the timber yard manager, Mr Ambrose Chin, as having stolen his shotgun the previous day, the police searched the yard and surrounding area. Ross left the *kumpit* at Batu Batu with a small rear party under the command of Dallimore while he joined Davies in the second *prahu*. The captured *prahu* was used to ferry five police officers.

As the small flotilla approached Lubok, Ross signalled to the other *prahus* to land the police, while he deterred several *prahus* from darting into a nipah swamp by ordering his four men to open fire into the river. This had the desired effect of the rebels sheepishly returning to Lubok, except for one who had a lengthy lead in front of the others and who reached the safety of the swamp. Ross's group landed and swept round the left hand side of the kampong while Davies carried out a similar sweep to the right and then drove the villagers out of their houses into two groups on the beach. A search of houses revealed a home-made bomb in the house owned by an ARAS lieutenant and, scattered around the surrounding area were six shotguns, a .22in and a .28in rifle, parangs, spears, jungle boots and TNKU uniforms, flags, insignia and other accoutrements of war, most of it concealed in boats, boat sheds and wells. The complicity of Lubok in the rebellion was obvious and sixty-eight men were ferried under guard to Batu Batu in the *prahus* and then taken to Weston in the *kumpit*. The arrest of the lieutenant was significant because he was one of the three TNKU company commanders in North Borneo.

When Parry returned to Weston, Police Headquarters asked if his force could go to Sipitang, but with his men needing rest and dry clothes, he convinced his superiors that he would be ready the next morning. Mr Lucarotti, who managed the train, then arrived in Weston and agreed that the prisoners should be taken to Beaufort that evening with the three remaining planters and police as an escort. The next day, the planters returned to their estates. When Ross learnt during the evening that one of the Weston raiders had returned to his house, he was arrested by the police and sent to Beaufort.

As Parry was returning to Sipitang and was passing through Lingkungan, he arrested a man armed with a gun. Parry felt it important to seed the idea among the TNKU that they were being pursued and so should feel discouraged from taking any initiatives. In Sipitang he disrupted unrest and dominated the TNKU by arresting and screening suspects. Intelligence assessments indicated that there were about thirty activists in the town. These local operations gave the reinforcements under Sergeant Salleh time to rest. Forty irregulars had also been recruited and a Mobile Force corporal gave them rudimentary training, which included live firing from a defended position. That evening Parry led a mobile patrol to the Palakat area in order to enlist recruits for the irregulars and during a search and question operation picked up two suspects. He increased his perimeter to beyond the bridge on the southern edge of the town and responded to persistent rumours of an imminent attack by vigorous foot patrols. He kept his vehicles as a mobile reserve. By this time the District Office Land Rover had been equipped as an armoured car with the ventilator shutters raised so that rifles and shotguns could fire over the bonnet. No contact with the rebels was made. He also sent a section of irregulars to guard the important telephone exchange at Masapol.

On 10 December, John Parry began planning to attack rebels suspected to be in Masapol Lama and Lubok Darot, two kampongs five miles north of Masapol, confiscate registered and known weapons and, hopefully, arrest two ARAS leaders. Leaving Sipitang, Parry divided his fifty men into three sections and had five four-wheel drive vehicles. Taking the kampong by surprise, while one section guarded the vehicles, Parry led the third section through the centre of the kampong and, marching four miles, arrested an ARAS leader and then doubled back to meet up with Sergeant Salleh, who marched three miles and arrested another ARAS leader at his house. Twenty-one suspects were arrested, seventeen from their homes, and a search resulted in eleven weapons, two bombs and a large amount of paraphernalia of insignia, flags and uniforms seized. One man fired at the Security Forces and then tried to get away.

Parry returned to Sipitang at about 10.00am and found that Superintendents Ross and Davies and Paul Dallimore had arrived from Weston. The group had left the port at 7.30am with Davies going by sea while Ross and Dallimore travelled by road in Public Works Department and Sipitang Transport Co. trucks and vehicles along a road that was in a poor state, and always under threat of ambush. Their arrival meant Weston and the area north of Sipitang were generally under government control. It was now time to dominate the area along the Sarawak border and prevent and deter TNKU penetrating either as activists or fleeing from the military operations in Brunei and Fifth Division.

Ross placed his HQ at Sindumin, a village almost on the border. Selecting Sipitang as the strongpoint, he ordered that the Government offices be further fortified and instructed Parry to continue dominating the town and rear area but not to encroach into the border area. The town would also be the collection point for prisoners. Ross was given the Marine Department launch *Sangitan* to patrol Brunei Bay.

Parry accompanied Dallimore to Beaufort with the prisoners captured at Masapol with an escort of several police and about twenty volunteers. Parry then continued the strategy of dominating the rear areas by arresting thirteen suspects around Masapol and Nalagun and recovering forty-three weapons as well as flags and uniforms. The arrests resulted in several TNKU officials surrendering in the knowledge that they would be picked up sooner or later. He assigned ten irregulars to reinforce the Home Guard and extended the town defence perimeter to include the bazaar and Telephone Exchange.

Ross and his force left Sipitang at midday on 10 December and drove west in Sipitang Transport Co. vehicles to Pantai, which was about six miles west of the border, where they met Inspector Mohammed Yassin, of the Mobile Force, who had been bearing the brunt of tension along the border long before the Brunei Revolt materialized. Tired but cheerful, Ross was impressed with everything that Yassin had done. He gave him two of the vehicles and arranged petrol and extra batteries for his radio. While Ross stayed in Pantai, Superintendent Davies and a detachment of police officers led by Inspector Ansibin left for Sindumin by river with instructions to search *kampongs* in the area and to pay particular attention to Mengalong, Sipotol and the border area bounded by Sindumin in North Borneo and Merapok across the border. Since Pantai was thought to have about fifty TNKU activists and was believed to be an assembly area for those who crossed into North Borneo, the afternoon was spent identifying ambush positions on cross-border tracks and improving defences.

The following day, 11 December, the police patrolled Pantai and, searching several houses, made arrests and recovered items associated with the TNKU. When activists from Ulu Sipitang surrendered to Parry, he despatched patrols into the area with the deliberate intention of causing anxiety and then sent a circular advising that anyone involved in the rebellion had two choices – voluntarily surrender or be arrested. Within twenty hours, more than fifty men had surrendered to a volunteer patrol and his own patrols were guarding more than eighty suspects.

Deputy Police Commissioner Plunkett visited Pantai and stayed overnight, leaving Police Commissioner Donald Matheson to control operations from Police Headquarters. The Resident, Mr John Wicksteed, visited Lingkungan with a police patrol and arrested several people. So far, about 120 TNKU and ARAS suspects had been picked up or had surrendered and had then been sent to police interrogation centres at Beaufort and Jesselton. Native Chief Haji Yacob was doing a good job building morale and organizing resistance in Masapol and Falakat while Native Chief Mulok was active in helping the colonial authorities in the Pantai and Sudamin area.

CHAPTER SEVEN

Singapore 8 December

After conferring with Lord Selkirk, at 1.30am Admiral Luce instructed HQ Far East Land Forces (FARELF) to activate Plan Ale Yellow placing 99 Brigade on notice. But the General Officer Commanding, Lieutenant General Sir Nigel Poett, was in the Philippines attending a scheduled military demonstration and command had been devolved to his Chief-of-Staff, Major-General W. Olding. An early member of the Parachute Regiment, Poett had commanded 5 Parachute Brigade during the D-Day Normandy landings. The notice came as something of a surprise because intelligence sent by/to HQ Far East had not been shared.

Olding instructed Brigadier Jack Glennie DSO, Deputy Commander, Singapore Base District, to assemble Initial Ale Force with orders from Admiral Luce that 'You will proceed to Brunei and take command of all land, sea and air forces for Borneo Territory and restore the situation.' It is reported, but not verified, that when the War Office was notified of the deployment, the duty officer had difficulty finding Brunei on the Operations map. Glennie had commanded 1 Royal Sussex during the unsuccessful storming of Monte Cassino in Italy in 1944.

The 99 Gurkha Infantry Brigade Group Officers Mess Guest Night was in full swing when, at about 1.30am, the news broke from Singapore District that Plan Ale had been activated, but no more. Brigadier Patrick Patterson, who commanded 99 Gurkha Infantry Brigade, was told that although HQ FARELF was aware of the political turmoil in British North Borneo and Indonesia's aspirations for South-East Asia, one intelligence assessment suggested the revolt might be connected with Chin Peng's Communist Terrorists, then lurking in southern Thailand, opening a front in Borneo. Nevertheless, Patterson was furious that Glennie was in command because he felt that since he was providing troops for Ale Force, he ought to command, but there was nothing he could do but instruct 1 Queens Own Highlanders to provide two companies.

The Battalion had been formed the previous year from the amalgamation of the Seaforth Highlanders and the Queens Own Cameron Highlanders. Recruiting from the Highlands of Scotland, the Western Isles and the Orkneys, the Regiment traced its history back to the raising of the 78th Highland Regiment in 1778, just thirty-two years after the defeat of Bonnie Prince Charlie at Culloden in 1746. In 1793, the 78th joined with the 72nd Highland Regiment to form the 78th Highland Regiment, which in 1881 became the Seaforth Highlanders. The Cameronian Highlanders was raised in 1793 as the 79th Foot. Both regiments saw service during the wars against the Napoleonic French, in India, Crimea, Afghanistan, South Africa and both world wars. Eighteen Seaforths and four Cameronians were each awarded a Victoria Cross.

In the internal security role in Singapore the Battalion retained the usual three rifle companies, each of three platoons, which were usually commanded by a subaltern, supported by the Platoon Sergeant and two radio operators, one carrying a rear link radio set to Company HQ and the second with a radio forward to the sections. Sections were organized into a Rifle Group of six riflemen and a 7.62mm Bren group of two, commanded by a lance corporal, who doubled up as the section second-in-command. Since battalions used for internal security had no need for reconnaissance, mortar, anti-tank and machine gun support, Support Company platoons were converted into rifle platoons and split between the companies giving each four platoons. HQ Company consisted of Battalion HQ, Signals Platoon, Intelligence Section and Quartermaster Platoons of drivers, storemen, cooks and a Medical section with a Royal Army Medical Corps medical officer and several regimental medical assistants.

The Commanding Officer was Lieutenant Colonel Charles McHardy MBE MC. Commissioned into the Seaforth Highlanders in October 1939 and posted to the 2nd Battalion in July 1940, McHardy fought in the newly-formed 51st Highland Division at El Alamein during the pursuit of the Afrika Corps to Tunis and had been awarded the Military Cross as a company commander at Wadi Akarit when the Germans fought a tough rearguard action to protect their retreat to Tunis. After landing in Sicily, he commanded the battalion for a short time after all the officers senior to him were either killed or wounded in stiff fighting near Mount Etna. Landing in Normandy, he was so badly wounded near Caen ten days later that his front line service ended. After attending the Haifa Staff College, he was appointed as Brigade Major 3 Infantry Brigade in Palestine and was awarded the MBE. McHardy then had a series of staff appointments dispersed with Regimental duty in Malaya, the Suez Canal Zone and with the British Army of the Rhine. He served for three-and-a-half years on the Directing Staff at Camberley Staff College before taking command of the 1 Queens Own Highlanders at Selarang Barracks in Singapore.

Although his battalion was the stand-by battalion, it was not on notice to move; indeed, McHardy was looking forward to greeting his in-laws due to arrive from the United Kingdom on Saturday, 8 December. Since August, one company and additional platoon had been in North Borneo as Chisel Force to help the police tackle piracy from the Philippines. In October A Company, plus a B Company platoon commanded by Major Ian Cameron, had rotated as Chisel Two and had been scheduled to rotate with Chisel Three of D Company and 7 Platoon, B Company in the last weekend of November; but the battalion had been placed on alert during that weekend and the rotation was postponed. When the alert was cancelled on 1 December, Brigadier Patterson confirmed that Chisel Three should rotate on 6/7 December. McHardy welcomed Chisel Two at RAF Changi and sent the Jocks on leave until 10 December. That evening McHardy joined friends for dinner at a restaurant on Orchard Street. He did not attend, as is sometimes suggested, the Mess Dinner. Soon after returning from the restaurant at about 11.30pm, his Duty Officer advised him to telephone Brigade HQ as soon as he returned. McHardy recalled:

> I spoke to the Brigade Major who told me that during their Guest Night, they had received Ale and I was to get two Companies ready to move at very short notice. I pointed out that there were only two Companies in Singapore and that one of them had only just returned a few hours earlier from British North Borneo and that many married men were now scattered in married Quarters across

> Singapore and it would take a little time to recall them. I then went, at midnight, to Ian Cameron's house to tell him that his Company was to be recalled from weekend leave and was to be ready to fly back to Borneo/Brunei later in the day.

At the office of Sir Geoffrey Tory, the British High Commissioner to Malaya in Phoenix Park, Kuala Lumpur, the situation was unclear and although the existence of the TNKU, as a uniformed military organization, was known, its intentions seemed muddled. No-one was quite sure of the rationale behind the unrest, particularly as the European executive of a car company based in Kuala Belait, who had left Brunei the previous day, had not reported any signs of trouble. When an Army spokesman at HQ Far East, Major J.H. Vaughan-Johnson, announced that 'Her Majesty's Government is placed in a position to carry out its obligations with the Brunei Government', it was a consequence to the build up of intelligence. He inferred that follow-up forces would be technicians and engineers to repair damaged infrastructure. The Malayan Government maintained that resolving the insurrection was a matter between the Brunei and British Governments.

With delays already creeping into Plan Ale, Brigadier Patterson instructed 1st Battalion, 2nd King Edward VII's Own Gurkha Rifles (1/2 Gurkha Rifles) to supply the two companies. He then telephoned McHardy at 4.00am and placed his Battalion on immediate notice to follow 1/2 Gurkha Rifles by air but said that no move was expected before 6.00am on Monday, 10 December.

Based at Slim Barracks, Singapore 1/2 Gurkha Rifles was commanded by Lieutenant Colonel Gordon Shakespear MC, another member of his family to continue the long association with the Regiment. He been awarded the Military Cross during the Battle of Monte Cassino in Italy. With four rifle companies, Gurkha battalions were stronger than their British counterparts. Support Company in the infantry role was sometimes titled E Company. Companies were commanded by British officers and the three platoons by Queens Gurkha Officers, who were commissioned from the ranks and usually highly experienced. Some in 1962 had seen battle in Burma and during the Malayan Emergency. British subalterns joining Gurkha battalions did not gain command experience at platoon level but were trained to command companies. The most senior Gurkha in the battalion was the Gurkha Major and an accolade from him was an accolade indeed.

But the Battalion was also below strength. One B Company platoon was 500 miles to the north on operations against the Communist Terrorists on the Thai border. Training eighty miles to the south in Kluang were the Assault Pioneers, in radio contact. The Mortar and Machine Guns Platoons were on the ranges in South Johore, while C Company, commanded by Captain Tony Lea, was scheduled to begin four week's basic jungle warfare training for a new intake of recruits who had recently arrived from the Brigade of Gurkhas Training Depot in Nepal. The previous week had been busy. On 3 and 4 December, B Company had combed the jungle in South Johore searching for the navigator of a crashed Javelin aircraft. More important, the battalion was midway through its annual Administrative Inspection.

Administrative Inspections took place in the autumn at the end of the training year. It was a formality that units dreaded because low assessments from a board of inspecting officers and technical experts could be career-limiting. Plans and procedures needed to be up to date and one was usually tested. Weapons, vehicles and clothing were checked for serviceability. Rooms and personal lockers were inspected, as were the Quartermaster and Technical Stores to check they were stocked with the relevant equipment, and cookhouses and messes for hygiene. It was a spring clean in depth. Unpopular though it may have been, the 'Admin' was to ensure that units were properly equipped and ready for any reasonable eventuality. For 1/ 2 Gurkhas several issues had been resolved on the Friday and Lieutenant Colonel Shakespear was anticipating a round of golf on Saturday afternoon. But when, at 5.00 am on Saturday, 8 December, he was telephoned by the Brigade Major, HQ 99 Gurkha Infantry Brigade Group and instructed that, under Plan Ale, he was to allocate two Tactical HQs and two companies, each of two platoons, for deployment to Brunei with the Initial Force and to be ready to move by 4.00pm, it did not make sense because the Plan was the commitment of the British Battalion not the Gurkhas. Initially believing that it was an 'Admin' test, he telephoned his Adjutant, Captain Digby Willoughby, and told him that the battalion was to identify two companies and asked that he obtain a copy of Operation Ale from Brigade HQ. Calling for an Orders Group for 7.00am, Shakespear then went to HQ FARELF where Major

General Olding briefed him on the situation in Brunei. But the Intelligence lacked detail. Assured that the deployment was not an 'Admin' test, Shakespear returned to Slim Barracks and alerted his Second-in-Command, Major Tony Lloyd-Williams, that he would command the deployment to:

Secure Brunei Town
Restore law and order
Recapture the Seria oilfield area and relieve Panaga Police Station

The paraphernalia of riot control equipment, such as batons, shields, bugles and the banner instructing the crowd to disperse, was to be left behind. When the banner was unfurled, mishaps were not unusual – upside down, the wrong way round or blown away in the wind, it often caused amusement among the rioters.

Since C Company was scheduled to depart on jungle warfare training during the day, when Shakespear instructed Captain Lea to allocate Company HQ and two platoons of his new intake for Plan Ale, Lea selected 7 and 8 Platoons. Lea had just returned to the battalion from a two-year secondment with the Singapore Police, then making deep inroads into the criminality of Chinese gangs. However, he was not particularly pleased because he had spent most of the night on a toilet with an upset stomach and was tired and weak. Nevertheless, he accepted that C Company was the logical choice. He then met with Lieutenant Peter Duffell, the Intelligence Officer, who confirmed the operation was for real but could only give him a map of Kuching, the capital of Sarawak, which Lea thought a little odd since he thought he was going to Brunei. He had recently spent a leave in the Protectorate and had some idea of its geography and culture. Major Bob Waterton commanding D Company provided the second Company HQ and two platoons. Both companies carried out a rapid re-organization to reform from the internal security order of battle, where Warrant Officers and senior sergeants commanded platoons, to Shakespear's insistence that the platoons be commanded by a Queens Gurkha Officer. Warrant Officer Two Lalitbahadur, who had been commanding a C Company platoon, stepped aside to become Company Sergeant Major. The consequence of this re-organization meant that the platoon commanders found themselves commanding men they did not know. When it became clear that Plan Ale stipulated an air-portable deployment, Lea mentioned to Shakespear that before being posted back to the Battalion, he had completed a Unit Emplaning Officers course with the Duke of Edinburgh's Royal Regiment in Tidworth and had learnt how to calculate the number of fully equipped men or vehicles or a combination of both that could be loaded into different types of transport aircraft. When he suggested that since a Unit Emplaning Officer would be required to deploy the remainder of the battalion, he should not also command C Company, Shakespear told him to get on with commanding his Company and be ready to act as Unit Emplaning Officer, if required.

By 9.00am the Initial Force was at Plan Ale Yellow – ready to move. General knowledge about the deployment was not well known in Singapore so that when the Regimental Quartermaster Sergeant arrived at 3rd Base Ordnance Depot to collect ammunition, he was told to return on Monday. At the FARELF Royal Engineer map store, Captain Duffell was told that the storeman man had a weekend pass. Although entry was made, there were no maps of Brunei. Transport to take Initial Force to RAF Seletar was available... after the school run had finished at 1.00pm. As Servicemen and their families looked forward to Christmas and the New Year break, very few anticipated that within days their idyllic postings would burst into life as the British helped the authorities in Brunei and would then become involved in the Confrontation with Indonesia that lasted until 1966.

Due to intelligence from Brunei indicating that the situation was extremely serious and that hostages had been seized, at 10.15am HQ FARELF ratcheted Plan Ale to Ale Red – immediate deployment. Brigadier Glennie planned to seize and defend Brunei Airport ready for the fly-in of the remainder of the Battalion and exploitation into the town. Eight hours after the rebellion had broken out at 2.00am, a British force was ready to move. Brunei Town appeared to be generally under police control. Police Headquarters, the Sultan's Palace, and the Prime Minister's house were in loyalist hands; however, there was fierce fighting around the power station. The road from the airport, two miles to the north of the town, was being threatened. The rest of the country was essentially in rebel hands, including the oilfields. Muara, Sengkurong, Tutong and Seria had all been seized. Hostages had been taken. Panaga and Kuala Belait police stations were resisting. Limbang was thought to have fallen, although information was very limited.

When, during the afternoon, Brigadier Patterson brought forward the deployment of the Queens Own Highlanders to 4.00pm on Sunday, 9 December, either by sea or by air and either as a two-company force or the strongest order of battle that he could muster, Lieutenant Colonel McHardy reformed the Medium Machine Gun and Assault Pioneers of Support Company and the Pipes and Drums into two rifle platoons, which he distributed one each to A and B Companies, giving them each four platoons. By 2.00am his Battalion was ready to move. It was a significant effort, particularly as A Company had returned from North Borneo just thirty-six hours before. Key to the deployment was that McHardy had followed the Battalion Air Portability Standing Instructions almost to the letter so that his men knew where they had to be, appropriately equipped, and when. Very few adjustments were required. A sea move was easier – board and land.

Aircraft were key to the rapidity of the deployment. HQ Far East Air Force at RAF Changi issued orders to Headquarters 224 Group, which controlled Royal Air Force, Royal Australian Air Force and Royal New Zealand Air Force operations from Singapore and Malaya respectively, to assemble as many serviceable aircraft as it could from its three bases at Singapore. The activation of Plan Ale Yellow had alerted 224 Group at 8.00am. When the Group ordered 209 Squadron to assemble its Twin Pioneers, Wing Commander Graves, who had spent the night in Kuching en route for a planned visit to Singapore, received the message at 8.00am and returned to Labuan. Squadron Leader Melville Bennett, who commanded 34 Squadron at RAF Seletar, was warned to have three Beverley transports ready by midday. The Blackburn Beverley was the largest transport carrier operated by the RAF. Specifically designed for parachute heavy drop operations, it was a stubby aircraft with a distinctive twin boom and fondly referred to as 'the furniture van' or insulted as 'a loosely assembled collection of spare parts'. Slow and lumbering with a maximum speed of 238mph, it could carry a payload of 29,000lbs or eighty troops a distance of about 1,300 miles.

Situated at the most eastern point of Singapore was RAF Changi, which had been built by Allied prisoners of war and forced labour during the Japanese occupation. Cooled by the Johore Straits sea breezes that reduced humidity, it had been modernized in the decade since 1952 into one of the most pleasant RAF stations. With the imminent demise of troopships and all Transport Command services in the Far East or en route to Australasia and Hong Kong transiting through Singapore, not only was its runway capable of taking the heaviest military and civilian aircraft, technical support was good. The Station had achieved international airport status. Its full range of services and facilities included decent accommodation, married quarters, a hospital, schools and social and recreational clubs, high on the wooded slopes leading from Ferry Point. Also based at RAF Changi was the Far East Communication Squadron and the Avro Shackleton Mark 1 and 2 Maritime Reconnaissance, plus anti-submarine warfare and search-and-rescue aircraft of 205 Squadron, and the Bristol Freighters of 41 Squadron Royal New Zealand Air Force. Recently, 48 Squadron Royal Air Force had converted from twin-engine Valettas to four-engine Handley-Page C3 Hastings transports, which could carry fifty passengers or a freight payload of 75,000lbs a distance of 3,280 miles at maximum speed at 22,200 feet. By chance on 8 December, Far East Air Force had more transport aircraft than usual on the ground, including a four-engined Bristol Britannia long range transport crewed by 99 and 511 Squadron at RAF Changi. It had a payload of 185,000 lbs and a cruising speed of 360mph and a maximum range of 5,334 miles.

RAF Tengah was nearing the end of extensive modernization and was busy with five operational squadrons; 60 Squadron was equipped with Gloster Javelin Mark 9 all-weather fighters. Rugged and efficient, armed with four Firestreak air-to-air missiles and two 30mm Aden cannon and equipped with sophisticated radar, it was the first all-weather fighter 'weapon platform'. Alternatively, it could fire four packs of 37.2in air-to-air rockets. Next, 20 Squadron, equipped with Hawker Hunter GA-9s day fighter/ground attack, had recently transferred from 2nd Tactical Air Force in West Germany. Armed with four 30mm Aden cannon and a capability to carry up to 1,000lbs of bombs or rockets, Hunters could dive at supersonic speed. Next, 45 Squadron was equipped with English Electric Canberra B-5 bombers (75 Squadron Royal New Zealand Air Force was also equipped with Canberras). It had spent a turbulent ten years with six different types of aircraft and had been moved around several times, most recently to Royal Australian Air Force Butterworth in Malaya. Finally, 81 Squadron was equipped with the long range Canberra PR7, the photographic-reconnaissance version.

RAF Seletar was the oldest and largest air station on Singapore and since its single runway could not be lengthened to accommodate post-

1945 fast and heavy aircraft, it was restricted to daytime flying on near minimum payloads. It suffered from humidity and substantial problems were experienced in keeping equipment and material free from corrosion. Nevertheless, technical support provided by 389 and 390 Maintenance Units was good. The base was also HQ 224 Group which, in 1962, was commanded by Air Vice-Marshal Headlam of the Royal Australian Air Force. The base housed three units. Apart from 34 and 209 Squadrons, 66 Squadron was also based there. Equipped with medium lift Westland Belvedere helicopters in June, its crews were still undergoing familiarization training.

In Malaya, 52 Squadron at RAF Butterworth was equipped with twin-engined Valetta medium range freighters providing VIP flights, air ambulances, flying classrooms and air despatch. With a maximum payload of 36,500lbs, it had a maximum speed of 258mph and a range of 1,460 miles. The Royal Australian Air Force was equipped with Lockheed C-130 Hercules medium range tactical transport. Not yet in service with the RAF, it had a maximum payload of 155,000lbs (ninety-two fully equipped soldiers), a range of 4,780 miles and a maximum speed of 385mph.

By 12.30pm, Initial Force HQ and C Company, 1/2 Gurkhas had arrived at RAF Seletar while D Company was on its way to Changi. But the Saturday had seen difficulties in assembling aircrew and ground maintenance teams from married quarters, shopping trips and recreation, and in resolving flight plans. Heavy rain hampered refuelling and thus it was not until 1.00pm that the aircraft were ready. The aircraft were ordered to depart by 224 Group first at 2.30pm, then 3pm and then 3.30pm.

In Labuan at 12.40pm, Wing Commander Graves instructed Pilot Officer Pearce and Flying Officer Garlick, who were supporting Chisel Force Three at Tawau in North Borneo, to fly a North Borneo Police Mobile Force company from Jesselton to Brunei. Three more Twin Pioneers, who had just spent the week searching for the Javelin crew, returned to Labuan.

Also included in Initial Force were Major W.J.B. Seager, who had been allocated from Transport and Barracks Branch, HQ 17th Gurkha Division to requisition billets and negotiate local purchases of fuel and other supplies, and Corporal Holdsworth and his three signallers provided by

249 Gurkha Signals Squadron to supply the rear link to Singapore in their Land Rover fitted with a C-53 High Frequency radio. Their Squadron Commander, Major Webb, was en route from the Thai border where he had been observing an exercise. The Force HQ Defence Section was provided by Corporal Sharpe and three troopers with two Land Rovers from the Queens Royal Irish Hussars. The regiment had arrived from Aden in October as the Theatre Armoured Reconnaissance Regiment. They were organized into three 'sabre' Troops, each of two Saladin armoured cars packing a 76mm main armament and four Ferret Scout Cars with a turret-mounted .30in Browning, plus an Assault Troop of dismounted cavalry in Saracen Armoured Personnel Carriers.

When Brigadiers Patterson and Glennie hurried to RAF Seletar to see Major Lloyd-Williams depart, they found Captain H. Higgins, an Air Transport Liaison Officer, and a small detachment of RAF movement staff, marshalling the Gurkhas into payloads by weighing them and entering their names on a manifest list as they waited to board the three 34 Squadron Beverley earmarked for Operation Ale. Captain Lea had provided the Movements staff with a nominal roll of his Company HQ and two platoons; however, it showed only surname. But some riflemen had identical names, as in some Welsh battalions with a proliferation of Jones, Williams and Hughes, where such soldiers were identified by the last three numbers of their regimental numbers. But Lea had omitted this. While Lea insisted his priority was to ensure that his Gurkhas embarked, Movements insisted that each man should be listed. However, further confusion developed when the nervous young soldiers whose English was limited were asked to spell their names. Lea's driver was about to load his Land Rover and trailer when he was instructed to empty the vehicle of petrol, as with peacetime regulations, until Lea reminded Movements that he was about to be landed on hostile territory and must have a full tank. Patterson, already irritated that he was not deploying with his Brigade HQ, seized the manifest list and told an RAF officer that since Gurkhas weighed less than the average British soldier, there should be no problem with the payload and instructed the Gurkhas to load.

At 2.42pm, a 48 Squadron Hastings left RAF Changi for the 750-mile flight for Labuan with about half of D Company and other assets, where it was planned that the troops would transfer to other aircraft for the seizure of Brunei Airport. The flight was scheduled to arrive at about 5.30pm. Three minutes later the remainder of D Company left in the Britannia, expecting to arrive at about 5.00pm. At 2.45pm Squadron Leader Bennett took off from Seletar in a Beverley overloaded with ninety-three Gurkhas and a four-strong RAF air traffic control detachment, with an expected arrival time of about 7.30pm. His orders were to proceed to Brunei Airport and, if free of obstacles and rebel activity, he was to land the troops; otherwise, he was to fly to Labuan and await orders. Commander of 45 Squadron, Squadron Leader M.J. Dawson, had been instructed to place his Canberras on stand-by as high speed transport. At 3.50pm, Flying Officers L.C. Warren and R.A.P. Burr took off from RAF Tengah with Major Waterton and Mr Pumphrey, the Assistant High Commissioner of Brunei, bound for Labuan. Arriving two hours later, Waterton saw a Brunei Airways DC-3 Dakota and two 209 Squadron Twin Pioneers on the ground. Learning from Singapore that Brunei Airport was still in loyalist hands, he began planning for D Company to be ferried there. The second Beverley, which was piloted by Flight Lieutenant J.J. Harvey and loaded with three Land Rovers, three trailers, thirty-five Gurkhas and five RAF ground crew, was delayed from taking off by rain until 4.35pm. The third, commanded by Flying Officer A.H. Hyland, was also delayed until 7.45pm, this time by the late arrival of two Land Rovers and their trailers, thirty-five Gurkhas and a mixed load of 5,000lbs of ammunition and rations.

Admiral Luce also instructed Commander-in-Chief, Far East Fleet, based at HMS *Terror,* to support the Operation. The 6th Minesweeper Squadron, which was commanded by Captain William Staveley, had returned to Singapore Naval Base for a refit during the day after a piracy sweep in the South China Sea. Staveley was warned two warships were required for immediate deployment. Although coastal patrol boats would have been ideal, the Royal Navy had disbanded Coastal Forces; nevertheless, the shallow draught of the Ton-class minesweepers enabled them to navigate rivers. After Staveley and his Half-Leader (second-in-command), Lieutenant Commander Jeremy Black, had been briefed at Naval Headquarters, they issued orders to HMS *Fiskerton* and HMS *Chawton*, that both were on immediate notice to steam under the Senior Naval Officer, Black, who commanded HMS *Chawton.* Lieutenant Peter Down was First Lieutenant on HMS *Fiskerton*:

> The extent of direct support for the insurrection from Indonesia was not clear. We anticipated some re-run of 'the natives are revolting' scenario which figured in the 'Aid to Civil Power' training. Opposition was expected to be in the form of spears, shotguns and the odd rifle, accompanied by the murder of officials and sabotage of power lines and communications centres.

Both warships were stored and, at about 2.00pm, departed from Singapore to the strains of the contemporary song *Speedy Gonzales* and set course through the north-west monsoon for the two-day voyage to Labuan. HMS *Fiskerton* was deeply into Nelson's Navy, probably as a result of the contemporary film *HMS Defiant,* which featured Alec Guinness as the kindly Captain and Dirk Bogarde as the unpleasant First Lieutenant and Black insisted on such cries as 'Avast There!' and 'Haul Away Handsomely!' The sea shanties *Trusty Boatswains* and *Heart of Oak* abounded. When the ship entered ports, two junior seamen dressed in Victorian-period uniforms manned an old Chinese brass cannon that doubled as the saluting gun. This eccentricity moulded his men into a close knit crew. The Inshore Squadron headquarters ship HMS *Woodbridge Haven* was also placed on notice to transport troops, as were the despatch ship HMS *Alert* and the destroyer HMS *Cavalier.* The commando carrier HMS *Albion* with 40 Commando on board off Mombasa was instructed to return at best speed.

General Poett arrived back in Singapore from the Philippines at about 5.00pm and confirmed, to Brigadier Patterson's continued intense disappointment, that Lieutenant Colonel Shakespear would assume command from Major Lloyd-Williams, once the Gurkhas were secure in Brunei Town, and that HQ 99 Gurkha Infantry Brigade Group should remain in Singapore on internal security duties until the situation became clearer. There was no point on committing more troops if the Initial Force succeeded in establishing internal security.

CHAPTER EIGHT

1/2 Gurkha Rifles Brunei Town and Tutong 8–9 December

In the Beverley commanded by Squadron Leader Bennett heading near east across the South China Sea to Labuan, Major Lloyd-Williams sat pondering the invidious position he was in. Intelligence was limited and little was known about the TNKU and yet his command was to be ferried piecemeal in Twin Pioneers from Labuan to a strange airport without any maps or guides. But at least it would be dark.

Captain Lea had a more pressing problem. He did not know how to use his Self Loading Rifle and, while being given weapon training by Company Sergeant Major Lalitbahadur in the boom of the Beverley, he managed to fire four shots through the fuselage. During his two year absence from the battalion, the L1A1 7.62mm SLR had replaced the .303in rifle and M1 .30in carbine. Ideally suited for picking off Soviet soldiers in West Germany, the British variant of the Belgian FN FAL introduced in 1954 had a twenty-round magazine and a rate of fire of forty rounds per minute out to 600yds and more. But its long barrel length was not entirely suited to jungle warfare. The 9mm Sterling Sub Machine Gun L2A3 had replaced the Sten and was issued to men carrying heavy equipment, such as radios. With a thirty-four-round magazine and a practical rate of fire of 102 rounds per minute, it was robust. The support weapon at section level was the Bren Gun. Fitted with its distinctive curved thirty-round magazine and noted for its accuracy, the original .303in barrel had been replaced by 7.62mm barrel and other parts replaced to accommodate the change in calibre of ammunition. It was later known as the Light Machine Gun or LMG.

En route, a member of the aircrew approached Lea and said that Squadron Leader Bennett had been informed that a Twin Pioneer flying from Labuan had landed at Brunei Airport without interference, but the airport buildings were under intermittent fire from the perimeter with the control tower hit several times. The sortie referred to had been flown by Flight Lieutenant Morris of 209 Squadron delivering the North Borneo Mobile Police Force. Lea was somewhat nonplussed because he had assumed he was going to Kuching, which was why he had been given a map of the city by Lieutenant Duffell. Conferring with Lloyd-Williams, they both agreed that since Bennett was the pilot and seemed to know what he was doing, they would rely upon him to deliver them to wherever they were meant to be going.

At about 7.30pm, Bennett approached the airport underneath a low cloud base. Below, it was pitch black – no moon, no lights. Bennett circled and then suddenly the darkness was split by the runway lights. The delays at RAF Seletar had cost valuable hours of darkness and, although landing was risky and no-one in the aircraft knew the exact situation on the ground, Lloyd-Williams realized that seizing the airport as an airhead was crucial for follow-up forces and decided to risk landing, in the hope that the lights had been switched on by loyal Bruneans. If not, the darkness would offer some protection. Advancing into Brunei Town could wait. As the Beverley approached at about 8.20pm, Mr Glass, the Brunei Controller of Civil Aviation, removed a few obstacles erected by the rebels. He was assisted by a few members of staff, the airport fire brigade and the North Borneo Police Mobile Force section, armed with shotguns. As Bennett applied the brakes and with the engines revving for an emergency take-off, the doors and ramps were thrown open and the Gurkhas plunged into the darkness to take up defensive positions. Lloyd-Williams despatched a platoon to deal with a few TNKU firing from the perimeter, the rest of the Company secured the airport, posted sentries and despatched patrols. Bren guns were placed on high buildings and a cook set about preparing supper. The four man RAF air traffic control detachment prepared to receive more aircraft. Twenty-two hours after the first news of the rebellion reached Singapore, British troops were in Brunei.

Flight Lieutenant Harvey landed at 9.05pm. Major Seager moved into the manager's office but as Corporal Holdsworth's Land Rover was unloaded from the Beverley, it slipped off the ramp and landed heavily on the tarmac, damaging the radio. With telephones liable to interception, Lloyd-Williams was now out of touch with Headquarters, Initial Force and Headquarters Far East Land Forces in Singapore. Harvey then collected a Gurkha Signals detachment from Jesselton.

At about 10.00pm, Lloyd-Williams and C Company set off for Brunei Town and, although some light resistance was encountered, by midnight he had established his command post inside Police HQ. Commissioner of Police Outram briefed him that about 300 TNKU had attacked soon after electricity was lost when the Power Station was recaptured at first light. The Sultan's Palace and the Prime Minister's residence had been successfully defended by the Police and the North Borneo Police Mobile Force platoon flown from Jesselton. Aggressive police patrols in the town had resulted in at least eleven rebels being killed, twenty-four wounded and about 150 taken prisoner, most held in the tennis courts on the *padang*. The police stations at Panaga and Kuala Belait were under major pressure.

Meanwhile, soon after the Hastings and Britannia had landed at Labuan, Major Waterton sent one of his two D Company platoons by Twin Pioneers to Brunei Airport. Should it be deployed independently of C Company, it was to be commanded by Lieutenant David Stephens. Stephens' father had recently retired as a major-general, having spent his career with 2 Gurkha Rifles. Major Waterton remained at Labuan to co-ordinate the move of the rest of D Company. When it arrived, they requisitioned a lorry and made their way to Brunei Town. Its arrival gave Lloyd-Williams three platoons but since it was politically critical to protect the Sultan, he sent Captain Willoughby and the D Company platoon to defend the Palace, leaving him with the two C Company platoons for military operations. With intelligence suggesting that a large force of TNKU was on its way from Limbang by river, Lloyd-Williams decided to secure Brunei Town and wait for first light before sending a force to recapture the Seria oilfields and relieve the siege of police stations at Panaga and Kuala Belait. When information then arrived from Seria that the TNKU was planning to use hostages as a shield for an attack on Panaga Police Barracks, he had no alternative but to try to rescue them.

With C Company his only deployable option, Lloyd-Williams instructed Captain Lea to rescue the hostages with Company HQ and the two platoons, totalling about seventy men, leaving the town to be defended by the police.

The sixty miles to Seria threaded through cultivated land, patches of jungle, past oil installations and along the coast. Intelligence on TNKU intentions and activity between Brunei and Seria was virtually non-existent but at least it was still dark. The plan was simple but full of risk: drive along the road, breach defences and roadblocks by shooting them up and keep moving, but the further west the column drove the greater the chances of being isolated. The good news was that communications between police stations seemed to have collapsed and therefore the TNKU would be unaware of Lea's intentions and strength. It is hardly surprising that Lea was somewhat nonplussed with the instruction; nevertheless, orders were orders. Outram gave him a map that he kept underneath a glass plate on his desk. When Lea asked for a medical orderly, Lloyd-Williams told him that none had been brought and that the First Field Dressings carried by every soldier should suffice. At his orders, Lea assured his men that the absence of a medical orderly did not mean casualties would be abandoned. The only suitable transport was two Public Works Department tipper trucks. As the Gurkhas were loading into the trucks, a Brunei Police inspector and three constables turned up as guides and interpreters. Lea insisted that the inspector ride with him in his Land Rover along with Company Sergeant Major Lalitbahadur, his orderly and his radio operator, Lance-Corporal Sombahadur Thapa.

Lea led the convoy in his Land Rover past an ineffectual rebel roadblock and then entered Sengkurong where more feeble obstacles were breached. Two TNKU were shot and several surrendered but were ignored. Driving fast into Tutong, the convoy came under fire from the Police Barracks but then near a garage in the town centre encountered heavier fire from TNKU positions in houses and shops in the bazaar. The road ran between the River Tutong on the right and the bazaar on the left and the only option was the simple counter-ambush drill of driving straight through the killing zone, with all weapons firing, and hoping that the road was not blocked. However, Lea's driver was shot in the shoulder and the Land Rover careered into a deep monsoon ditch running alongside the riverbank and came to a crunching halt in the water. Everyone scrambled out and returned fire and then, rushing a house that they could fortify, they gained a foothold on the veranda only to find it occupied by TNKU. During a brief but fierce close range firefight, they drove the rebels out by firing into the ceilings. The radio was recovered from the Land Rover but Lea was unable to raise anyone. Isolated and with no idea what had happened to his two platoons or where they were, the group then found a better position in the fish market and used the concrete display platforms and concrete pillars as cover. The market was also big enough to expose anyone who entered. Handing over its defence to Company Sergeant Major Lalitbahadur, Captain Lea dressed the shoulder of the wounded driver and, in order to keep him occupied, allocated him a defensive position. When Lance-Corporal Sombahadur Thapa then mentioned that his backside hurt, Lea told him to drop his trousers and noted that he had two bullet wounds in his buttocks. By chance, Lea had grabbed a tin of morphine phials from his desk drawer as he left his office in Singapore and had stuffed them into his pocket. Jabbing Sombahadur in the buttock, he extracted one bullet but was unable to find the other one. Also needing to keep him occupied, Lea told him to keep trying to raise his two platoons on the radio until he was successful. The radio operator would keep trying all night. When Lalitbahadur then mentioned to Lea that two TNKU were creeping along the riverbank toward their position, they allowed the rebels to get close and then swiftly despatched them without a shot being fired, their bodies falling in such a way as to give some protection to Lea's men.

Meanwhile, the two platoons had blasted their way through Tutong and seized the bridge on the western outskirts of the town where, for the rest of the night, the two platoon commanders tried to contact Lea, without success. The ambush had allowed the TNKU to exploit fully the use of their shotguns and several Gurkhas had buckshot wounds.

In Brunei Town, Major Lloyd-Williams was consolidating his position. At about 2.00am, when an observation post reported a man creeping along the monsoon ditch near the State Secretariat Offices across the road from Police Headquarters, he instructed Lieutenant Stephens to investigate. As Stephens was leading a patrol across the road, it came under heavy shotgun fire from the Secretariat and the Post Office which very seriously wounded him in the chest and killed Constable Batty of the Brunei Police. While Stephens' orderly, Rifleman Muktiraj, dashed to Police

Headquarters to report, the D Company platoon returned fire at TNKU positions across the football field. In anticipation of an attack on the north-east perimeter of the Police Headquarters, a section and a half were moving into position when they also came under heavy, close range shotgun fire that wounded Lieutenant (QGO) Thapa Gurung and four men, one, Lance-Corporal Dalhabadur Gurung, very seriously. When the firing died down Stephens and Dalhabadur were rushed to Brunei Hospital where the Gurkha died. Stephens died during the early evening of 12 December of pneumonia as a consequence of his wounds.

Meanwhile, HQ D Company and its second platoon had arrived at Labuan and immediately flown to Brunei Airport then advanced toward the town. It had reached the eastern end of the Secretariat when the firing broke out. Major Waterton, mistakenly believing that they were Police Headquarters, halted and radioed Lloyd-Williams to agree a plan to attack the Secretariat from the rear and dislodge the TNKU. His leading platoon had just moved when matters became more muddled in the darkness when the rear section was fired on from behind and had to turn around and deal with the threat. D Company had advanced a short distance when a group of uniformed armed men was seen crossing the road. Without maps and with such confusion in the town, Lloyd-Williams and Waterton agreed that D Company would go firm until daylight.

It was essential to get a situation report to HQ FARELF. Major Lloyd-Williams prepared a short account, which was taken to Brunei Airport in the hope that its radio could reach Singapore. Instead, Mr Glass arranged for the control tower staff to transmit the details to the pilot of a British Overseas Airways Corporation Comet airliner, then on its regular flight from Australia to London via Karachi, and asked him to relay it to Headquarters Far East Land Forces. When the Headquarters read that a Gurkha officer had been killed and Lieutenant Stephens and several others were wounded, it was clear that the situation in Brunei was serious.

The situation remained tense all night with rebels taking pot-shots at Gurkha patrols hunting them. At about 6.45am, Brigadier Glennie, a Royal Army Service Corps corporal clerk and the Queens Royal Irish Hussars defence section had arrived at Brunei Airport in a Twin Pioneer from Labuan. Glennie had left RAF Seletar in a 45 Squadron Canberra at 4.00pm the previous day. After arriving at Labuan at about 6.00pm, with the priority to fly-in Gurkhas, he had decided not to fly to Brunei Airport that night in case he became caught up in fighting. Corporal Holdsworth's radio was still not working. At 6.30am the next day, Lieutenant Colonel Shakespear arrived and found a large map of Brunei Town on a wall but noted that it was mounted sideways, so that north was on the left; this momentarily upset his orientation because north is usually at the top of maps. He instructed the D platoon inside Police Headquarters to start securing Brunei Town by clearing the buildings east of its position, toward the river, and then advance towards the Brunei Hotel. Fourteen police officers suspected of being TNKU were turned over to Special Branch and later released. At the same time, Major Waterton and his platoon captured four rebels while searching the State Secretariat. Within forty-five minutes, D Company had completed its tasks and two hours later Brunei Town was firmly in the hands of the Gurkhas – with the Chartered Bank, the Secretariat, the Post Office, the Telecommunication Centre, the Power Station, the river front and Brunei Hotel all cleared of TNKU. Observation posts were installed on the roofs and top floors. Lloyd-Williams' achievement in planting a footprint was considerable in that the entire operation had taken place mostly in darkness in a town about which he knew nothing; nevertheless the situation was still fragile with outbreaks of firing.

Collected soon after dawn by two police Land Rovers and a Black Maria, Brigadier Glennie, Major Seager, a Royal Army Service Corps corporal clerk and the four-strong Queens Royal Irish Hussars defence section arrived at Police Headquarters, and by 7.30am had taken over the control of operations from Major Lloyd-Williams. The next major task was to ensure the safety of Sultan Omar. Accompanied by Acting High Commissioner Mr Pumphrey, Glennie advised the Sultan that he had insufficient troops to guard him in his Palace and escorted him to Police Headquarters, where he was given the cells as his accommodation, remaining there until moving to the State Secretariat the following day. During the day, the Royal Air Force flew in a C11/R210 radio set to replace Corporal Holdsworth's defective C-52 and, in between exchanging occasional shots and giving blood, they managed to contact Headquarters Far East Land Forces for the first time.

As the reports from Brunei began arriving at Headquarters Far East, it was clear that the emerging Intelligence picture indicated that the rebellion was far more serious and widespread than originally thought and had nothing to do with a resurgence of Communist Terrorist activity. The level of public support for the rebellion was not clear but seemed to be ambivalent. In fact, most people had stayed in their homes or had returned to their *kampongs*. The Seria and Miri oilfields, Muara, Sengkurong, Tutong, and Limbang appeared to be in rebel hands; however, Brunei Airport was held by Initial Force. Labuan was providing a valuable forward operating base.

It was clear that more troops would have to be sent. In Singapore, Brigadier Patterson was directed to place Lieutenant Colonel McHardy on standby to move with his Battalion Tactical Headquarters and two rifle companies but no move was expected before 6.00am on 10 December. The battalion set about recalling its high number of married men back to barracks. Lieutenant Colonel Robin Bridges, the Commanding Officer of 42 Commando, was briefed during the morning by Brigadier Billy Barton, who commanded HQ 3 Commando Brigade, the Theatre Reserve. He was informed that a situation was developing in Brunei which might require his Commando to move at short notice and, although no action was to be taken, contingencies were to be made to move key personnel quickly. Singapore-based 42 Commando was sited at Royal Naval Air Station Sembawang, later known as HMS *Simbang*. Of the three Commandos of 3 Commando Brigade in December 1962, 40 Commando was on HMS *Albion* off the East African coast and 45 Commando was in the middle of a seven-year tour in Aden under the operational control of HQ Middle East Command. During the afternoon Brigade HQ issued orders that the Queens Own Highlanders were to be ready to move, either by sea or air, as the two company group or as large a force as possible, by 4.00pm on the 9 December.

Unsure of enemy strength or organization and assuming the rebels to be as effective as the Communist Terrorists in Malaya, Shakespear decided to evacuate European women and children by flying them to Labuan when reports emerged that TNKU in Limbang intended to cross the border and attack Brunei Town. He could not afford to waste troops. All were evacuated except for two Australian women employed by the Brunei Government who decided to remain at Police Headquarters where they supplied Gurkha sentries with food and tea and carried out other tasks. Hamstrung by the lack of transport aircraft and helicopters, and without sufficient men to crew requisitioned boats, Shakespear had no alternative but to accept he was in danger of losing the initiative and, assessing that it was critical to protect the Sultan, he decided to concentrate his resources on the town and airport. Brunei Airport was defended by men from Headquarters Company, two Royal Army Service Corps Air Traffic Liaison Officers and a small Royal Air Force detachment with air-portable communications equipment. Next day, B Flight, 15 Squadron, Royal Air Force Regiment flew in to Labuan and strengthened its defence.

At 7.00am, A Company, which had arrived during the night, was tasked to recapture Miri. After being briefed by two Special Branch officers, Mr Anderson and Mr Head, two hours later it flew to the town in a Brunei Airways DC-3 Dakota and seized the town against very little opposition; 3 Platoon secured Lutong. When Major Terry Bowring's B Company arrived from Brunei Airport, Lieutenant Colonel Shakespear deployed it to the north of Brunei Town with particular emphasis on guarding Edinburgh Bridge, which was a key road bridge over the River Kedayan leading to Tutong. A small TNKU group lurking on high ground opened fire but was wiped out. Bowring then ordered his men to clear the town of rebels, which the Gurkhas did with considerable thoroughness. By the time the fighting had died down, TNKU casualties amounted to seven dead, twenty wounded and more than 100 captured, at the cost of eight wounded, including Lieutenant Stephens.

Meanwhile, a patrol from 8 and 9 Platoons had reached Captain Lea in Tutong fish market. Lea had acquired a Sten gun, a weapon he was more familiar with than the SLR. At the Police Barracks, which had been abandoned by the TNKU, when Lea was cheerfully told by the corporal-in-charge that the police radio network was active, he strongly suspected that the TNKU knew about his convoy and had anticipated that it would take the main road. The corporal connected Lea with Police Headquarters and, after first being put through to the office of Commissioner Outram, he explained to Lieutenant Colonel Shakespear that, although he was secure in Tutong, he was sufficiently isolated to believe that he might be attacked. He also had several wounded requiring hospital treatment, including a colour sergeant badly wounded in the chest, and about 150 TNKU suspects. Shakespear told him he must stand firm and hold the road to Seria open. Anticipating he would be withdrawn at some stage, Lea requisitioned four Public Works Department lorries and armoured them by welding metal sheets around their cargo spaces. The Land Rover was dragged out of the ditch and, although damaged, it was serviceable. At about midday, Shakespear instructed Lea to withdraw to Brunei Town and at about 3.00pm Lea reached Battalion HQ, without incident. The prisoners, who had been crammed into two lorries, were delivered to the tennis courts where they joined other suspects, whose low spirits were being dampened by rain sweeping across the river and jungle. During the night they were moved into the holding centre in the town cinema.

By now, Lea's men had been without sleep for more than thirty hours and, after a meal, most found spaces underneath the stairs in Police Headquarters to rest. Suitably rugged, unshaven and carrying his Sten, Lea attended an Orders Group chaired by Shakespear, after which the Battalion Gurkha Major Pirtilal said to him 'Well done'. Such a comment from the senior Gurkha officer and a veteran of the Second World War was an accolade that Lea treasured.

Applying internal security framework principles developed during the Malayan Emergency, Lieutenant Colonel Shakespear spread 1/2 Gurkha Rifles around Brunei Town and, acting on information from Special Branch, helped the police to round up those either known to have taken part in or who had supported the rebellion, including those who had expressed sympathy with the Brunei People's Party. Brunei was now under military control but intelligence reports persisted that up to 300 TNKU directly posed a risk to the town with about 300 more available from Limbang. After a second night of several clashes, the Battalion conducted rigorous searches and recovered a substantial quantity of arms, ammunition, equipment and documents, and made a large number of arrests. The next night the clashes continued and several curfew-breakers were shot. C Company later defended the southern part of the town with aggressive patrolling, protected the bridges, manned rooftop observation posts and enforced the twenty-four hour curfew. The Battalion also dominated the Brunei-Tutong-Muara triangle and regained the confidence of the inhabitants.

On 12 December, the day that the Royal Marines landed at Limbang, D Company, 1/2 Gurkha Rifles reoccupied the police station and jail in Sengkurong against no opposition. The next day, C Company and Tactical Headquarters, supported by two Queens Royal Hussars Ferret Scout Cars passed through D Company and cleared Tutong of rebel activity and released several police officers from the cells in the police barracks. The following night, a force of twenty-six TNKU infiltrators in seven longboats was ambushed by a combined C and D Company on the waterfront. There were no survivors. C Company was then joined by the Medium Machine Gun Platoon and, by 21 December, had rounded up about 300 known TNKU.

In Singapore, Brigadier Patterson had suggested to Major General Olding that HQ 99 Gurkha Infantry Brigade should move to Brunei. He had a point. Although Brigadier Glennie had managed the immediate crisis with a small headquarters, it was logical that with more units being deployed, a Brigade HQ should control operations. HQ 3 Commando Brigade was not in a position to command Army units, HQ 28 Commonwealth Brigade Group could not be deployed for political reasons, and HQ 63 Gurkha Infantry Brigade had responsibility for the defence of, and should remain in, Malaya. This left HQ 99 Brigade. Although structured to address civil disturbances in Singapore, it was appropriately staffed and, since there was no unrest in the city that the Singapore Police could not manage, General Poett relented. On 10 December, Patterson and his Tactical HQ flew to Brunei where he was subordinated to Glennie, now appointed Commander British Forces, Brunei still reporting direct to the Commander-in-Chief, Far East. Police Headquarters had become so crowded that Shakespear moved his Battalion Headquarters to the Civic Centre, along with the Assault Pioneers as the Battalion Reserve.

However, 99 Brigade was structured for internal security and lacked some service support units and logistics associated with the Army in the field. The theatre of operations also lacked stockpiles.

The Royal Army Ordnance Corps (RAOC) in Singapore had been looking forward to a quiet run-up to Christmas after the hectic activity during Corps Week, the previous week of parades, a two-day study period, cocktail parties and formal Mess dinners in the Officers' and Sergeants' Messes. When news of the emergency was passed by the Ordnance Branch, Headquarters Far East Land Forces to Brigadier G.C.H. Wortham, the Command Director of Ordnance Supplies, on Sunday, 9 December, he was attending a curry lunch at the 3 Base Ordnance Depot Officers' Mess. Then informed that HQ 99 Brigade was deploying, knowing that it lacked a Brigade Maintenance Area to house logistic units and the hub for processing supplies and returns, he instructed that the 'ready to move, shadow' Ordnance Field Park (OFP) on notice to deploy to Laos be mobilized as 99 OFP. It was to be reinforced by twenty clerks and storemen from 3 Base Ordnance Depot and based on Labuan. The District Officer, Mr Richard de la Poer Beresford-Pierce, eased the labour recruitment and other administrative issues.

Group Captain R.D. Wilson, the RAF Seletar Station Commander, arrived on the island to control air operations, which increased from twelve transport moves on 8 December to sixteen the following day and twenty-eight on 10 December that, between 8 and 13 December, delivered 167 military and sixty-nine civilian sorties carrying 3,209 passengers, thirteen dogs, 113 armoured, light and medium weight vehicles, seventy-eight trailers and bowsers, two Auster aircraft, an aircraft refuelling bowser and 624,308lbs of equipment and supplies. Passengers flown – including wounded, sick and prisoners of war – numbered 4,751. Inevitably, under such intense flying, aircraft were frequently flown beyond their regular maintenance schedules; nevertheless, the ground and technical crews in Singapore and in theatre ensured that all serviceable aircraft were ready. Commander C.A. John was appointed the Naval Officer in Charge, Victoria Harbour, Labuan. Naval Party *Alpha* deployed with powerful radios to set up reliable communications to Singapore. Hitherto, HMS *Fiskerton* was still passing messages or relaying them through HMS *Woodbridge Haven*, and later HMS *Albion*, to Headquarters Far East Land Forces. The naval radio communicators staff became virtually 'Watch on, stop on' – a vital contribution that has not been sufficiently acknowledged.

The Royal Army Service Corps played an extremely important role in supplying and ferrying additional vehicles and vehicle parts, ammunition, rations, clothing and medical supplies. As Major Seager in Brunei handed over logistic command to Lieutenant Colonel B.H.J.A. O'Reilly MBE, of 3 Army Air Supply Organisation, over the thirteen days from 8 December, Army and RAF movement staff worked without interruption to organize airlifts. The Organisation had been assembled in 1960 from 5, 6 and 7 Air Supply Control Sections, 55 Company RASC and 21 Air Maintenance Platoon Royal Army Ordnance Corps (Royal Army Ordnance Corps) to support FARELF operations.

On the ground initial responsibility for the delivery and collection of supplies fell to 31 Company, Gurkha Army Service Corps, which had been formed in July 1958 to provide four companies to support 17th Gurkha Division and its Brigades. Commanded by Major A.W. Blackmore, he and his advance party had arrived on Labuan on 10 December. Part of the main body, thirty-two British and Gurkha soldiers, were mistakenly delivered to Brunei Airport in a Shackleton during the late evening of 12 December but not for long. They hitched a lift in a Beverley on a supply run to Labuan. Initially, the Company confined itself to the Land Rovers and trailers flown in by Beverley. Matters significantly improved with the delivery by sea of its 4-tonne Bedford RL lorries and four Massey Ferguson forklift tractors that the unit happened to have on loan. Lieutenant Robin Marston's platoon established a Forward Supply Point in the concrete works adjacent to Brunei Airport, after they had neutralized TNKU interference. The Brigade Administration Area was later reinforced by Composite Platoon, 3 (28 Commonwealth Brigade) Company, 28 Company from Hong Kong and 34 Company from Malaya. The drivers were about to be committed into a very different environment from Singapore, that of landing on beaches and negotiating jungle roads under active service – conditions in which ambushes and civil disturbances were an ever present threat. Repair support was provided by a Royal Electrical and Mechanical Engineers Workshop.

At sea, the Landing Ship Tank HMT *Kittiwake* delivered first-line scales of clothing, technical stores, war stores (such as barbed wire), groceries, medical stores and engineer stores. Two 46 Squadron Landing Craft Tank, the *Ardennes* and *Arromanches*, sailed on December 10 with orders to unload at Brunei Town. The voyage normally took about two days but they encountered poor weather in the South China Sea. About twelve hours behind schedule the *Ardennes,* loaded with a Ferret troop, the forklift trucks and general cargo, was intercepted by the Royal Navy guard-ship at the mouth of the River Brunei. Not only did its commanding officer express concern that the landing craft was at the 'sharp end', the Senior Naval Officer, Labuan ordered *Ardennes* to report to Naval Headquarters, Victoria Harbour before unloading the Ferrets in Brunei. *Ardennes* contacted the *Arromanches* and both vessels entered Brunei River, selected a hard standing and unloaded the Ferrets. Their sister ship, the *Ajedabia*, reached Labuan on December 18 with general cargo. Thereafter, the three landing craft were busy ferrying men and supplies, with one of them tasked for the 14-hour daily delivery run from Labuan to Brunei. The day began at 6.00am when loaded lorries were driven onto the landing craft. They were driven off by the 31 Company Composite Platoon in Brunei, who then delivered the vehicles to the Forward Supply Point for onward disposal to unit echelons. The landing craft took back returned and damaged stores to Labuan. The extent of the logistic build-up is demonstrated by the fact that, in December, the three steamed 6,200 miles and carried 1,300 passengers, 862 vehicles and 2,892 tons of ammunition.

The Royal Engineers of the Lighterage and Stevedore Troops, 10 Port Squadron, Royal Engineers and 1204 Pioneer Corps Labour Unit, unloaded supplies from ships. Forces Post Offices were established by 368 Postal and Courier Unit at Brunei, Brunei Airport and Labuan, not only for the delivery of personal and unclassified post but also for the transmission of classified mail through protected channels. It worked closely with Brunei General Post Office.

No. 656 Squadron, Army Air Corps had a long history of Far East operations going back to 1943. Based at Ipoh in Malaya, it consisted of two flights of Sioux helicopters and a third flight of fixed wing Austers and Beavers. Co-located with the squadron was 16 Reconnaissance Flight, which was the Air Troop of the Queens Royal Irish Hussars. It would spend most of 1963 supporting the Malayan 2 Federal Infantry Brigade and supporting police operations mopping up Communist Terrorist activity on the Malay/Thai border.

The 16 Commonwealth Field Ambulance Royal Army Medical Corps, which included three Queen Alexandra's Royal Army Nursing Corps Sisters, took over two wards in Brunei Hospital and established the Medical Reception Station, Brunei to stabilize casualties before flying those who required further attention to the British Military Hospital, Singapore.

With Brunei Town now secure, in the next stage of Operation Ale, Brigadier Glennie asked that the Queens Own Highlanders be sent to liberate hostages held in Seria and recapture the oilfields. As more units and individuals arrived, they were accommodated elsewhere in the town, with the Police Headquarters nominated as The Keep in case there was a major rebel incursion. When Major Webb arrived with elements of 249 Gurkha Signal Squadron, he was disappointed to find that several officers in Headquarters 99 Brigade did not seem to appreciate that logistics assets and resources would be needed. He also searched for a more suitable site in which to base the HQ and its Signal Squadron and settled on Brunei Girls' High School with its offices, classrooms, kitchen and dormitories. After some wrangling with the local authorities, the girls were sent home and the Army moved in. One drawback was that the beds were only 5ft long. Telephone communications were linked to the Brunei Posts and Telecommunications switchboards and Morse links to Singapore were established at Rear HQs in Kuching and Jesselton.

CHAPTER NINE

1 Queens Own Highlanders Seria

Soon after having being given the latest time that 1 Queens Own Highlanders should be ready to move, namely at 4.00am on 9 December, Lieutenant Colonel McHardy received orders that his battalion would start moving to Brunei in the early afternoon.

At 2.15pm, the advance guard of twenty-four men of 2 Platoon, A Company, commanded by Second Lieutenant Alastair McCall, left RAF Seletar on board a 34 Squadron bound for Brunei Airport. On arrival, the Highlanders proved a handy reinforcement for Major Seager and the small RAF communications team and a section from HQ Company 1/2 Gurkha Rifles defending the airport. Meanwhile, B Company, commanded by Major Neil Wimberley MBE, the Medium Machine Gun Platoon of Lieutenant Simon Taylor and three Land Rovers and trailers embarked on the destroyer HMS *Cavalier* at Singapore Naval Base. She sailed at 8.00pm. Wimberley's father had commanded the reformed 51st Highland Division in North Africa, Sicily and Normandy after it had been forced to surrender in 1940.

As the remainder of the battalion assembled at RAF Changi during the afternoon, McHardy had the impression that the airlift to Brunei was not being effectively co-ordinated by HQ FARELF and that more attention seemed to be being paid to embarking naval and military personnel and their dependents bound for the United Kingdom in a RAF Comet. When he tried to requisition the Comet, the RAF movements staff were not entirely in favour of his proposal. At 11.30pm 3 Platoon, A Company, commanded by Second-Lieutenant Jeremy Mackenzie left RAF Changi in a 48 Squadron Hastings, and was followed by the rest of A Company and Battalion HQ in a Britannia that left at 12.05am on 10 December and arrived in Labuan at about 2.20am that same morning. McHardy was briefed by Brigadier Glennie that he was to join 1/2 Gurkhas at Police HQ in Brunei Town and 'To get into Seria and Kuala Belait, clear them of rebels and free all hostages.' Glennie emphasized that the size of his force meant that speed and surprise were critical in executing the mission. But McHardy had no maps and his only knowledge of the area had been gained during a cricket tour to Seria in July. As far as intelligence was concerned, it was known that the TNKU had seized the most important towns in Brunei and that Seria Police Station had surrendered to the rebels on 7/8 December, and that about fifty Europeans and Indians, mostly oil workers, had been captured. Kuala Belait and Panaga Police Stations were under siege, although there were unsubstantiated reports that both had surrendered during the night. If Panaga had fallen this was serious because it had the largest police armoury in Brunei.

At 3.55am Tactical HQ and A Company arrived at Brunei Airport in a Beverley and, linking up with 2 Platoon, were then driven to Police HQ where McHardy learnt from Lieutenant Colonel Shakespear, a colleague from his days at Sandhurst, that Captain Lea had been ambushed at Tutong. Since the bridges over the Sungei Tutong and Telamba were at risk from demolition, McHardy concluded that a land approach to Seria was too risky. A landing from the sea was also out of the question because there were insufficient ships to lift the battalion. After telling Glennie that the only alternative was air assault, Glennie allocated him a Beverley with the possibility of a Twin Pioneer. By now, McHardy had acquired a torn but detailed map of Seria, removed from a wall in the office of the Commissioner of Police Outram.

At 7.40am, McHardy, Major Cameron, Outram and two Shell representatives, one of whom was Captain Peter Gaskell, a Shell pilot on local leave, took off from Brunei Airport in the Force Commander's Twin Pioneer to recce Seria and Kuala Belait. Soon after take-off, they received the reassuring news that the police stations at Panaga and Kuala Belait were still holding out but were short of water. From the air they saw the ten mile long and a mile and a half wide coastal stretch encompassing Anduki Airfield, Seria, Panaga and Kuala Belait and the Brunei Shell Petroleum complex clearly occupied by the TNKU, judging by the number of red and white rebel flags in evidence. The north was bounded by a strip of scrub and then sandy beaches. Jungle was to the south. The tarmac road from Brunei and Tutong ran past Anduki Airfield, through the oil installations and then led to Seria, the expatriate married quarters at Panaga and west to Kuala Belait at the mouth of Sungei Belait. Also noted was the absence of the Shell fixed wing aircraft that were usually parked near the control tower. The World Wide helicopters could be seen; four of the pilots were hostages in Seria. A red fire engine parked not far from the control tower blocked the 1,450ft Anduki runway.

When, at about 6.00am, a 209 Squadron Twin Pioneer piloted by Flight Lieutenant Lamb and Master Navigator Boyko flew McHardy over Anduki airstrip, in the dim light of dawn they noted the red fire engine blocking the runway and were puzzled when rebels at the terminal buildings did not fire. They later learnt that the rebels had seen the red and white fuselage roundels and assumed that the Twin Pioneer was an Indonesian Air Force aircraft delivering arms and ammunition. Lamb then flew over Seria and Panaga to reconnoitre Panaga Golf Club, which Wing Commander Graves had suggested might provide a possible landing strip. Lamb also noted a strip of ground near a patch of jungle that would screen rebel interference which could originate from the *Istana Kota Menggalela* (Sultan's Country Palace) that overlooked the western perimeter. There was a damp patch in the middle of the field. The approach would have to be from the sea and steep, in order to avoid rebel fire. Following the sortie, a 45 Squadron B5 bomber Canberra crewed by Flying Officer J.A. Thomas and Flight Lieutenant D.N. Sleven carried out a medium recce along the coastal strip. Any notion by the rebels that they were not going to be attacked disappeared.

Lieutenant Colonel McHardy planned to launch simultaneous seizures of Anduki Airfield and the Panaga grass strip and then use Anduki as his airhead for subsequent operations. The immediate task for the Anduki fly-in was to seize the Brunei Shell Petroleum store and deny the TNKU access to explosives, and then capture the Bailey Bridge over the River Bera and ensure lines of communications to Seria. Available to him was a Beverley and a Twin Pioneer. While considering his options, Flight Lieutenant Lamb mentioned to McHardy that there were four more Twin Pioneers at Labuan. When he returned to Police Headquarters, Brigadier Glennie agreed to allocate them for his operation. With twelve men per aircraft, this would give him the ability to land sixty lightly-armed men. There was no room for mortars and Vickers medium machine-guns. McHardy linked up with Wing Commander Graves to plan his attack. McHardy reduced the size of his HQ and filtered the remainder into rifle sections.

For Anduki Landings, McHardy allocated a strong platoon of forty men from HQ A Company and 1 and 4 Platoons to be commanded by Captain Johnnie MacDonald, the Company Second-in-Command. His tasks were the Bailey Bridge and Shell Explosive Area, some two miles west of the airfield. The platoon assembled from Battalion HQ and HQ Company placed under command of the Adjutant, Captain Johnnie Langlands, was to secure Anduki Airfield and man a roadblock on the Tutong to Seria road and disrupt rebel movement between the two towns. Squadron Leader Bennett assigned Flight Lieutenant Mike Fenn to fly the Beverley. In support was a Canberra bomber crewed by Flying Officer Thomas and Flight Lieutenant Sleven. Once the airstrip was secure, Battalion HQ would then fly in. Fenn and his Beverley crew had already been busy. They had left Singapore at 7.40pm on 9 December with a payload of Gurkhas bound for Labuan and the next morning, at Brunei, had given blood to a Gurkha sergeant who had been wounded in the fighting in Tutong, because the medics had run out of plasma, before taking him on to Labuan.

For the Panaga fly-in, McHardy allocated the task to sixty men from 2 and 3 Platoons, A Company commanded by Major Cameron. They were to land from the Twin Pioneers on a strip of grass near the golf course, relieve Panaga Police Station and capture the Telecommunications Centre. It had originally been planned to land on the golf course but this was rejected because there were too many bunkers. The Company was to enter Panaga from the west, raise the siege of Panaga Police Station and recapture the Telecommunication Centre. The problem was this force would be isolated and difficult to reinforce quickly; McHardy's other company, B Company, was still at sea and its arrival time not known. Wing Commander Graves decided to lead the Twin Pioneers with Flight-Sergeant Buxton as his co-pilot. In the second Twin Pioneer would be Lamb and Squadron Leader Slade; in the third Flight Lieutenants Dabin and Bedford; in the fourth Flight Lieutenants Morris and Garlick; and in the fifth Flight Lieutenant Arrowsmith and Pilot Officer Pearce. Graves was happy with the plan but one pilot suggested that it would be difficult to land the Twin Pioneers in such a small area without first developing an approach. Graves cut him short with the comment, 'If the Queens Own Highlanders want us to land on this strip, then we shall do all we can for them.' Meanwhile, the doors of the Twin Pioneers had been removed and Cameron's force began a very short training session in rapid disembarkation. They soon found that the only way to move fast was to discard packs and for the Jocks to cram everything that they needed in the skeleton order of two Bren gun pouches, and a water bottle into their pockets. Extra ammunition was taken in bandoliers.

Since the operations were ten miles apart, Lieutenant Colonel McHardy elected to co-ordinate the landings from a 656 Squadron Army Air Corps Beaver flown by a sergeant. H-Hour was 1.15pm. The forecast was cloudy with rain squalls.

By noon, the ninety Jocks, in light battle order, landing at Anduki had boarded the Beverley, making it considerably over the accepted payload. With the need to achieve surprise, the flight would have to be low level, out to sea and of sufficient distance from the coast to screen its purpose. This meant that Fenn would be unable to see Anduki Airfield over the palms and trees lining the beaches and therefore he would be reliant upon the combination of the skills of his navigator, Flight Lieutenant Ken Kime, and the local knowledge of Captain Gaskell. With the Jocks standing on the lower deck, Fenn took off from Brunei at 12.05pm and, flying at 50ft roughly due west, Kime plotted bearings using a military prismatic compass and watched the sea state. He followed the tree-lined coast west with Gaskell muttering 'A bit further, a bit further' until he indicated a distinctive gap in the trees through which the runway could be seen. The Beverley banked to port and skipped over casuarina trees bordering the beach and, at about 12.15pm, crunched onto the runway about 600ft from its eastern end and came to a halt, engines protesting in reverse thrust. The rebels had helpfully removed the fire engine because they thought the Beverley was an Indonesian aircraft bringing arms and ammunition. Within a minute and forty-eight seconds, 1 Platoon had de-bussed and was in cover from desultory shotgun fire coming from the control tower. Meanwhile, Fenn gunned his engines and raced along the runway in a short field take off but, even so, the aircraft was hit twice in the fuselage and tail as it passed the control tower. Kime later reckoned that if the aircraft had been flying a fraction slower or the gunman had fired a second later, the shotgun bullets would have torn among the flight deck crew. Flying low over Seria and Mrs Bennett's house, Fenn was back on the ground at Labuan at 12.35pm.

Both 1 and 4 Platoons had advanced to within about 250yds of the airport buildings when they came under fire from the control tower. In command of 1 Platoon was Second Lieutenant Donald Monro. He had arrived in Singapore on 8 December fresh from a year at the Mons Officer Cadet School and had been told by McHardy that he was on forty-eight hours notice to move. Supported by Sergeant Lewis, within forty-eight hours he was leading his platoon into action! Covered by Corporal Scott's section, 1 Platoon cleared the apron of TNKU, and then provided fire support for Company HQ and 4 Platoon, commanded by Sergeant Joe Mahady, attacking the control tower and the airport entrance police post, killing two TNKU and capturing five. While A Company were re-organizing, Lieutenant Colonel McHardy and Commissioner Outram landed in the Beaver with the knowledge that Kuala Belait Police Station had just surrendered; however, Panaga was still holding out. The news was grave but at least Anduki Airport was in British hands. Searching the airport buildings, McHardy found a detailed map of his area of operations. While the Regimental Signals Officer, Captain Neil Sutherland, organized communications, the Intelligence Officer, Lieutenant John Duncan, was analyzing information on the approaches to Seria through which the Battalion would be advancing. In a natural act of faith by soldiers burying the dead in the tropics, the eight or nine dead TNKU were buried in graves, each marked with a cross carved from compo ration boxes. Outram later ordered the bodies to be disinterred so they could be identified.

Captain Macdonald handed the road block to Captain Langland's Battalion HQ platoon and then advanced in two columns on both sides of the road west toward the Bailey Bridge. Nine fully armed TNKU en route to Anduki in two cars were captured, along with several rifles, shotguns, parangs, ammunition and tear gas grenades. Several minutes later, as 1 Platoon scrambled into a ditch to ambush a Land Rover seen driving fast down the road, they were spotted. As the Land Rover screeched to a halt, reversed and accelerated, Sergeant Lewis jumped out of the ditch and fired a shot which burst the right hand rear tyre. The Land Rover slewed across the road and, as three rebels jumped out, Lewis shot one in the groin. One rebel disappeared into the undergrowth; however, two who had been wounded surrendered and were sent back to Anduki. By 3.00pm, 1 Platoon was dug in astride the Bailey Bridge while 4 Platoon had seized the nearby Explosives Area. Back at Anduki, a rebel was killed trying to breach the road block and a rifle, ammunition, military respirator and TNKU flags were found in his car.

Meanwhile, at 12.10pm, ahead of another rainstorm, Flight Lieutenant Lamb had taken off from Brunei Airport in the first of five Twin Pioneers packed with HQ A Company and 2 and 3 Platoons. By 12.25pm, the remaining aircraft were heading out to sea. Fifteen minutes later, ahead of yet another rainstorm, Wing Commander Graves in a steep-angled approach leading two aircraft, hopped over the high trees bordering the beach and, nose up, air brakes full on, landed on grass soaked from a recent torrential downpour, and pulled up barely 10yds from a ditch and a sign declaring 'Halt. Major Road Ahead'. The area was quickly secured by a section. Flight Lieutenant Vic Dabin in Twin Pioneer 3, temporarily bogged down in the damp patch in the middle of the field, was pushed to firmer ground by the Jocks. Alastair Ker-Lindsay happened to be near the area and was nearly shot by a soldier with orders to shoot anyone wearing a bush hat. Several minutes later, after heavy rain had cleared, the remaining two aircraft landed on a mess of churned-up mud; nevertheless, by 12.50pm, the five Twin Pioneers were heading back to Labuan.

Mrs Bennett and her friend, Ann, heard the Beverley pass low over her house and then watched the Twin Pioneers land. A few minutes later she was telephoned by an excited friend, 'You know those chaps who didn't manage to get over here for St Andrew's Night? Well, they have just arrived!'

HQ A Company and 2 and 3 Platoons advanced along the road to Panaga Police Station, about two miles away. Offers of help from several expatriates were declined. Major Cameron recognized his axis of advance from the information gleaned after the July cricket tour. At 3.00pm, his Jocks relieved the besieged policemen and took the TNKU by total surprise. He then established Company HQ inside. Cameron then decided to create a roadblock and asked the officer-in-charge to establish one at the most westerly roundabout of the town. However, the latter said that he had orders not to leave the Police Station and refused to take orders from anyone who was not police. Unfortunately, Outram was not available. With his main threat from Seria, Cameron despatched 2 Platoon, commanded by Lieutenant Alastair McCall, to establish a roadblock about three-quarters of a mile east at a crossroad on Jalan Tenga, which was the main road from Panaga towards Seria.

At the same time Cameron sent 3 Platoon to establish a roadblock on Jalan Utara in the area of the Telecommunication Centre, a block directly north of 2 Platoon. Jalan Utara ran parallel to Jalan Tengah. In between the two platoons was the monsoon ditch, which, after the heavy rains, was free flowing. Moving in bounds with two of its sections leading, 3 Platoon edged forward in fire and movement until, within sight of the Communications Building, shots were fired from an upper window to the right of the entrance. The leading Section Commander, Corporal Shepherd, instructed his Bren gun group to provide fire support for Lance Corporal Walkinshaw's Section as they dashed to a ditch from where they then engaged the heaviest rebel fire coming from the two windows on both sides of the entrance. Second Lieutenant Mackenzie decided to enter the compound from the rear. He and Lance Corporal Ward were scaling the wire fence when two rebels came out of the building to surrender. Mackenzie instructed one to open the front perimeter gates, which he did, but firing broke out again. He entered the compound with other members of the platoon and, while attempting to locate the enemy, was lucky not to be killed when he unwisely poked his head through a window and was wounded by a shot fired from the back of the room, grazing his ear. Two rifles were then thrown out of the window followed by two rebels surrendering. Hearing movement from inside, 3 Platoon fired several shots into the ceiling. However, this produced no appreciable result until the two captured TNKU were persuaded to invite their six colleagues to surrender. Four hostages were released.

Then 3 Platoon occupied the Communications Centre and also established the roadblock on Jalan Utara. A car soon approached from the west and three rebels were captured, along with a .303 calibre Lee Enfield and a shotgun. Ten minutes later a Hillman Hunter van flying three People's Party of Brunei flags approached from the west and flashed its headlights three times. This turned out to be the rebel recognition signal. The occupants apparently thought that the Centre was still in rebel hands until they drove toward the roadblock and realized their error. A window was wound down and a shotgun thrown out. However, the driver reversed and Lance Corporal MacDonald's 8 Section Bren Group opened fire. As the driver tried to turn, the van toppled backwards into the ditch. A man crawled out and was shot as he tried to run away. Three TNKU surrendered, one severely wounded – a .38in revolver and thirty rounds of ammunition were seized. At 5.00pm a black Ford saloon driving towards the roadblock also flashed its headlights three times. The Jocks replied with three flashes but, as the car approached, the occupants saw the Bren gun and fired a single round. The Bren gunner fired a burst and two TNKU rebels were taken prisoner along with another .303in rifle, a full Bren magazine, a respirator and several items of police uniform. Another wounded rebel was also captured. Within fifteen minutes, Second Lieutenant Mackenzie stopped a pair of uniformed TNKU on a Vespa scooter, one of whom was armed with a .303in rifle. Fifteen minutes later, a captured police Land Rover approached the road block and flashed three times. The Jocks again replied and when it stopped at the roadblock, two rebels, one in uniform, were captured, and five Lee Enfields, a .38in revolver, 200 rounds of .303 ammunition, fifty tear gas grenades and several items of police uniform. All was quiet until 11.10pm when another Land Rover approached and gave the rebel signal. This was answered by the 8 Section Bren and the vehicle crashed into the ditch. One rebel escaped and two were captured, one of whom was wounded. Inside the vehicle were found two Lee Enfields, tear gas grenades, .303 ammunition and two bottles of acid.

With 1 Queens Own Highlanders well established with the Tactical HQ and two platoons and A Company to the west effectively isolating Seria, Lieutenant Colonel McHardy ordered his Battalion to go firm for the night, which was very welcome for his tired, wet and hungry men. Although the weather was dreadful, at 5.00pm a Beverley had landed at Anduki with three Land Rovers and trailers containing rations, the Jocks' packs and Company Sergeant Major Burns and his Assault Pioneer Platoon. At 6.15pm, as dusk turned into night, a Twin Pioneer brought Padre John Stuart. Stuart very nearly did not accompany the Battalion to Brunei when the Chaplains Department, Singapore District instructed that he was to remain in Singapore, an order that Lieutenant Colonel McHardy quickly countermanded. In fact, Stuart had just arrived from Brunei Hospital where he had been comforting the wounded. With the logic beloved of British padres and chaplains, Stuart justified his appearance by bringing a consignment of Tilley lamps claiming he was 'bringing lamps to lighten the darkness', in reality to illuminate Anduki runway. He subsequently used this phrase as a basis for several sermons in his ministry. Three Twin Pioneers then arrived at Anduki with Major David Lochhead MC, the Battalion Second-in-Command, who reported to Lieutenant Colonel McHardy that B Company would fly in from Labuan at first light after a fast but very rough trip on HMS *Cavalier*. It had secured alongside a Victoria Harbour jetty at 11.00pm.

Conditions for the hostages in Seria Police Station were still grim. Starved of information and anxious about the outbursts of firing, the appearance of two 45 Squadron Canberra bombers was a huge morale-booster to the hostages, the expatriates confined in their houses and the oil workers still permitted to work in the refineries. One Canberra was sighted at about 7.30am reconnoitring Kuala Belait, and the other at about midday checking Anduki and Seria, flying low level over the town. When a guard asked Mr Bennett if they carried bombs, he replied only small ones but they were atomic. Few, if any, rebels had much experience of the British and their appearance made a deep dent in TNKU aspirations. The initiative began to slip from the rebels. There was considerable relief during the evening when Jean Scott, a Scottish nursing sister employed by the Brunei Government, negotiated the release of the women and children in exchange for tending the rebel wounded. Using an ambulance, Jean Scott drove the freed hostages to their homes and then returned to the Barracks. One of the freed hostages telephoned Mrs Bennett and said: 'I do not think the rebels will dare to repeat last night's performance.' The remark puzzled Mrs Bennett because she had no idea to what it referred.

CHAPTER TEN

Seria and Kuala Belait 11–12 December

At 7.00am on 11 December, B Company duly arrived at Anduki Airfield in two Beverleys and was pitched into operations. At 9.30am McHardy issued his orders for the next phases of the operation; B Company was to link with A Company. At the same time A Company was to form a roadblock on the outskirts of Panaga to prevent incursions from Kuala Belait and recapture the Summer Palace, which was known to be occupied by the TNKU and presented a threat.

After crossing the Bailey Bridge, Wimberley planned to turn north and clear the coast road through three report lines named 'Perth', 'Inverness' (Brunei Shell Petroleum Materials Area) and 'Aberdeen', as far as the River Seria. He would then turn south to 'Angus' (Seria Community Centre) and link up with A Company. Company HQ was to set up in the Shell Transport Area.

At 9.00am 6 Platoon, commanded by Second Lieutenant Alastair McGregor, leading, crossed the bridge and passing through 1 Platoon, swung north and advanced west along Utara Jalan, with the thin strip of land bordering the beach on their right and oil installations on their left. In a show of force to deter several cars shadowing the column, Corporal Robertson's Section opened fire. The unenthusiastic occupants of another car surrendered. Corporal Walker's Section, leading 6 Platoon, ejected light resistance in an oil installation, most of the rebels smartly withdrawing, some on foot and some in a car, including a wounded TNKU. Meanwhile, B Company continued advancing through oil derricks and machinery and passed Shell Brunei employees waving white flags and claiming that TNKU had instructed them to keep working to maintain local electricity supply.

Elsewhere A Company had experienced a relatively quiet night; 3 Platoon at the roadblock heard the firing as B Company advanced from the east and then at 9.25am, rebels in a green Shell Oil Land Rover appeared from Panaga and engaged the roadblock. It crashed into the ditch as 3 Platoon returned fire. Four rebels were captured and a fifth killed. Six Lee Enfield rifles, .303 rounds of ammunition, bayonets, documents and police clothing were recovered. By this time 3 Platoon had captured fifteen rebels and enough stolen vehicles for a dealership. During the morning 3 Platoon moved east and took up positions near the Roxana Cinema, four blocks east of the 2 Platoon roadblock, with the intention of linking up with B Company in the area of Angus.

At about midday B Company reached 'Inverness', the crossroads near the Brunei Shell Petroleum Materials Area, and established a stronghold held by Company HQ, the Medium Machine Gun Platoon with its Vickers, and the Mortar Section. Several Europeans and Brunei Shell employees, who had been confined in their offices since 8 December, hung out Union flags at their approach and supplied Wimberley with valuable intelligence on rebel positions and details of other Shell employees worth contacting. The remainder of the Company, commanded by the Second-in-Command, Captain Jonathan Nason, advanced towards Angus at the Seria Community Centre with 6 Platoon leading and 5 Platoon in reserve. Near the Roxana Cinema, a Land Rover suddenly appeared and Private Walker (86), a Bren gunner in 5 Platoon, opened fire, killing the driver, and it careered out of control into the ditch with its two-way radio still working. As a result of information from a Malay schoolmaster, several rebels were captured by 5 Platoon, along with several knives and *parangs*, and escorted to the Materials Area. By 2.00pm contact with 3 Platoon at the Roxana Cinema meant that the Battalion now had control of ground from Anduki airstrip to the western suburbs of Seria. The only rebels in the town were still holed up in the Police Station.

Shortly after 9.30am in Panaga Police Station, Major Cameron wanted to establish a strong military/police roadblock in the area of the Brunei Police Mobile Reserve Unit Barracks, located at the mouth of the River Mumong at the extreme west end of Seria, west of the Sultan's Country

Palace. His aim was to block TNKU activity from Kuala Belait, but the police were reluctant to do anything without military support. Taking them under his command, Cameron recalled 2 Platoon from the roadblock east of Panaga Police Station and placed them at the new roadblock. They arrived in several police and requisitioned Land Rovers. Although Alastair Ker-Lindsay and his squad of hard-drinking Iban had been freed by B Company the previous day, they had joined A Company.

When McHardy then ordered Cameron to recapture the Country Palace using 2 Platoon and two police sections, Ker-Lindsay agreed to act as guide. At 11.00am Cameron's force left Panaga Police Station in Land Rovers but, when a four-wheel vehicle was seen to take evasive action in the distance, Cameron instructed his men to debus. With Corporal McGovern's Section leading, as 2 Platoon advanced in broken arrowhead formation on both sides of the road for about half a mile, Cameron noted that the police were reluctant to follow. Badly needing every man, he persuaded them to help him. At the most westerly roundabout of Seria, McGovern's section doubled-up across the open area and then set off along the road to Kuala Belait. They were within about 100yds from the drive into the Palace grounds when a car appeared from the grounds. Cameron instructed McGovern to open fire and the car rolled into a ditch, spilling out the driver as it did. Although severely wounded, covered by determined resistance, in particular from a Bren gun, he stumbled back to the Palace. At the same time, Cameron ordered the two rear sections to advance through light undergrowth in extended line using the drive as the axis. Still wary of their commitment, he instructed the two police sections to cover the beach.

Lucky not to take casualties from the Bren gun, the sections of Corporals Hoddinott, on the right flank, and Turner on the left, leapfrogged through each other until they reached the driveway and went firm to 'Watch and shoot' and cover McGovern's section as it moved to a better firing position to cover the approach to the Palace. Fire control was initially ragged but as the battle developed it improved markedly. Under covering fire from Turner's section, Cameron, Lieutenant McCall, Ker-Lindsay, and Privates Cowle and Firmstone ran to the Palace, where the two officers and Ker-Lindsay threw tear gas grenades through ground floor windows. McCall, hugging the wall close to a corner, clashed with a rebel armed with a Lee-Enfield No. 4 rifle and shot him at very close

10 June 1945. Australian infantry and a Matilda tank landing on Green Beach. (*Australian War Memorial*)

9 December 1962. Part of D Company, 1/2 Gurkha Rifles wait to board a RAF Transport Command Britannia at RAF Seletar in Singapore. (*Courtesy of the Gurkha Museum*)

10 December 1962. Major Tony Lea, Major Tony Lloyd-Wiliams, Lt Col Shakespear and a QRIH officer shortly before C Company, commanded by Major Lea, left for Seria. On the way, he was ambushed in Tutong. For the only time in the campaign, the Gurkhas wore helmets. *(Courtesy of The Gurkha Museum)*

Tutong. The town in which C Company, 1/2 Gurkhas was ambushed on its way to Seria and took cover in the market. In the centre, a QRIH Ferret. *(Courtesy of The Gurkha Museum)*

A small Police Station outside Tutong that held out against the TNKU being visited by a 1/2 Gurkha Rifles patrol. (*Courtesy of The Gurkha Museum*)

11 December. A 1 Queens Own Highlander Mortar Platoon Bren gunner at the road block outside Anduki airstrip. Across the road is a car that attempted to breach the block. (*Courtesy of Colonel McHardy*)

Alastair Ker-Lindsay, one of the hostages who escaped during a TNKU attack on Seria Police Police Station. He later helped the Security Forces with a group of Brunei irregulars and was awarded the MBE for his contribution. (*Courtesy of Lady Annie Ker-Lindsay*)

About 3.30pm, 12 December 1962. Several of the hostages released from Seria Police Station by the Queens Own Highlanders.

13 December 1962, Seria. In a show of force, the Queens Own Highlanders march through the town. (*Courtesy of Colonel McHardy*)

About 9 December 1962, Sipitang. Acting District Officer John Parry's 'Private Army' of loyalist irregulars and one or two military personnel. (*Tom Kajer*)

Sipitang, North Borneo. Six truckloads of captured insurgents just prior to despatch to Jesselton Prison. (*Tom Kajer*)

About 9 December 1962, Sipitang. Acting District Officer John Parry addressing volunteer militia outside the District Office. (*Tom Kajer*)

North Borneo. When they were released from detention, many insurgents were involved in reparation and rehabilitation tasks, for instance building this bridge in Sipitang. (*Tom Kajer*)

Mr Richard Morris and his wife, Dorothy, who were held hostage in Limbang for four days until rescued by L Company, 42 Commando.

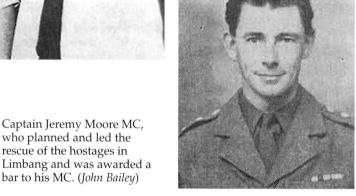

Captain Jeremy Moore MC, who planned and led the rescue of the hostages in Limbang and was awarded a bar to his MC. (*John Bailey*)

TNKU leader Salleh bin Sambas who led the defence of Limbang.

1962. Brunei Town showing the Brunei Hotel that was used by 42 Commando before the Limbang attack. (*John Bailey*)

Arriving in Sarawak on minesweeper
H.M.S Chawton - 1963
M 206

HMS *Chawton*, one of the two ton-class minesweepers that provided sailors for Z-Craft. (*John Bailey*)

A Vickers machine gun, which was still in service in 1962, manned by two Royal Marines.

THE LANDING
AREA. MORNING
AFTER THE DAY
BEFORE!!

12 December 1962, Limbang. The landing place (at the palm tree) used by L Company, 42 Commando to attack the Police Station. (*David Thorp*)

12 December 1962. Limbang Police Station. Note the bullet holes in the wall. (*David Thorp*)

12 December 1962. Limbang Hospital in which the hostages were held for two days. The photo is taken from the point where Major Moore landed. (*John Bailey*)

12 December 1962. The first of the two Z-Craft return to Brunei Town with the casualties after the 42 Commando attack on Limbang. *(Captain Derek Oakley)*

12 December 1962, Brunei Town. Lieutenant Commander Jeremy Black talks to Lieutenant Peter Waters after he had been wounded at Limbang. (*Capt Derek Oakley*)

13 December 1962. A Green Jacket and a police officer examine weapons captured from the TNKU. (*Courtesy of RGJ Museum*)

13 December 1962. Green Jacket church service at Bekenu. (*Courtesy of RGJ Museum*)

A QRIH Ferret Scout commander watches as a Wessex helicopter takes off from a landing site near a kampong. (*QRIH Museum*)

13 December 1962. A Green Jacket patrol in hired boats. (*Courtesy of the RGJ Museum*)

Two 66 Squadron Belvedere helicopters embark Gurkhas. On 4 May 1963, a Belvedere crashed nearby in the Trusan Valley, Sarawak, killing the crew, four members of the SAS, a Foreign Office official and Mr D. Reddish of the Borneo Company. (*The Gurkha Museum*)

A Queens Own Highlander radio operator carrying an A41 radio crosses a river on patrol. (*Courtesy of Colonel McHardy*)

December 1962. Major General Walker talking to Colonel McHardy (on right), CO 1 Queens Own Highlanders, and Major Cameron, OC A Company. (*IWM*)

Corporal Bob Rawlinson, who was awarded the MM at Limbang, leads a patrol across a river in Brunei. (*John Coombes*)

A Queens Own Highlander patrol land from a launch to visit a longhouse. (*Courtesy of Colonel McHardy*)

January 1963. Captain Parker and Reverend Wood of 42 Commando paddle a canoe down the main street during the floods that swept through the Limbang Valley. (*John Coombes*)

HADIAH $15,000
YASSIN AFFANDY RAHMAN
alias DJASIM
alias IASSIM RACHMAN
alias MOHAMED YASSIN
alias JASIN
alias MOHAMED JASSIN bin ABDUL RAHMAN
Kerajaan Brunei menawarkan hadiah $15,000 kerana kenyataan yang membawa pada tertangkap atau tertawan Yassin Affandy Rahman. Sa-barang orang yang mengetahui di-mana ia berada hendak-lah ber-hubong dengan pasokan keselamatan dengan serta merta.
Hadiah ini akan di-bayar kapada orang awam sahaja. Ia-nya tidak di-bayar kapada anggota2 pasokan keselamatan atau pegawai2 kerajaan yang mendapat gaji bulan.

Wanted poster for Affendi.

A Border Scouts platoon being briefed by a European police officer of the Sarawak Constabulary. The Scouts played a key role in providing an intelligence and patrol tripwire along the border with Indonesia. (*The Gurkha Museum*)

A flight of 20 Squadron Hawker Hunters being marshalled after a sortie. These aircraft played a valuable psychological weapons role in quellling the rebellion. (*RAF Museum*)

3 September 1966. Lieutenant Sumbi after being captured deep in Brunei. (*Major Alan Jenkins*)

range in the stomach. Cameron then withdrew 2 Platoon into the undergrowth to give the the rebels the opportunity to surrender and also for his men to fill their magazines. However, the continued firing indicated that the TNKU were not showing signs of surrendering.

After about five minutes, Cameron sent Hoddinott's section through some trees parallel to the beach and, then covered by Turner's section, they ran to the Palace, threw a teargas canister and an irritant grenade through the ground floor bay windows and returned to their positions. But the grenades had no effect on the resistance. Cameron realized that he would have to break into the building and clear it room by room. Instructing the two sections to take up firing positions along a garden balcony covering the bay windows, Cameron and McCall smashed a window and entered a large, empty room and began clearing two other rooms on the ground floor. In one, the rebel shot by McCall surrendered. Meanwhile, Turner's section had clambered through the windows. Of five TNKU who rushed out and headed toward the beach, Sergeant McLeman, the Platoon Sergeant, shot two. The police failed to open fire. Inside, Cameron was going upstairs when he was confronted by a rebel wanting to surrender. He handed him over to Turner and then encouraged five more trapped in a room to surrender by firing a shot over their heads. Meanwhile, Turner's section was systematically searching the rooms by the simple expedient of firing a round into every bed and cupboard. A dead sniper shot in the face was found on the roof. Corporal Hoddinott's section cleared outside buildings and captured another rebel. After a three-hour operation, Cameron had captured nine TNKU, eight Lee Enfield No. 4 rifles, a Bren gun, a Sten gun, tear gas grenades, a large supply of ammunition and police uniforms. Two Brens had suffered misfires. For his gallantry, Major Cameron was awarded the Military Cross.

With the Palace secure, B Company advanced the half mile west to the Mobile Reserve Unit Barracks located to the west of Panaga. Lieutenant McCall and a section moved through jungle while Sergeant McLeman and the rest of the Platoon advanced astride the road and recaptured the Barracks. Two rebels driven out of the jungle were shot at. McLeman had just finished repairing the second of the Brens when a car approached. Deciding to test the weapon, he fired a single shot at the windscreen and grazed the passenger in the head. The driver leapt out with a shotgun and a bandolier and, in a rather unwise display of courage, ran towards 2 Platoon. However, he had hardly taken a few steps before being felled by a volley from the disbelieving Jocks. The Platoon then searched the ransacked Barracks and surrounding houses and, after removing a rebel flag, withdrew to the roundabout and took up night defensive positions to cover the western approaches to Seria.

At 11.30am, B Company, 1/2 Gurkha Rifles commanded by Major Terry Bowring, strengthened by the Assault Pioneer Platoon, and ten buglers from the Pipes and Drums arrived by Beverley at Anduki Airfield from Labuan to reinforce the 1 Queens Own Highlanders and give it the standard three rifle companies. Lieutenant Colonel McHardy instructed B Company to release hostages in Kuala Belait. At 1.15pm, in a convoy of ten military Land Rovers, nine with trailers, and two police Land Rovers recaptured from the TNKU, the Gurkhas drove through Seria and met up with 2 Platoon. Here they waited until Mr Linton, the Managing Director of Brunei Shell Petroleum, was collected from his house in order to brief Bowring on the situation in Kuala Belait. Arriving on the eastern outskirts of the town at 4.00pm, the convoy encountered intermittent sniping and so the Gurkhas dismounted and advanced toward the town centre. When the leading platoon came under fire from the right, it assaulted the enemy position, which was held by about eight TNKU, who left in some haste, although one slower than his colleagues was captured, as were several weapons and some ammunition. Exchanging fire with retreating rebel groups, B Company advanced in bounds and by 6.00pm had recaptured the Government offices, which dominated the town. Bowring formed a perimeter encompassing the Shell Petroleum Hospital and the Post Office. The Gurkhas were refused entry to the hospital in case it came under fire. When the prisoner said that the Police Station was held by about sixty TNKU, McHardy reinforced the Gurkhas by sending 5 Platoon, B Company, commanded by Second Lieutenant James Cassels as a reserve based at Mobile Reserve Unit Barracks with Major Cameron. Ker-Lindsay had joined the Gurkhas but fell out favour with Major Bowring when he borrowed a military Land Rover so that he could see his parents, who had recently been held hostage in the Public Works Department. They were overjoyed to see him, not only because he had brought food and medical supplies but because they had been told that he had been killed.

Throughout the afternoon, McHardy tightened his grip on Seria and laid siege to the Police Station where the TNKU and their hostages were.

Intelligence that the bazaar was thought to contain about fifty hardline rebels was confirmed when several patrols came under fire of ranges up to 300yds and an observation post on top of an oil derrick overlooking the bazaar, manned by Medium Machine-Gun platoon commander, Lieutenant Simon Taylor, became a distinctly uncomfortable place when it was subjected to accurate sniper fire. The total armed TNKU strength was thought to be 200. Under intermittent but annoying sniper fire, B Company and 1 Platoon, from A Company, escorted engineers to check the vital main water valves and deep freeze temperature gauges of oil storage tanks and other equipment. Arrangements were made to feed the many Shell employers at work with rice and boxes of military 'compo' rations. As light fell, the Queens Own Highlanders had surrounded Seria:

East of Seria
Tactical HQ – Anduki Airport and blocking the road to Tutong
1 Platoon, A Company – Bailey Bridge over the Sungei Bera and the crossroads 400yds to the west
4 Platoon, B Company – Explosives Area

North of Seria
HQ B Company and Medium Machine Gun and Mortar Platoons – the Shell Transport Compound (Inverness)
6 Platoon – Community Centre (Angus)

West Seria
HQ A Company – Panaga Police Station
2 Platoon – western roundabout
3 Platoon – Roxana Cinema

Police Mobile Reserve Barracks
5 Platoon, B Company

Kuala Belait
B Company, 1/2 Gurkha Rifles

Lieutenant Colonel McHardy had every reason to be pleased. With just two companies he had seized the oil installations, Seria, Panaga, the

Summer Palace and Kuala Belait without suffering any serious casualties. Several TNKU had been killed and about 300 had been captured, as well as arms, ammunition and other paraphernalia.

Mrs Bennett and the other expatriates knew from the BBC World Service and news bulletins broadcast from Australia that military operations to rescue the hostages were in their final, and most risky, stages but there was nothing they could do. At about midnight Mrs Bennett took a telephone call from a Malay who told her not to worry as her husband and the other hostages would be home next day and then rang off. The night dragged on and then, at dawn, the Malay again called and told her not to worry. It appears that Ah Chuen, the Bennetts' amah, had told the caller that she was not at home but knew where she could be contacted. It later transpired he was one of several TNKU who had decided that enough was enough. Others were painting red crosses on their uniforms.

By 11 December it was absolutely clear to A.M. Azahari that his attempt to create a federation of North Borneo had failed. There had been no general uprising, and civil resistance to the rebellion in Sarawak and North Borneo had hardened, particularly as British troops had arrived. In Brunei, the population were still reeling from the shock of the rebellion and the TNKU was being systematically destroyed by the rapid British response. But he was still fighting a hopeless propaganda campaign and when he claimed that Sultan Omar was his friend and that all he, Azahari, needed was half a battalion to support the revolution, his appeal fell on stony ground. Realizing that assistance was not forthcoming and having outstayed his welcome in Manila, he went into exile in Indonesia, where he remained until he died. The rebel cause now lacked a political figurehead.

Throughout the night at Tactical HQ, Lieutenant John Duncan, the Intelligence Officer, had been collecting intelligence indicating that the Battalion was faced by at least 200 armed rebels in Seria, of which fifty 'hardcore' were active in the bazaar. The hostages were held in the Police Station, which was reinforced by bunkers underneath timber bungalows to the south of the compound. Several rebel strongpoints had been identified on the roofs of tall shops and houses in the centre of the bazaar. Rumours had emerged during the evening that the hostages held by the TNKU in Seria and Limbang would be executed the following day. The

Shell Public Relations Officer, Mr B. Levick, was particularly helpful in giving local information.

The Canberras of 81 Squadron at RAF Tengah had been alerted to support the Brunei operation on 10 December. An aircraft was tasked to support the Kuala Belait operation by distracting rebel attention by making a fake run over the town. Arriving at about 7.00am on 11 December, Flight Lieutenant Brown and his crew, Flight Lieutenant Armstrong, settled down in a medium to low-level profile but as the Canberra streaked along the coastal strip in yet another rainstorm, it clipped a radio mast that seriously damaged a wing. Brown coaxed the aircraft back to Labuan where the wing was completely replaced several days later. Meanwhile, Major Bowring had launched an attack on Kuala Belait Police Station and, although a few rebels offered token resistance near the Hong Kong Bank, by 10.00am the Gurkhas had liberated the hostages against very limited opposition. The Police Station, a shambles of discarded arms and ammunition and ransacked cabinets, was occupied. The Police officer-in-charge was contacted and by 12.30pm the following day, he had persuaded twenty-seven of his colleagues to return to work. Initially anxious about TNKU reprisals against their families, they were assured by the presence of the Gurkhas and were soon accompanying patrols.

Lieutenant Colonel McHardy prepared to deal with the TNKU in Seria by sending Major Wimberley and Captain MacDonald on an aerial recce of the area. Before departing for Anduki Airport, Wimberley instructed the Medium Machine Gun Platoon and Mortar Section to join 6 Platoon at the Community Centre and prepare for the assault. Company HQ and the Assault Pioneer were to remain at the Materials Area under the command of Company Sergeant Major Burns.

When McHardy gave his orders for the attack on the Police Station at 8.30am, he said that it was important that his Jocks were not seen to be surrounding the Police Station and to divert attention would be four 20 Squadron Hawker Hunters commanded by Squadron Leader R.A. Calvert. The Squadron had been on standby since 11.00am on 9 December, when it was warned to have four aircraft for deployment to Labuan at 1.00pm. However, poor weather over the South China Sea prevented deployment. It eventually left RAF Tengah at 6.48am on 11 December, arriving at Labuan at 8.42am. The plan of attack was:

> 11.00am. Captain MacDonald to move from the Explosive Area, make his way through the scrub and establish cut-off ambushes astride the narrow gauge railway that ran south-east to the water-pumping station at Badas. He was also to cover a wide track about a mile to the south. The idea was to offer the TNKU a funnel through which they could escape from Seria and then be trapped by ambushes.
>
> By 11.45am, B Company to establish strongpoints on the roofs of the Malay School and a block of flats about 200yds west of Seria Police Station.
>
> As soon as the strongpoints were occupied, Inspector Mustapha, of the Brunei Police, was to invite the TNKU to surrender.
>
> 12.00 noon. Supported by 20 Squadron, B Company to advance, seize the Police Station and release the hostages. McHardy emphasized that the Company was to use the Hunters and a Voice Twin Pioneer as distraction and that the British had total air superiority.

In a sortie to demonstrate British air power to the TNKU, between 7.29am and 8.20am, Calvert's three Hunters made low level passes over the Police Station – one of the Hunters opening fire with four Aden cannon, the 30mm rounds ripping in tall spouts into the sea – followed by a Voice Twin Pioneer inviting the rebels to surrender.

At 11.15am, 6 Platoon leading, the Medium Machine Gun Platoon and Mortar Section left the Community Centre, moved south for one block and swung left to approach the Police Station from the west. In spite of wrecked cars and lorries littering the road preventing clear observation, several TNKU were seen taking up defensive positions. Covered by the Machine Gun Platoon, 6 Platoon reached the Malay School and the flats without opposition and then took up position while the Mortar Platoon mounted Bren guns on the rooftops of both buildings. The Police Station was 200yds away and B Company was in position.

At 11.45am Inspector Mustapha, inviting the rebels to surrender, told them that resistance was pointless, but there was no response. The

Machine Gun Platoon then advanced, the Sections leapfrogging through each other, the leading one acting as fire control. Fifty yards short of the Police Station it came under fire at a range of 20yds from a Sterling sub-machine gun, shotgun and teargas from a fortified position under a house on the right of the road. Heavy suppressive fire was immediately returned with Mortar Section engaging at least two men running across the road. On time, the Hunters of Flight Lieutenants Carpenter and Marshall zoomed in from the south at low level and 'beat up' the bazaar and Police Station. A Voice Twin Pioneer again invited the rebels to surrender. The leading section of the Machine Gun Platoon had used the commotion to occupy a monsoon ditch 25yds from the Police Station perimeter and then Platoon HQ and the reserve section under the command of Sergeant Smith, the Platoon Sergeant, covered the crossroads in front of the building. When movement was seen inside the building, Lieutenant Simon Taylor, the Platoon Commander, and the reserve section made their way to the rear of the Police Compound, scaled the 7ft perimeter fence and rushed into the building, scattering the surprised TNKU and releasing thirty hostages from the Arms Store and sixteen crammed into a cell designed for one person. Five rebels, two of them wounded, were found sheltering in a room being used as a first aid post by a Brunei Shell Petroleum doctor and the Scottish nurse, Jean Scott. Taylor opened the compound gates for 6 Platoon to double forward and, searching the rear, found discarded equipment, including weapons. The majority of the TNKU who escaped withdrew through the funnel to the south and ran into MacDonald's ambushes.

Before the area around the Police Station could be properly searched and secured, near chaos broke out when a horde of journalists arrived in a fleet of Land Rovers. They had arrived at Anduki in two groups earlier in the day although one, representing the *Daily Express*, had managed to stow away on board a Beverley bringing in supplies earlier in the morning. His initiative led him to being locked up by Regimental Sergeant Major Hamilton. The press had been supervised by a Public Relations Officer staff officer from HQ FARELF but when they had arrived at Anduki, they had been prevented from going to Seria by Lieutenant Colonel McHardy because he was keen that their presence should not interfere with his operations. Nevertheless, he briefed them on the situation and as soon as he heard that Seria Police Station had been captured, he had sent them by

Land Rover to witness the release of the hostages. However, the journalists were disappointed not to be at the actual act of release but were determined to get their stories. It took until 3.00pm for B Company to clear the Police Stations and surrounding houses of TNKU.

Mrs Bennett and her friend Ann heard the Hunters beat up Seria Police Station and the Voice Twin Pioneer not only inviting the rebels to surrender but also sending a message to the hostages to keep away from windows and doors. Shortly after the Police Station had been recaptured, the British Shell Petroleum Company Information Officer telephoned the two women that the surviving hostages were safe. Later, a 1 Queens Own Highlanders Land Rover arrived at the Panaga married estate and dropped tired and hungry hostages at their homes.

After five days concealed in the house not far from the Shell radio station on a diet of rice and lentils, and in spite of persistent rumours of a large Indonesian force marching to Seria, they had seen the rebel morale dissipate when the Canberras and Hawker Hunters appeared. And then shortly after the Police Barracks were recaptured, Herbert Blanche and his friend were rescued by the Jocks, amid intermittent firefights. The next morning the early morning faithful in Kuala Belait were treated to a rendition of 'I belong to Glasgow' by two cheerful Scotsmen who had persuaded the Imam to allow them to offer a prayer over the mosque tannoy. Later, British Shell Petroleum gave each of the hostages a gold watch.

Major Bowring secured Kuala Belait by placing Company HQ and a platoon in the Government Offices, the second platoon in the Police Station, a third platoon in the offices of the Brunei Press and brought up Cassels' platoon to cover the River Belait ferry crossing. During the day four TNKU were killed, fifteen captured and the one wounded was taken prisoner. Twenty-five No. 5 Lee Enfield rifles, two shotguns, a .22 rifle, two 9mm automatic pistols, two boxes of Bren magazines, teargas grenades and .303 and 9mm military ammunition and shotgun cartridges were recovered in searches. Gurkha casualties were nil. Two Ferret Scout Cars from B Squadron, Queens Royal Irish Hussars, joined the Gurkhas after being unloaded at Miri from HMS *Tiger.* However, the TNKU continued to harass the town by crossing the river to attack patrols and cause concern. On 15 December, two troops supported the Gurkhas in a major cordon and search operation and prevented anyone using a boat to escape by crews machine-gunning them. In two days of internal security operations and firefights, the Gurkhas had killed six more TNKU rebels, including two shot by Second Lieutenant Cassels Jocks. Thirty-five were captured along with weapons, ammunition, documents and other equipment. When suggestions of Indonesian subversion emerged among the timber camps in the Tawau District of North Borneo, Brigadier Glennie ordered B Company, 1/2 Gurkha Rifles be deployed from Kuala Belait to support the North Borneo authorities. On 17 December, Bowring handed Kuala Belait over to Cassel 5 Platoon, 1 Queens Own Highlanders and flew to Tawau with his company.

Alastair Ker-Lindsay and his Iban stayed with A Company and over the next few days helped with cordon and search operations and provided valuable local knowledge and guides. They were later flown to the interior, helped release more hostages and then returned to Panaga to assist with the interrogation of prisoners. Ker-Lindsay left Brunei in March 1963 and was awarded not only the MBE for his contribution, but also the Sultan's personal honour, the Brunei Campaign Medal (silver) and a Gallantry commendation from the High Commissioner for Brunei, Sir Dennis White.

CHAPTER ELEVEN

42 Commando Brunei Town 9–11 December

At 1.30pm on 9 December, Lieutenant Colonel 'Todd' Sweeney, who commanded 1st Battalion, The Green Jackets (1 Green Jackets), was warned by Headquarters 17th Gurkha Division to prepare for immediate deployment to Sarawak. The 1 Green Jackets was originally raised in 1741 as the 54th Foot and renamed 43rd Foot seven years later. In 1757 the 52nd Foot was formed. Both regiments were amalgamated in 1881 to form the 1st and 2nd Battalions, The Oxfordshire Light Infantry and were then converted in 1908 to Oxfordshire and Buckinghamshire Light Infantry ('Ox and Bucks'). In 1958, the Regiment was named 1 Green Jackets along with the 2 Green Jackets (Kings Royal Rifle Corps) and 3 Green Jackets (The Rifle Brigade). The 'Ox and Bucks' had an illustrious history in the Seven Years War, the Peninsula War against Napoleon, in South Africa in the mid-1850s, the Indian Mutiny, against the Maoris in the 1860s, followed by the Boer War. During the First World War battalions had served on the Western Front and in the Middle East, and during the Second World War it saw service in France, North Africa, Italy, North-West Europe and Burma. Six members were awarded the Victoria Cross, all to non-commissioned officers, including Private Addison in the Indian Mutiny. Since 1945, it had served in the Suez Canal Zone and Cyprus.

As a platoon commander with D Company, 2 Ox and Bucks, Sweeney had taken part in the historic glider assault on the Orne Bridges on D-

Day, an event that, in 1962, was playing to packed Services Kinema Corporation audiences in *The Longest Day*. Based at Penang in Malaya, the battalion was part of 63 Gurkha Infantry Brigade Group. As with other commanding officers, Sweeney's first problem was to assemble his men. Major David Mostyn MBE, who commanded B Company, was playing polo 100 miles away, the Intelligence Officer was in hospital and the Regimental Signals Officer was with the 1st New Zealand Infantry Battalion on the Thai border. The platoon guarding the Commander-in-Chief's residence and the demonstration platoon at the Jungle Warfare School were both recalled and, by midnight, the entire battalion bar four, who could not be found, were on their way by lorry for the 640-mile journey to Singapore Naval Dockyard escorted by Royal Military Police, the convoy drove through the night, stopping every two hours or so. Sweeney received orders that the convoy was to make its way to Singapore Naval Dockyard.

The cruiser HMS *Tiger* was scheduled to dock at Singapore Naval Base at 8.00am on Monday, 10 December, after a visit to Australia, when late on Sunday signals arrived that she was required to lift troops to Brunei. Preparations for the ceremonial entry and the awning for the Admiral's farewell cocktail party on the quarter deck were replaced by awnings covering the decks and forward deck. All boats, except the whalers, were landed and then a composite troop of six Ferret Scout Cars commanded by Lieutenant Cramsie from B Squadron, Queens Royal Irish Hussars, nine Land Rovers, ten trailers, a tractor and two water bowsers were swung on board, as were forty tons of stores. The remainder of the Squadron were loaded into the two 46 Squadron LCTs for what turned out to be an extremely bumpy voyage across the South China Sea. During the evening, 1 Green Jackets and elements of HQ Company, 42 Commando, embarked. The ship was designed to accommodate 400 troops but as the last of the 634 men filed on board, the captain was heard to exclaim, 'For God's sake, let's sail before we sink!" At 10.45pm, the cruiser set a course for Borneo on a flat sea but in heavy rain. The next day the chefs prepared 5,000 meals, starting with breakfast at 5.30am, lunch at 10.00am and the evening meal at 3.00pm. The troops were also entitled to a tot of rum.

Formed in 1943 from 1 Battalion, Royal Marines, 42 Commando was part of 3 Commando Brigade, an Army formation, during the Battle of Kangaw in Burma. When the Army Commando units were disbanded in

1946 and the Royal Marines took over the amphibious warfare role, 3 Commando Brigade reformed from 42 Commando with its Far East knowledge and 40 and 45 Commandos with their Mediterranean and North European experiences respectively, and in 1962 were the Far East floating Theatre Reserve.

In September 1962 the Royal Marines was in transition as it discarded its Second World War order of battle of five 65-strong rifle troops and a heavy weapons troop and adopted the Army structure of three rifle companies and a Support Company. The original structure was designed for raiding and special assault and had been retained by the Royal Marines determined to be independent of the Army, but it had proved operationally awkward during rotations. Now 42 Commando consisted of K, L, M, Headquarters and Support Companies, each of three Troops commanded by a Royal Marines captain, who equated in status to an Army major. Troop strengths were similar to Army platoons of three eight-man sections, one of which was sometimes commanded by a sergeant, and the other two by corporals. Troop Headquarters consisted of the Troop Officer, Troop Sergeant and two radio operators. There was also a Support Section of a 2in mortar-man and two-man 3.5in M2 Bazooka anti-tank rocket launcher crew. When Second Lieutenant Richard Targett-Adams took command of 5 Troop, he did something that he had never been able to do before – interview the men in the Troop. His Troop Sergeant was Sergeant John Bickford, a physical training instructor and noted football player. In Support Company were the Assault Engineers, Reconnaissance Troop, Mortar Troop with six 3in mortars, Anti-Tanks and the Medium Machine Gun Troop of six .303-inch Vickers Mark 1 medium machine-guns. Introduced into service in 1912, the Vickers was synonymous with reliability. During the Battle of the Somme, one gun fired 10,000 rounds an hour for twelve hours without a failure. The rate of fire of was 450 rounds per minute. Crewed by three men, the Number One and commander on the trigger fired four-second bursts by counting 'One banana, two bananas, three bananas, four bananas – stop' in order to keep the gun on a steady platform. The Number Two fed the 250-round ammunition belt onto the feed tray and prevented jams. A feature of the barrel was that it was kept cool by water fed from a condenser. It was the job of the Number Three to keep the condenser topped up with water and ensure the Number Two was supplied with ammunition. The Medical

Officer, Sick Berth Attendants, the Padre and Education Officer were Royal Navy. Instructor Lieutenant Colin George doubled up as an additional Intelligence Officer and would be Mentioned in Despatches for his operational work during the follow up phase of the rebellion.

Although the Royal Marines had an advantage over the Army of being in postings longer than two years, unlike the infantry and cavalry which retained regimental structures, its policy of 'trickle' draftings meant that units had to cope with frequent changes of personnel.

In September, Captain Jeremy Moore MC took L Company on the four week Exercise Dervish in North Borneo to become familiar with the new organization. Training was progressive with the first week concentrating on individual battle skills. Since Targett-Adams was relatively new, Moore transferred him to 6 Troop to work with the experienced Sergeant John French. The second week was devoted to section drills, the third to Troop battle drills and the fourth in company attack and defence profiles. Supporting Moore as his second-in-command was Lieutenant Peter Waters.

At midday on Sunday, 9 December, Headquarters 3 Commando Brigade placed 42 Commando on four-hour notice. Captain Jeremy Moore was writing Christmas cards in his cabin when a steward told him that Lieutenant Colonel Bridges wished to see him in his room in the Officers' Mess. Born in Staffordshire to a colonel who had won the Military Cross during the Battle of the Somme in 1916, Moore was commissioned into the Royal Marines in 1947 and had also been awarded the Military Cross in April 1952, while serving with 40 Commando in Malaya, when his patrol killed two Communist Terrorists in an ambush. Assuming that Bridges was expecting him to entertain a guest, he found that he was the only company commander present. Bridges briefed him about Operation Ale and told him that since the K and M company commanders could not be found, L Company was to be the advance guard for the 42 Commando deployment to Brunei. Bridges agreed to a request from Moore that the L Company weapons being serviced in workshops be returned immediately and that he be allocated a range at first light next day to zero them.

Meanwhile, Major John Taplin, the second-in-command, had initiated Operation Round Up by announcing on the Station tannoy 'The CO is away at a briefing and the unit is on four hours standby to go to Brunei where there is a revolt'. Sergeant Walter Macfarlane had arrived in

November from the Royal Marine Reserve in London and was attached to Company Headquarters; he was waiting to take over as the 5 Troop Sergeant from Sergeant Bickford. When the 21-year-old commando-trained L Company Sick Berth Attendant Terry Clarke returned to barracks from a weekend in Johore Bahru, he was told by Petty Officer Platt that since he had not been in camp when L Company mobilized, another Sick Berth Attendant was going in his place. When Clarke argued that he had been the Company medic since being drafted to 42 Commando in May and it was his job to go, Platt agreed provided he was ready by the time that L Company deployed. Sergeant Les Wakeling was about to go swimming with his family when he was instructed to return to Support Company and prepare No 1 Medium Machine Gun Section for deployment with L Company. Number One gun was commanded by Marine Peter Stubbs and Number Two by Marine Tony Daker, then on fatigues for the day in the Sergeants' Mess. Several months earlier Daker had been one of about sixty Royal Marines who had been extras during the *The Longest Day*. He had 'stormed' ashore on Omaha Beach to be 'met' by Henry Fonda, who had flown in by helicopter and while playing a British infantryman on Sword Beach had had the dubious distinction of being told to 'Piss off' by the not yet so famous Scottish thespian, Sean Connery, acting as an infantryman.

By 5.00pm on 10 December, Bridges told his Orders Group that L Company was to move to Brunei on light scales of ammunition with its 3in Mortars and Vickers Medium Machine Guns for a 'shooting war'. Only fighting order and a small kit bag containing a change of clothing, towel and other basic items, were to be taken.

In the six weeks since the exercise in North Borneo, the Company order of battle had changed. The 5 Troop Officer, Lieutenant Paddy Davis, was experienced but the remaining two officers, Second Lieutenants Derek Lloyd of 4 Troop and Targett-Adams of 6 Troop, were not. Company Sergeant Major Cyril Scoins was experienced as were Sergeants French and John Russell, the 4 and 6 Troop Sergeants respectively. Moore sent Sergeant Macfarlane to 5 Troop to support Bickford; 4 Troop had experienced few changes since Exercise Dervish. When Marine Mike Bell rejoined Corporal Bill Lester's 4 Section in 5 Troop after a spell at Company Headquarters, the only person that Lester knew had sufficient experience was Bell and he told him that 'If anything happens to me, you're in charge'. But 6 Troop was at about half strength and was being reinforced by marines from other companies, including two cooks, Corporals 'Powder' Horn and Parrish, now section commanders. Moore instructed Russell to remain at Sembawang and send men to join 6 Troop in Brunei. Attached to Company was a detachment from the Commando Intelligence Section of Sergeant David Smith and Marines Ken Fyffe and Darryl Needham. Fyffe had been playing golf at RAF Seletar when a Royal Military Policeman in a Land Rover told him he was to return to barracks at once and offered him a lift. He found the sedentary nature of the Intelligence Section to be a 'square number', in other words, boring.

L Company began deploying during the early evening when a Beverley flew fifty-six men from RAF Seletar to Brunei Airport. Expecting a hostile reception, as the ramp and doors opened, the Royal Marines charged out and took up defensive positions only to be greeted by 1/2 Gurkha Rifles defending the airport. Captain Moore telephoned Headquarters 99 Brigade and was told by the Brigade Major to stay at the airport overnight in order to avoid 'blue on blue' contacts with the Gurkhas, who had imposed a dusk-to-dawn curfew and were inclined to shoot first and ask questions later. When he was then told that L Company would be guarding the Residency, he advised the Brigade Major that he had not brought the best company that he was likely to have at his disposal for it to be used for a task that could be carried out by a few police officers. During the night more L Company travelled in a Transport Command Britannia to Labuan and were then flown to Brunei by a Beverley.

Lieutenant Colonel Bridges left RAF Changi with his Reconnaissance Group and the balance of Support Company at 9.00pm and arrived at Labuan at midnight, where he remained until 6.30am the next day. Captain Moore was shaving in the gents' cloakroom when his Marine Officer Assistant said that a brigadier wanted to see him. It was Brigadier Patterson, who gave him two tasks:

> Plan the rescue of hostages in Limbang, a task he was to hand over to Lieutenant Colonel Bridges when he arrived and 'to carry it out, whichever was the sooner'.
>
> Find accommodation in Brunei, and transport and river craft for 42 Commando.

Moore despatched Lieutenant Waters to find a hotel for the Commando, which he did – the Brunei Hotel. Among those who also appeared was Captain Derek Oakley, the GSO 3 (Intelligence), Headquarters 3 Commando Brigade, who had made his way to Labuan on HMS *Cavalier* and had then scrounged a lift to Brunei. Moore borrowed a vehicle and, accompanied by a 5 Troop escort and Sick Berth Attendant Clarke, drove to Headquarters 99 Gurkha Brigade at Police Headquarters to learn as much as he could about Limbang. He met Superintendent Millington, the Sarawak Police Field Force commander, who said that he had motored up the river to Limbang and had been fired on from the Police Barracks, where, he believed, hostages were being held. Moore also assumed it was the rebel command post and, if there was protracted fighting, the hostages could either be shot or used as human shields. When Bridges arrived at Brunei Airport at 7.00am, Patterson told him that while Brunei Town was more stable than twelve hours previously, the situation in Seria and Panaga was confused, although the Queens Own Highlanders were regaining control. He instructed that 42 Commando was to attack Limbang as quickly as possible. Moore briefed Bridges and Captain Benjie Walden, the Commando Intelligence Officer, of his conversation with Millington and then left to requisition transport. While returning to Brunei Town with several Public Works Department lorries, the convoy was ambushed as they approached a tree felled across the road. Swift anti-ambush drills cleared the immediate area.

Limbang sits on a bend on the eastern banks of the River Limbang. The only road from Brunei Town was on the Sarawak side, but it was thought to be in very poor repair. The only approach was by the river. Approaching the town from downstream there were houses, some on stilts, a bazaar and, further to the south, the Divisional Police Barracks, and then about 60yds of open ground scattered with a few trees and buildings to the hospital, which was also brick built. To the south there were more government buildings and houses, which included the Residency. The waterfront frontage was about 1,000yds long and 500yds wide. The Barracks had been built in 1958 and consisted of two single storey buildings of the Police Station connected by an overhead rain shelter to the sleeping quarters and a recreational room.

When Bridges learnt that 42 Commando was to be deployed on other tasks, he instructed Moore to rescue the hostages and capture the town.

Undertaking to gather information he and Walden carried out an aerial reconnaissance in a Twin Pioneer and, although the cloud base was low, obtained visual information that confirmed that an air photograph taken in 1959 was still accurate. Below them, Richard and Dorothy Morris had been escorted to the Residency for a bath, change of clothes and to collect food and medical supplies. When the Twin Pioneer circled overhead they noted that their escort were suddenly anxious and, by the afternoon, several told them that they no longer supported the rebellion and hoped the Resident would deal with rebels when the British were in charge again. Increasing numbers of Red Cross visitors brought food and cigarettes and passed news of the British successes in Brunei Town, Seria and Kuala Belait. During the evening, the Morrises were escorted to the hospital, accompanied by more assurances from disloyal TNKU, and were placed in a locked consulting room that had two beds. They met the six fellow-hostages who had also been moved from the Barracks. In anticipation of rescue, the Morrises believed that it would either be by the Royal Marines or the Parachute Regiment and, to help them identify friend and foe, they composed a ditty based on the nursery rhyme *She'll Be Coming around the Mountain*, which they intended to sing with all the vigour they could muster. They changed the verse to *They'll be wearing dark green/red bonnets when they come, when they come.* They also planned to move a bed into a corner of the room near the door as a shelter.

At 12.30pm, Bridges and Brigadier Patterson discussed the options available to L Company, with the latter emphasizing that the hostages should be released unharmed as soon as possible. The strategy assumed that the TNKU would defend the Police Barracks. Captain Moore then gathered the L Company officers and SNCOs in the Brunei Hotel and explained that it was thought that there were approximately eleven hostages and, although their exact location was not known, it was likely to be either at the Police Barracks or the Jail or both. Poring over a map which had large areas titled 'Not surveyed', Moore said that the undulating nature of the ground and the lack of detail on the map would make planning difficult and, even if they used the road, they still had to cross the river. He had therefore concluded that a dawn landing from the river was the only option. Even so, if things went wrong, L Company would be isolated and rescue difficult. The landing had to succeed. Hardline rebel strength was estimated to be about thirty. Moore was unaware that when the Twin Pioneer flew over Limbang, the leaders had instructed their men to conceal themselves inside houses. No defensive positions had been identified; however, monsoon drains alongside the road made good trenches and the undergrowth and jungle gave good cover. The rebels most likely had access to automatic weapons liberated from the police armoury, although their weapon handling was likely to be superficial. A few probably had shotguns, which were useful in close quarter fighting, while beyond 100yds, the Royal Marines could bring down heavier fire.

With a landing accepted, Captain Oakley and Lieutenant Davis searched for suitable boats along the town jetty and requisitioned two Z-Craft belonging to the Brunei Government, named *Nakhoda Manis* and *Sindaun,* that they found at the north end. Both had been ordered in 1958 by Richard Morris, then Commissioner of Development in Brunei, for the development of the interior. Not dissimilar in appearances to landing craft, they were commercial craft about 120ft long with a 30ft beam and drawing about 9ft, and were flat-bottomed. The wheelhouses were covered in canvas and the well deck consisted of wooden planks. There was also a ramp. On board the *Sindaun* were two new yellow Mitsubishi bulldozers. Their seats were still covered in plastic. The Royal Marines were trained to land from Landing Craft Infantry with their steel sides and ramps but all that was now available was an unarmoured civilian landing craft with very little protection. Oakley and Davis were wondering how to crew them when, at about midday, HMS *Fiskerton* and *Chawton* berthed alongside the jetty, bringing more 42 Commando collected from Labuan.

During their two-day transit across from Singapore to Labuan, all weapons were exercised, including the Lanchester sub machine-guns. Even cutlasses were sharpened. When the ships reached Labuan on 10 December, Midshipman Rupert Best on board HMS *Chawton* had seen the Twin Pioneers delivering the Queens Own Highlanders to Anduki. After being delayed by a violent thunderstorm, the warships anchored in Victoria Harbour during the evening. Following a telephone conversation with Brigadier Glennie, in which he was instructed to support operations in Brunei and provide long range communications, Lieutenant Commander Black left the following day with the Royal Marines. Also on board was Captain Mouton, the Brunei Director of Marine. Since Brunei

Town was about twenty miles from the sea along a winding jungle-clad river and opposition was expected, Black ordered the two ships to clear for action – Condition Yankee – watertight doors shut, clips thrown and the Bofors and Oerlikon and bridge-mounted Bren manned, with the Royal Marines taking up stations on the upper decks as best they could. Mechanical Engineer Tony Standish, the 'Freshwater Tanky', recalls:

> I observed from my action stations (steering gear compartment aft) that the Royal Marines were on full alert, safety catches off and eyes scanning the jungle foliage on both banks of the river. Not a word was spoken and the tension could be felt as we slowly sailed up river. Although very much alert, the Marines relaxed slightly and one young Marine offered me a packet of Spangles from his rations and, being a stoker, I was partial to a bit of 'nutty.' The Royal Marine sergeant observed this transaction and some leg pulling and lamp swinging broke the tension.

The Ton-class minesweepers were unable to distil drinking water from sea water and so a mechanical engineer had the vital job of topping up the drinking water tanks at every opportunity. 'Tanky' was the first man ashore and the last on board before the ship sailed.

As Brunei Town came into sight as the ships rounded a bend, those on board saw a town dominated by the domed mosque while to port lay the Kampong Ayer of wooden houses with rush roofs that stood in the shallows on stilts and were connected by narrow twisting walkways. Black announced his arrival flying a large battle ensign and with the HMS *Fiskerton* tannoy playing *Heart of Oak*. Lieutenant Down was delighted that he had managed not to run aground. After the Royal Marines had disembarked, the ships agreed arcs of fire, posted armed sentries fore and aft, manned the main armaments and rigged a necklace of lights to deter swimmers planting limpet mines. With Captain Oakley acting as an intermediary, Lieutenant Colonel Bridges contacted Lieutenant Commander Black to advise him of the situation, in particular of the dusk to dawn curfew and, outlining the situation in Limbang, then asked him for naval help, emphasizing that time was short. Black immediately agreed and both minesweepers supplied complements commanded by their First Lieutenants to operate the two Z-Craft:

Nakhoda Manis. Crewed by HMS *Chawton* personnel with Lieutenant David Willis in command. Midshipman Rupert Best was his second–in-command with Petty Officer David Kirwin as the stoker, Leading Seaman Maher as the coxswain and Able Seaman 'Gabby' Hayes as the deckhand.

Sindaun. Crewed by HMS *Fiskerton* personnel, Lieutenant Peter Down commanded with Petty Officer 'Taff' O'Leary as the stoker, Acting Leading Seaman Mike Taylor as his coxswain and Able Seamen Laurie Johnson and 'Pincher' Martin as the deckhands.

Lieutenant Willis, appointed as the Senior Naval Officer largely because he was Black's First Lieutenant, was to ensure that the assault force arrived off Limbang but, once the landing was under way, the Z-Craft were then under the tactical direction of the senior Royal Marine on board. None of his men had any experience in handling the Z-Craft or landing craft operations but they were now being committed to an opposed landing. It was a daunting prospect. Willis and his detachment were given strict instructions by Lieutenant Harry Mucklow, second-in-command to Black, not to do anything rash. The Royal Navy began familiarizing themselves with the Z-Craft by checking engines, controls and lighting but, when they found that the ramp was lowered manually, troops charging ashore seemed out of the question. Lieutenant Downs noted that cables and wiring were not in armoured sleeves. Metal sheeting was erected around the well deck to provide some shelter for the Royal Marines. The Vickers section had yet to arrive. They were to be fitted on the Sindaun. Marine Daker remembers:

> During the afternoon, it had been decided that my Vickers would be mounted up front on the port side and the second Vickers port side by the bridge. The bridge was quite high with lots of glass. At the centre of the craft there was a bulldozer, which would hopefully offer cover from the starboard side. Some of the planking was removed from the side and the decision was made to have both machine guns in the 'lowest service position'. It was at this time that it started to rain, as only it could in this part of the world.

A near full moon was predicted, which would ease navigation; however, the rains meant that the river state was high. There were no Ordnance Survey maps or Hydrographic Office charts extending to Limbang and, since local boat traffic did not move after dark, there were no buoys or navigation lights. Mouton had previously marked his preferred channel by placing spars on the main mud banks, but these were prone to shift after the monsoon rains. Depths could not be confirmed. Navigation was problematic; however, Captain Mouton did have a large wall-mounted map from which sketches and notes were made by the two First Lieutenants. Down recalls:

> It was back to the techniques of Nelson's navy when approaching an unknown shore. Our attack chart was a postcard-sized sketch with pilotage directions of the nature:
>
> 'Take main channel out of lagoon for approx 8 miles. As river bears right, take second tributary on left. Limbang town is on the left bank of a wide right hand bend. Residency and police post at far end of the town on a grassy slope, about 25 yards from the riverbank. Wooden jetty with a boathouse opposite police post. Believed one fathom clearance alongside.'

Throughout the afternoon, Bridges, Moore, Black and Oakley detailed the attack with the principal aim being to capture the Police Barracks, thereby disrupting rebel command and control and also rescuing the hostages. Surprise and speed. The concept developed was:

> Sergeant Smith, who spoke Malay, would invite the TNKU to surrender.
> If this failed, 5 Troop and Company Tactical Headquarters were to land from *Nakhoda Manis* opposite the Barracks under covering fire provided by the remainder of the Company.
> 4 and 6 Troops to land and conduct subsequent operations, according to the intelligence collected, and expand the beachhead by clearing south toward the Residency and adjacent government buildings.

It was hoped that the TNKU would be too busy surviving the battle or running away to think about the hostages. It was assumed that news of the requisitioning of the Z-crafts and battle preparations would reach Limbang. This appears not to have been the case.

Shortly before Richard Morris took up his appointment as Resident, Fifth Division, he was requested to call at the offices of the Sarawak Red Cross in Kuching, where he was asked to revive the Limbang Branch, which had lapsed due to lack of support and funding. Agreeing to do so, he said that he would wait until he was more familiar with the people of the district. No sooner had he arrived in Limbang when he received a letter from Michael Manggie, an Iban who was the Honourable Secretary of the Limbang Red Cross, asking if he could stay overnight in the Residency so that he could attend a meeting of the local group. On 25 November Mrs Morris chaired a well-attended Red Cross meeting at the Limbang Recreation Club and when it was agreed that a headquarters was required, a Chinese businessman undertook to provide building material and an English former nurse, Mrs Helen Brake, agreed to develop a training programme in First Aid and home nursing. Links were to be established for cadets and the Voluntary Aid Detachment.

As soon as the rebellion broke out, the embryonic Limbang Red Cross swung into action. Under the inspired leadership of the Limbang Postmaster, Awang Omar bin Abang Samaudin, who was on leave pending retirement, he and his wife restored the authority of the International Committee of the Red Cross by making a uniform complete with Red Crosses sewn onto pockets, sleeves and the backs of several white shirts. Determined to impose its authority on the TNKU, on 9 December, wearing a Red Cross cadet beret of one of his daughters, Awang and a helper presented themselves at the Jail and asked Salleh bin Sambas if they could inspect the conditions under which the hostages were being held, as was his right under the Geneva Conventions. Mrs Morris writes:

> Later that same day (Sunday) our spirits rose considerably when members of the hastily re-constituted Limbang Red Cross appeared, with coffee, rice, towels, codeine, bandages and ointment for the wounded Police Inspector in the next cell, and friendly smiling faces. These tireless brave and devoted few did more than they will ever know for the morale as well as for the comfort of all of us behind the bars. One of the most unsettling

> aspects of our incarceration was the very distasteful business of being stared at and glared at by our guards through the bars of our only window, which looked onto the short passage between the cells. Expressions varied, but even when one turned one's back to the window it took great strength of will not to turn round and glare back when a new guard took over and the scrutiny was more prolonged.

Sambas agreed to further Red Cross visits. When Awang asked that Mrs Brake, who was being held under house detention with her husband, should accompany him, he agreed and also granted permission to other officials, including an Iban anti-malarial sprayer and a Senior Hospital Assistant. The sprayer was employed by the Medical Department to spray DDT in longhouses in a programme devised by the World Health Organisation to rid British North Borneo of malaria. He had originally wanted to join the Sarawak Constabulary Field Force but had been rejected because he was an inch below the required height. During the afternoon, Awang and Mrs Brake appeared at the Jail and, although not permitted to enter the cells, passed bottles of drinking water, rice, a blanket and some English language magazines to the hostages. The appearance of the Limbang Red Cross brought a major rise in the morale and hope of the hostages but even so the future for the hostages appeared uncertain. Mrs Morris describes how she felt:

> During the night I had heard whispered discussions in Malay between the guards sitting at the top of the steps, and just outside our cell door. Although I only heard snatches, there was frequent mention of prisoners, sunrise and shooting. I will never know, nor do I really want to know now, whether it was just my over-taxed imagination, or wishful thinking on the part of our guards, but I do know that I took a good whack of codeine tablets about midnight, prayed as I'd never prayed before that we would all be given courage to face bravely whatever lay ahead, and then I prayed for our children. Then I did sleep and so effective was the codeine that when I woke the sun was shining through the chinks in the walls; it was long past sunrise, and Dick and our other cell-mate, Dayak Constable Bisop Anak Kunjan, were both very alive

> and there were the usual greetings being called from cell to cell, and even to add to all this a familiar whuffling and chinking under the gaol.
>
> Our dog Spatter had found us. Spatter-the-Indestructible, whom we were fairly sure had been shot on the night of 7/8 December, after helping to give the alarm that our compound was being surrounded. However, being an old and a wise dog he had presumably headed for the jungle when the firing came too close, and bided his time before emerging to see how the new regime was acquitting itself. Finding no joy at the Residency where twenty-six rebels were making themselves at home, he had continued his search and finally smelt us out. We received a tremendous welcome when we emerged for our early morning escorted stroll to the loo, and from then on he never left the premises. Some of our guards were actually feeding him with rice and he was soon allowed to sit at the head of the steps. So possessive did he become that on several occasions he even growled at the incoming new guard, and we would have to shout to him to lie down before he got shot, the clot!

During the night of 9/10 December, Superintendent George Millington, the Sarawak Police Field Force commander, led a reconnaissance patrol in the police launch *Lefee* to Limbang but did not approach too close for fear of coming under fire. However, he glided past twice. Ashore, Sambas instructed his men not to take any action and remain hidden. Millington also met several local Malays paddling from Limbang in their canoes and gained a considerable amount of information, in particular that hostages had been captured, including the Resident. He persuaded one of them to take him to Limbang and, on the edge of town, he saw about twenty armed rebels. The future of the Limbang hostages was still in the balance. Mrs Morris recalls:

> The guards on the first few days were fairly cocky and the reciprocal glares were a mixture of triumph and dislike on their parts and of assumed indifference on ours. By Monday the tougher, more dedicated elements had been despatched to the outskirts and upriver as rumours spread of Dayaks coming down to 'do over' the TNKU. We had suggested when we could that

> they should see that their wives, children and homes were adequately protected in this event, and by Monday with each change of guard there appeared to be more of the older men, of less aggressive men, and including some who appeared to be genuinely distressed at the turn of events and even ashamed of the role they were being forced to play. Many of these had, in fact, been beaten up and threatened with harm to their families and homes, if they refused to join the cause. With these the photos of our children were always a talking point, and many of them echoed our own heart-felt relief that Geraldine and Adrian had not yet arrived in Limbang for their Christmas holidays.

Still at liberty was Fritz Klattenhoff, of the Peace Corps. Warned by a local that something was going to happen during the night of December 8, he had not slept in the Government Rest House and had found a barn. Woken by the battle at Police Barracks, at first he thought the shooting was firecrackers from a Chinese wedding scheduled that day. He was careful throughout the day not to be seen but then learnt that a friend, a police officer, had been killed and his body was lying on the road. That night, Klattenhoff and a Malay, in an act of considerable courage, found some shovels, crept to where the police officer's body lay, and dragged it to a grave. The next night Klattenhoff found accommodation in a barn of a family he thought friendly, but it seems that the rebels were alerted by the disappearance of the body. They knew that the Peace Corps worker was in the area and carried out an intensive search, focusing, in particular, on families known to be friendly with Klattenhoff. Even though he knew the risks, during the morning of Monday, 10 December, Klattenhoff was feeding thirteen cattle and pigs at the farm project and chatting to a Chinese friend when he was challenged by a Chinese-Malay TNKU. His friend advised him to run but Klattenhoff believed that, as an American and a member of the Peace Corps, he would be immune from arrest until another Chinese-Malay and about six rebels armed with shotguns seized him and prodded him into a captured police Land Rover. Driven to the Barracks, when he was interviewed by Sambas, Klattenhoff showed his Peace Corps identity card and reminded him that he was an American, an admission that resulted in him being locked up in the Jail with the Roman Catholic priests.

By 10 December the number of rebels in Limbang had increased to an estimated 300 but this included a sizeable portion conscripted from *kampongs* close to the town and in Temburong District. The Limbang Company was expected to reinforce the TNKU elsewhere and ensure that there was a hardcore defending Limbang. Not all were willing and a number slipped into the jungle and returned to their families.

In the late afternoon several more L Company boarded the Royal Australian Air Force C-130 Hercules at RAF Changi. Inside was the Vickers section. Two hours later, after the pilot laconically announced that he was short of fuel and would be landing at Brunei Airport, the Royal Marines were driven in a commandeered lorry to the Brunei Hotel and rejoined L Company, as it was completing its battle preparations. For the first time for many, ammunition was limitless. Marine Brian Downey, a 4 Troop Bren gunner, had twenty-five magazines, each with twenty-eight rounds and 800 rounds in his pack. His Number Two had twenty-six magazines and 500 rounds; 1/2 Gurkha Rifles provided additional ammunition for the Vickers. As dusk took over from daylight, Moore issued his orders. Second Lieutenant Targett-Adams remembers that it was detailed with contingencies built in:

> I got my section commanders together and briefed them not in as much detail obviously as Jeremy Moore had given us. I did not want to confuse people with too many 'what ifs', so I stuck to the immediate objective which was how we were going to land and what everybody was going to do immediately on landing. Jeremy gave us about an hour to actually sit down and think about what all this was going to give. Whilst I was formulating my particular briefing, the acting Troop Sergeant got the Section Commanders together and told them we would be having a briefing in an hour and in the meantime to get back to their sections and check their kit and make sure the lads had their weapons, ammunition and we knew where we were expected to be and that we would be moving off at about 10.00 pm. At that stage, as far as I remember, that is all the information that the troop had until I actually came and gave them my briefing in detail.

At about 10.00pm, L Company paraded outside the hotel. It had recently rained and SBA Clarke caused some amusement when he slipped and his

Sterling accidentally discharged. 'Thank god it was you and not us,' he was ribbed. The roll was called and, as L Company marched on the jetty, Black recalled how heartening it was to see the Royal Marines silently appear, faces blackened, a few quiet orders and then they filed onto the Z-Craft. All wore their Green Berets with their glinting cap badge to help identification. Each marine used his large pack as a sandbag. On board *Nakhoda Manis* was:

> 5 Troop.
> The Company 'R Group'. Captain Moore, his signaller, Marine Officer Assistant escort and Sergeant Smith of the Commando Intelligence Section. They were stationed in the wheelhouse.

On *Sindaun*:

> 4 Troop.
> 6 Troop. Although a section short, it had been brought nearly up to strength by men from Company Headquarters.
> The Medium Machine Gun Section. Each gun had 6,000 rounds of ammunition.
> Company Headquarters commanded by Lieutenant Waters.

Targett-Adams recalled:

> Everybody got on board in a very disciplined manner. Unusually for Marines there was not a lot of joshing around and that made me feel, 'Yes, these guys are taking this seriously' and at some level it had got through to the jokers if you like that this was serious and that something serious was going to go down. We did not know for certain how long the journey would take and that was one of the hardest bits.

On HMS *Fiskerton*, Lieutenant Commander Black converted his cabin into a Tactical Headquarters staffed by Lieutenant Peter Ford RN, the ship's gunnery officer, and Captain Oakley. The ship also provided communications between Singapore and Brunei, relaying signals through HMS *Woodbridge Haven*, and later HMS *Albion*.

At midnight under a steady drizzle, the Z-Craft slipped from the jetty, butted into the River Brunei with the *Nakhoda Manis* leading, without lights and in a silent routine. The only navigational aid was a military prismatic compass. Lieutenant Willis followed the advice of Captain Mouton and kept close to the bank in order to identify the channel that led south to the River Limbang but, in the darkness, missed the jungle-clad turning. He then took several attempts to turn the lighter around, in confined waters, with poor astern performance. *Sindaun* took over the lead. Both discovered that mangrove trees roots can extend some several yards from the bank and are so low that openings to tributaries are screened. Lieutenant Down recalled, 'We bumped our way upstream.' After about ten miles *Nakhoda Manis* misjudged a corner and crashed into dense mangrove swamp, sending the sound of snapping branches echoing through the silent jungle and losing an engine. At about 5.00am, a mile north of Limbang, Willis laid up in an area of nipa palm. The jungle was silent and thus minimum movement was needed to prevent sounds created by a careless collision between a rifle barrel and part of the vessel, slapping whining mosquitoes and ants or the shock of the occasional rat falling from branches, ringing like a church bell through the stillness. There was also anxiety. Marine John Genge, normally the Company armourer, was attached to 4 Troop:

> The feeling was very apprehensive and the lads on the boat, the sailors, came round and gave us tea and various things. How they managed to rustle it up, I will never know. You had a good feeling amongst yourselves, like a brotherhood. You did not know what was going to happen to you the next morning and you wondered if you would see the sun come up the next day.

CHAPTER TWELVE

The Battle of Limbang and Bekenu 12 December

During the night of 11/12 December, HMS *Tiger* received orders to land part of 1 Green Jackets at Miri. Steaming at 30 knots, the cruiser arrived offshore in the drizzly gloom of first light on 12 December and prepared for an opposed landing.

At about 5.45am, the two Z-Craft stirred and some forty-five minutes later they glided into the main channel. In the half light of dawn, it was still silent – no barking dogs, no crowing cocks, no screeching monkeys and no swooping birds – just silent mist rising from the jungle and river surface. Salleh bin Sambas would claim, when interviewed in 2004 for the DVD *Return to Limbang*, that at 5.30am he received a message to expect the Royal Marines.

One of the navigational unknowns was the current and when it became clear that this was quicker than expected, speed was reduced so that L Company could take advantage of a dawn landing. The Royal Marines fidgeted with their final preparations – weapons loaded but not yet cocked, sights adjusted and comfortable firing positions adopted. Marine Daker slotted his Vickers on Pin One to give full traverse and elevation for firing over open sights. Lieutenant Davis ordered 5 Troop to 'Fix bayonets'. Midshipman Best on the bridge commented to Moore 'I didn't know they still did that'. For many in L Company the day would be their first action. As the Z-Crafts chugged upstream there was no sign of life in Kampong Ayer to starboard. Marine Fyffe on *Sindaun* recalls:

> As we rounded a bend in the river we could see the glow of the lights above the trees and, just as that registered, the lights were suddenly extinguished – they knew we were coming.

In fact, the lights had been turned out because it was getting light. As the Z-Crafts closed on the Customs wharf, the bazaar suddenly sprang to life with people running in all directions, some into the jungle and others into houses. *Sindaun* briefly beached on a midstream sandbank and then took up a position about 50yds offshore of the bazaar. Marine Daker continues the story:

> I was lying on my back with the legs of my Number 2, Marine Shoebridge, tucked under my head. He was lying on the right side of the gun to enable him to feed in the canvas belt of 250 rounds. Our large packs were in front and our personal weapons were to hand on the deck. It was now starting to get light and we could see the town on the riverbank. I looked to the bridge, where the Number 1 (Vickers) was with my mate Pete Stubbs, and we gave one another the nod waiting for the order to 'Fire'. We could see several targets.

The Royal Marines were calling out TNKU positions in the bazaar and around the Police Barracks – 'Two men with shotguns upper window of barbers!' About 200yds from the town, Sergeant Smith announced in Malay through a loudhailer, 'The rebellion is over. You should lay down your arms.' The few shotgun shots being fired were joined by automatic fire from a Bren in the concrete monsoon ditch in front of the Barracks. Diplomacy a failure, Smith laid aside the loudhailer and picked up his weapon. Second Lieutenant Targett-Adams describes the scene:

> Fire was initially opened at 06.02 on the morning of Wednesday, 12 December 1962. The medium machine guns from our craft began to open up on the shops and Police Station. A large volley of shotgun and rifle fire whizzed overhead and smacked into the water.

Such was the weight of enemy fire that some Royal Marines thought the TNKU had at least two Bren guns and several .303in rifles. They knew that they had a fight on their hands. Marine Daker continues:

> The order was given to open fire and all hell was let loose. People were shouting out directions where to fire, at windows and doorways, as we moved up towards the town. Sergeant Wakeling was walking up and down the deck looking after his lads as though we were on the ranges.

Captain Moore then instructed Lieutenant Willis to land 5 Troop opposite the Police Barracks as planned. Willis directed his coxswain, Leading Seaman Maher, to go alongside the jetty near the boathouse about 50yds from the Barracks. Corporal Bob Rawlinson, the 5 Section Commander, instructed his Bren gunner, Marine Fred Powell, to give covering fire from a higher point at the rear of the Z-Craft so that he could fire over the top of his colleagues. On *Sindaun,* Lieutenant Waters heard from Moore that he intended to land 5 Troop and instructed Lieutenant Down to get the Z-Craft into position so that the machine-guns could give covering fire, but just as Sergeant Wakeling was about to order them to switch from the bazaar area to cover 5 Troop, the Z-Craft swung in the current. CSM Scoins calmly asked Down to harden up. Down, true to the culture of his warship, replied, 'Sarn't Major, Nelson would have loved you.' As *Nakhoda Manis* closed on the jetty, the TNKU opened very heavy fire. A Bren gunner on a spit of land jutting into the river fired a full magazine into the well deck as the Z-Craft smashed into the planks of the jetty and crunched on to the bank, the starboard forefoot hard up against a tree. But the burst had caused havoc. Marines Jennings and Powell were both mortally wounded and Leading Seaman Maher, the coxswain, and Able Seaman Hayes were both injured. Midshipman Best was on the well deck:

> For a moment it seems unreal and detached. Until the sudden shock of spattered canvas stinging me in the eyes, across the neck; until the gasp of a young Marine as he drops his rifle with a clatter – unheard above the noise of spitting carbines and breaking glass – and slumps on the deck, spread-eagled, mouth foolishly open, trying to close it, gargling helplessly. War at the moment suddenly became rather serious and terribly futile. No time for philosophy. It was the Bren that did the damage against our slow moving close range target. It must have raked the bridge and well deck. We discovered that luck was with us.

Willis used a megaphone, 'Troops out'. Covered by 6 Section, 4 and 5 Sections led by Lieutenant Davis and Sergeant Bickford scrambled over the side and made for the monsoon ditch. The plan was that they would cross the road and provide for two Royal Marines to cut a hole in the Barracks fence. It was assumed the gate had been barred. But Lieutenant Davis was quickly cut down, badly wounded. Salleh bin Sambas, firing a Bren, had been wounded in the arm and chest. He recalls:

> I saw one Marine fall from the ship. Then the ship landed at the jetty so I fired more but I could not sustain our defence when we came under fire from the present Custom's office which shot up the Police Station.

Marines Sykes and Roberts, who at about 6ft 3in, 18 stone and aged about 30 years was the 'old soldier' of 4 Section, were debating how best to climb the steep riverbank without being shot when a sudden burst of firing concluded that conversation. Beneath the steady 'thump, thump' of the Vickers, Corporal Bill Lester and his 4 Section hauled themselves out of the ditch, hurtled across the road and overran several rebel positions north of the Barracks and went firm at the rear. To Marine Mike Bell's frustration, his rifle kept jamming, probably because the gas regulator that governed it had been damaged. Sergeant Bickford and 5 Section then landed. On the flimsy bridge, Captain Moore was watching:

> We had just had a major training period and it really was, I would use the words 'very beautiful' to watch. Every time a Corporal gave an order I knew, not because I could hear them, because there was a battle going on and a hell of a din, but because you could see all the Marines taking the right actions and coming down under cover, changing their magazines, checking things, rolling to one side and getting up and going.

With Leading Seaman Maher collapsed on the bridge wounded in the knee and no-one at the wheel, *Nakhoda Manis* drifted off the riverbank, effectively marooning 4 and 5 Sections from the Troop reserve of Corporal Mervyn Jones' 6 Section.

When Salleh bin Sambas realized that his inexperienced TNKU were no match for the Royal Marines and that resistance was pointless, he immobilized the Bren, as he had been taught by Captain Lewis, and, with his brother, made his way over the hill to Temburong District. He had no idea how many of the Limbang Company had been killed.

On *Sindaun* stationed midstream firing at anything that moved, Marine Downey, a 4 Troop Bren gunner, had seen Lieutenant Davis collapse and was itching to get ashore. The craft then came under fire from Chinese shops north of the Barracks with bullets ricocheting off the bulldozers. In the wheelhouse, Lieutenant Waters was wounded in the left knee and as Leading Seaman Taylor, the coxswain, took off his leather belt to apply a tourniquet, CSM Scoins instructed Lieutenant Down to lay *Sindaun* alongside the jetty in order to land 4 and 6 Troops. Down told Taylor to forget Waters. A ricochet had dented Down's hip flask in his rear trouser pocket. SBA Clarke, who was sheltering behind one of the bulldozers, was told that he was needed on the bridge and he describes how, running to the stern, he threw himself into the first opening to find that it housed the 'heads'. He was then directed to a ladder that led him to the wheelhouse where he treated Lieutenant Waters and found a broom for him to use as a crutch.

Virtually everyone was firing. Down had picked up Water's rifle but when his magazine emptied and he had no idea how to reload, Scoins gave him some rapid weapon training. On the well deck, Midshipman Crombie was helping the Vickers gunners to change sides as the boat swung round for another run and discovered that the barrel gets very hot. Able Seaman Martin earned his pay as a marksman from the horns of the bow ramp. The Vickers of Marine Stubbs then suffered a stoppage caused by the lack of water not cooling the barrel jacket, which meant changing the barrel. Meanwhile, Second Lieutenant Targett-Adams had ordered 6 Troop to 'Fix bayonets' and as *Sindaun* came alongside the jetty Lieutenant Down shouted 'Go, Marines'. First out was Stumpy, HMS *Fiskerton*'s ship's dog, who scampered across the jetty and disappeared into the small beachhead created by 5 Troop. Second Lieutenant Lloyd shouted '4 Troop with me' and leapt onto the gunwale only to find the bank too far away to reach in one leap, and stumbled ashore. Knowing that 6 Troop was following, the Troop ran 150yds to a dip in the ground facing Limbang. To the right was the steep hill. Lloyd deployed the Troop in a square formation with 1 Section on the right supported by 3 Section to deal with counter-attacks from the jungle and 2 Section on the left with Troop Headquarters behind.

Second Lieutenant Targett-Adams and 6 Troop landed and ran across the monsoon ditch in front of the Barracks and took up positions, on the left of 4 Troop, facing Limbang and the river. Targett-Adams went into the Barracks and noted the cells were occupied by Malays, all shouting and yelling. He had no idea if they were rebels or hostages. As he left the building, Corporal Parrish's composite section were clearing the rooms. Outside, he saw Marine John Coombes emerge with two rebels, one of whom then made a break and ran towards the river. Coombes shouted in Malay 'Stop! Hands up!' But the rebel did not stop and he was shot. The surviving TNKU turned out to be the Limbang Company second-in-command and he was very frightened. Surprisingly the Police Barracks had not been trashed and money was still in the desk. Not long afterwards Sergeant Bickford came down the road carrying a wounded marine on his back. With Davis wounded and Sergeant Macfarlane yet to appear, he reorganized 5 Troop, which had suffered five killed and four wounded, and created an inner defensive position centred on the Police Barracks.

Soon after 6 Troop had landed, Moore realized that he had been slightly wounded. Then, noticing that Leading Seaman Maher had been wounded and Lieutenant Willis was firing a rifle that he picked up, Moore shouted to him, 'Hey! Get us back in the bank!' Willis grabbed the wheel but by the time he had regained control of the Z-Craft it had drifted about 150yds upstream opposite the school. Moore then ordered Sergeant Macfarlane to land with 6 Section, from 5 Troop, and clear the area of the hospital and rejoin 5 Troop. Marine Peter Caress was the Section Bren gunner. Marine David Fermoy was his No. 2. Unfortunately, some of the Section jumped into waist-high muddy slime, which drew the usual colourful language. The Section reaching the road and skirmishing, with the Rifle Group on the left and Bren Group on the right in fire and movement, set such a fast pace under Macfarlane that Caress barely had time to find a position to cover the Rifle Group before he was on the move again.

As 6 Section reached the hospital and came under fire, Marine Caress opened fire from the hip, killing a TNKU and wounding another. When Corporal Jones then radioed that he could hear English singing from inside the hospital, this was unexpected because it was thought that the hostages were at the Barracks. It was a relief that they had not been caught up in the fighting. When Richard Morris had seen the Z-Craft, he and Dorothy had just crawled underneath the bed they had moved as a shelter when the window disintegrated under a hail of Vickers fire. It was then they began to sing their song at the top of their voices.

Under intermittent fire, 6 Section advanced toward the hospital and then split, with the Rifle Group taking cover in dead ground on the left while Macfarlane led the Bren Group, on the right, around the hospital to find a position to give suppressive fire. But as they reached the back, they had to dive for cover in undergrowth at the bottom of the hill from short range fire, but were unable to pinpoint the enemy. As Sergeant Macfarlane then edged along the hospital, Richard Morris put his head out of a window and told those inside, 'They are wearing green berets! They are Commandos!' Morris then said that the hostages were inside. Macfarlane told him to 'keep low and you won't get hurt' and then knelt at the corner of the building and saw a privet hedge across several yards of open ground. Behind it was an outhouse of the Police Barracks. Almost immediately, they came under close range shotgun fire from the hedge and Marine Fermoy was killed. As Sergeant Macfarlane rose from his kneeling position to cross the space, he was also killed. Caress was badly wounded in the legs and collapsed in the space. As a hostage encouraged the dazed Royal Marine to crawl to safety, a Vickers fired over his head into the undergrowth. As the Marine reached the corner of the hospital, he was dragged inside by one of the hostages, a priest.

Then 6 Section attacked the attap house from which TNKU had shot the three Royal Marines. Meanwhile, Captain Moore had told Willis to return to midstream so that he could see what was happening. Willis told him that the Z-Craft was lodged on the riverbank. Moore landed with his Tactical Headquarters and made his way to the hospital. Sergeant Smith had gone to the back of the hospital and found the Morrises in the consulting room. Mrs Morris later wrote:

> 'Out you come, old girl', whereupon 'old girl' clambered out in Dick's wake through the rather jagged aperture of the window obligingly broken by Sergeant Smith. He looked so large and calm and capable, crouching down with gun aimed at the thickly wooded slope immediately behind the hospital into which the guards who had survived had fled. We didn't waste time in pleasantries but darted into the ward to find our fellow hostages all present and correct and, like us, a trifle dazed.

Fritz Lloyd Klattenhoff had picked up a SLR and wanted to use it. Moore then met Morris and learnt that other hostages were also being held. However, the first priority was to secure the Barracks and its immediate grounds against rebels, but the jungle reaching close to the building gave them plenty of cover.

Moore and his Tactical Headquarters then followed 6 Section to the Barracks. It was about 7.00am. From interrogations of prisoners, Sergeant Smith arranged the release of the hostages held in the Jail while Mortar Troop released an expatriate water engineer and his family held under house arrest. Meeting up with Lloyd and Targett-Adams, he ordered them to widen the beachhead and secure an east-west defensive line by clearing the row of Chinese shops up to the bazaar. When they looked puzzled, he asked, 'Have you not covered street fighting in your training at this stage?' When they replied, 'None', he led them to a place where they could see Limbang and gave them a short lesson. A Bren gunner lying behind a tree advised them not to stand in the open because he had just been shot at from a building. The trio took cover and after Moore finished the lesson he gave them their orders.

On board *Sindaun* Sick Berth Attendant Clarke had been given an escort by Company Sergeant Major Scoins and had landed. Going to the monsoon ditch, he found that Lieutenant Davis was badly injured with a high velocity entry wound in his chest and a large exit wound on his back. He administered first aid and then patched him up as best he could and made his way to the hospital, where he found several casualties and some of the dead Royal Marines. Helped by Mrs Morris and a Malay nurse, Fanny Tan Anek, he made Marine Caress comfortable and, after checking the back of Corporal Rawlinson for shrapnel, earmarked him for evacuation.

As 4 and 6 Troops began to widen the perimeter, they were covered by Sindaun cruising up and down the river, the Vickers machine-gunners watching for Royal Marines waving their Green Berets to indicate the progress of their advance. On several occasions, they poured fire into suspect buildings indicated from ashore. A fast motorboat that tried to cross the river was sunk. Since throwing grenades risked injuring civilians, the marines generally cleared houses by entering through the roof, the idea being to drive any occupants outside into the covering force, but most houses were decidedly rickety and several Royal Marines were injured falling through roofs. Marine 'Nobby' Clark fell through a corrugated roof and so badly gashed his hand that he was invalided out of the Royal Marines, and Marine Steve Whitchurch fell through a floor and cut his leg, adding to the casualty list. Several times the Troops came under fire. A TNKU wounded by a 4 Troop Bren gunner could not be reached and every attempt to pull him into cover drew fire. A TNKU gunman using a room full of women and children at the eastern end of a block of shops was dislodged. A young couple, both dead, were found in a house that had been used as a firing position. It was during the clearance that the only civilian casualty occurred, when a grenade thrown into a suspect house killed an elderly lady. After several hours and radio communications becoming intermittent, Second Lieutenant Targett-Adams crossed open ground, chased by bullets hitting the ground around him, to confer with Lloyd. They agreed that 4 Troop should secure the area around some Malay houses at the southern suburb of Limbang and engage anyone trying to cross into the bazaar area and through the jungle.

Meanwhile, Sergeant Smith was screening the people of Limbang before they were escorted to the town cinema. Several suspects assembled on the *Nakhoda Manis* helped clear up the shattered glass and blood of the British casualties. Identified TNKU were detained by the Sarawak Constabulary in the wired compound of the Public Works Department. Several prisoners were detailed to dig a large grave at the rear of the hospital for the dead TNKU, most of whom had been searched by the Intelligence Section. When the hospital came under fire from the high ground to the east, CSM Scoins acted as No. 2 to Marine Downey while another searched for more ammunition. Three TNKU were flushed out and captured.

At about 10.15am, Sergeant Wakeling landed with the two Vickers sections to cover the southern perimeter, the only sector that had a field of fire of more than about 50yds. To most of those who fought at Limbang, the Vickers had been a battle-winning weapon. In 1963 an English newspaper featured a mock memorial service held by the Army to mourn the passing of the Vickers as it was phased out in favour of the 7.62mm General Purpose Machine Gun. The Royal Marines sent a terse letter to the editor informing him that in the opinion of the Royal Marines, the service was a 'trifle premature and, if proof was needed, S Company, 42 Commando would be delighted to oblige.'

During the course of the day, the heat became oppressive and the dead, wounded and hostages were sent to Brunei Town on the Z-Craft.

Those left behind in Brunei had experienced an anxious night. After seeing the Z-Craft depart, there had been silence until the dawn and distant gunfire was heard. Thereafter, Captain Oakley used a Land Rover to relay information to Brigadier Glennie from Lieutenant Commander Black's Headquarters on HMS *Fiskerton*. When messages indicated that there had been casualties and then that the two Z-Craft were returning, medical teams and ambulances were directed to the jetty. Dorothy Morris rested on board HMS *Chawton.* The casualties were triaged at Brunei Hospital and the seriously wounded flown to Labuan to be stabilized for the flight to the British Military Hospital in Singapore the next day. When casualties were notified on the radio, it was usually by the regimental number of the casualty to save time on air and avoid confusion with names. In Sembawang Barracks, Corporal Alan Jarvis, the 42 Commando Movements NCO, was at the Children's Party in the NAAFI when he was told that L Company had suffered several casualties in Brunei and, in order to identify them, there was a need to match their regimental serial numbers to his strip index list.

The five killed and eight wounded was the largest number of Royal Marines casualties in a single day between Korea in 1951 and the Falklands in 1982. Sergeant Macfarlane had been intending to run a corner shop in his home town of Middlesborough. Marine Fermoy left a widow and 5-month-old son. Marine Jennings, from Bourne in Lincolnshire. had joined 42 Commando from the Depot in January 1962, having enlisted in 1961. Marine Gerald Kierans from Widnes had been in the Corps a year. Powell came from Bradford. The wounded were Lieutenant Waters and Davis, Corporal Rawlinson and Marines Richard Taylor, Peter Caress and Roy Clarke.

At about midday, a low level flight by the four 20 Squadron Hawker Hunters over Limbang which then split into pairs over the jungle, was another timely reminder of British firepower. During the afternoon two requisitioned launches, commanded by Sub-Lieutenants Chris Jarrett and David Mayo of HMS *Chawton* and *Fiskerton* respectively, delivered Brigadier Patterson, Captain Oakley and the Assault Pioneers plus a section of 81mm mortars, both acting in an infantry role, to Limbang. The reinforcements had arrived at Labuan in HMS *Cavalier* during the morning of 11 December. Also on board was the naval Chaplain Noël Jones, who had been standing at the stern of Mayo's launch, clutching a Sterling sub machine gun, when suddenly it hit an underwater sandbank and he disappeared and surfaced, coughing up river water but still clutching his gun. Since the Commando Medical Officer had not yet reached Brunei, the Regimental Medical Officer of 1/2 Gurkha Rifles arrived to help SBA Clarke.

By the end of the day, L Company was secure to the south of Limbang. The Royal Marines had not rested for nearly thirty-six hours and since house-clearing at night is not recommended, Moore halted operations. The first east-west street south of the bazaar was held by 4 Troop, while 6 Troop faced east to the Jail and west to the river. Corporal Parrish's section was the Troop reserve in the Police Barracks. Support Company and the Vickers machine-guns covered the river to the west and 5 Troop was in the Company reserve at the Police Barracks. Parrish's section included the Company chef, Corporal Horn. With a couple of colleagues he searched shops and prepared a meal. During the night noises were heard in the roof and when the missing PC Essa bin Meratim was released from the loft, it was after four days of surviving on rain water and listening to the TNKU conversations. During the evening of 11 December, they had been discussing killing the hostages the next day. During the night several shots fired from the bazaar were not returned because the firing positions could not be identified. On the other hand, anything moving in the jungle covered by 6 Troop was engaged – men, animals, shadows, and banana plants. One enemy was killed about ten yards from the attap house. To the south, Mortar Troop threw a grenade at a TNKU seen on the riverbank and who refused to surrender. Next morning, 13 December, 4 Troop and Support Company advanced into Limbang without encountering opposition. During the afternoon, K Company, on board HMS *Woodbridge Haven*, and Commando Headquarters arrived, with the former taking over the defence. The 42 Commando Chaplain padre, Bob Wood, armed with his personal weapon, a LMG, appeared telling the bemused Royal Marines, 'Whoever smiteth my flock shall be smited by me.'

In his post-operation report, Captain Moore assessed TNKU strength at Limbang to have been more than 300, a figure given to him by Mr Morris. About 150 TNKU are thought to have defended the Police Barracks and thirty had held the hospital. Fifteen were killed, three wounded and eight captured. The majority were armed with shotguns. The police Bren, a Sterling sub machine-gun and fifteen .303 Lee Enfield rifles were recaptured, plus a variety of .22 rifles, muzzle loading muskets and other pieces. In his conclusion for the operation, Moore wrote:

> Although some casualties would have probably been avoided by a landing further down stream and an advance on foot it is not considered that the hostages' lives would have been saved if this course had been adopted.

Captain Moore was awarded a bar to his Military Cross. Corporals Lester and Rawlinson were awarded Military Medals. SBA Clarke received a Commander-in-Chief's Commendation and the 5ft 4in Marine 'Ginge' Underwood, in Company Headquarters, received a Mention in Despatches for sheltering wounded while under fire, in spite of being wounded himself.

The Royal Navy contribution was critical but is largely an unrecognized element of the operation. Had it not provided the crews for the two Z-Craft, it is doubtful the operation could have been mounted at the speed it was. By then the hostages may well have been executed. For all, it had been a shock. Midshipman Best's words several weeks after the action were:

> We were all shaken. This was not a sailor's war. The war we had been trained for was one of 6in shells and flooded boiler rooms; HQI, anti-flash gear and ABCD. The idea of a personal vindictive was something new. A war where you could see your enemy; where he could see you and aim his rifle at you; and fire at you. A war where it was only too obvious that a canvas screen offers no protection against a Bren bullet.

Lieutenant Willis was awarded the Distinguished Service Cross and Petty Officer Kirwin the Distinguished Service Medal.

Reflecting on Limbang, Captain Oakley later wrote:

> In the 1950s and 1960s the colonial empire was still at its height and just beginning to be handed over to independence. The sort of

> situation that arose with the rebels at Limbang was one of many throughout the world at that time. We happened to be there. We were involved. All we knew, as far as Servicemen were concerned, was that we were carrying out a job on behalf of the Government policy. This was our job. We weren't there to reason why or to ask why, we did it. This is what we were paid for, what we were trained for.

On 3 August 1963, the Limbang Memorial to the five Royal Marines and the four Sarawak Constabulary officers overlooking the waterfront was unveiled by Governor Waddell. The bronze plaque with the names is mounted on a plain stone plinth and was funded by public subscription at the express request of the residents of Limbang. Lieutenant Waters was Commander of the Guard provided by 5 Troop. Terence Cuneo painted a depiction of the landing from the point of view of the defenders in the monsoon ditch. In 2005, Martin Spirit of Brush Fire Films produced a DVD entitled *Return to Limbang* for which veterans of the action from both sides were interviewed. The Morris family commemorate their debt to the L Company and annually post on *The Times Register* on 12 December 'In Memorium – War 42 Cdo RM. In grateful memory of those who fell at Limbang on 12th December 1962'. Throughout the 1970s, the 1980s and most of the 1990s when they returned to England, which was almost every year, their itinerary included staying with Royal Marines. Richard Morris died in 1999 and Dorothy in 2002.

During the night of 11/12 December, HMS *Tiger* received orders to land part of 1 Green Jackets at Miri. Steaming at 30 knots, the cruiser arrived offshore in the drizzly gloom of first light on 12 December and prepared for an opposed landing. Ashore, Mr Fisher, the Fourth Division Resident, assembled as many craft as he could, mostly from Shell, to land 310 men, the first group welcomed by the Mayor of Miri, his entourage and a welcoming speech. A Company remained on board in reserve. HMS *Tiger* then proceeded to Labuan where it went alongside a wooden jetty at Victoria Harbour and disembarked the remainder of the troops and the vehicles. The Ship's Royal Marines Detachment took over defence duties at the airfield until the ship then returned to Singapore. The Green Jackets were then flown to Seria to help in mopping-up operations between the town and Tutong. Two Ferrets joined 1/2 Gurkha Rifles in Brunei Town, where they occupied the Ministry of Education. The remainder of the battalion joined 1 Queens Own Highlanders at Seria. With Miri clear of rebel activity, Lieutenant Colonel Sweeney was instructed to deal with the TNKU at Bekenu and Niah where there had been reports of hostages.

Sweeney selected B Company, commanded by Major David Mostyn, for the attack on Bekenu and allocated him a Sarawak Police Field Force detachment, commanded by Superintendent B. Lewis. As the men were preparing to depart, news of the Royal Marines' action at Limbang arrived, in particular that five had been killed and several others wounded. Anticipating that the rebels would expect a landing from the sea, with an approach of twenty-five miles, Mostyn decided to use a Shell Oil Company Z-Craft to take 4 and 5 Platoons to a point about ten miles from Bekenu and then they would approach the town from the jungle. Meanwhile, 6 Platoon were to use two launches to steam upriver to give them flank protection, act as a fire support group during the attack and cut off escape routes. There was hope that the departure of the Company would be reported as going to land at or near Bekenu. At 10.30am, B Company departed in the Z-Craft that was towing two requisitioned launches. By 4.30pm, the Z-Craft had arrived off a beach near a small coastal village but it was still loaded with oil drilling equipment and it grounded on a sandbank 50yds from the shore. When the skipper claimed that his vessel was in 4ft of water, the first man stepped off the ramp and disappeared into 7ft of water. Using the launches, it took an hour to land the Riflemen.

With 6 Platoon in the launches protecting their flanks, the Sarawak Police Field Force led 4 and 5 Platoons through thick jungle and mangrove swamps. By 8.00pm, B Company had reached a house on the banks of the River Mumong. A full moon had risen. Calculating that it would take four hours to reach the outskirts of Bekenu by first light, at midnight the two platoons set off, but it soon became apparent that sixty men filing in column along jungle tracks in the darkness would cause delays. As the column approached a bridge over the Jongalus, the police scouts reported that it was held by six TNKU. Deciding to avoid it, Mostyn sent Superintendent Lewis and his police to ambush a likely approach route in case the TNKU decided to investigate. The Company was ferried across in two small boats which took eight men at a time. It later turned out that the police report was inaccurate and the bridge was undefended. In spite of the detour and delays, by about 9.00am on 13 December, fourteen hours after leaving Miri and having covered the last half mile balancing on tree trunks laid over a marsh, the weary platoons formed up on their start lines hidden in pepper and rubber plantations about 400yds from Government offices on the outskirts of Bekenu. Meanwhile, 6 Platoon reported that it was ten minutes from the town, so far undetected. The night had been extremely tough and the delay gave the platoons a brief opportunity to rest. Lieutenant Colonel Sweeney flew over the town in a Voice Twin Pioneer and noted TNKU waving and saluting and their flags flying from Government offices and the Police Station. Like their colleagues at Anduki, they believed the aircraft to be Indonesian because it had red-painted wing tips.

Moystn planned that when the platoons reached the outskirts of Bekenu, Superintendent Lewis would use a loudhailer to invite the TNKU to surrender. At 9.45am, 4 and 5 Platoons crossed their start line and, advancing through the pepper plantation, were 200yds short of the Government building when the leading sections were spotted by a group of TNKU appointing a rebel administration inside an office who opened fire with shotguns. With the hostages now at high risk, Mostyn dispensed with Lewis inviting the TNKU to surrender and the Green Jackets surged into the town, catching most rebels by surprise. Some fled into the jungle, some scrambled into the river and a few sheltered in houses. Several who boarded a boat were ambushed by 6 Platoon. Lieutenant Robin Everlegh used the ears of a garden gnome to steady his rifle to shoot a man escaping in a canoe. When it capsized and he swam ashore, he proved a valuable source of intelligence. By the end of the short battle, six TNKU were dead, five had been captured and about a dozen had escaped. 'How many will there be for lunch, sir?' enquired a government official. 'We had no casualties,' replied Mostyn, 'So it will be 90.'

Clearing the town over the next twenty-four hours, the Green Jackets arrested 328 suspected TNKU and seized 327 weapons. The interrogation of a wounded TNKU led to sufficient information for 4 and 5 Platoons to land at Setap, where they captured eight TNKU and released a local held as a hostage. Several weapons were found in the house of a TNKU captain. The prisoners were assembled at the Police Barracks where a few police officers beat some, which proved to be counter-productive in the search for information.

Meanwhile, C Company commanded by Major Mark Pennell had been ordered to seize Niah. Also departing from Miri in a Z-Craft and reinforced by a Sarawak Police Field Force section and two Brunei Police constables, the Company motored up to the river, then transferred to two requisitioned launches and at 6.00pm entered Niah to find that two European survey officers, Mr Noel and Mr Walley, had formed a Home Guard to defend the *kampong*. Police Corporal Saini bin Bakar was involved in forming the Home Guard and refused to abandon the Police station so that he could send daily incident summaries.

A platoon motored upstream to Rumah Pasang where another member of the survey team and Mrs Harrisson, the wife of Tom Harrisson, had formed another Home Guard. The appearance of the Green Jackets had an important psychological effect on the locals.

CHAPTER THIRTEEN

Aftermath

The Brunei Revolt was over. Although the Indonesian dissident, Pramoedya Ananta Toer, claimed the activities of British Intelligence were 'reprehensible', the fact is Indonesia's ambitions were exposed and the people of British North Borneo were spared her ruthlessness. The British also brought stability to a region in turmoil, as communists attacked South Vietnam. Opposition parties in British North Borneo, who had largely rejected Azahari's claim as an opposition mouthpiece, condemned it. The local population had generally not supported the rebellion; indeed it highlighted their vulnerability to interference from Indonesia and even the Philippines. In elections held in North Borneo that year, the Sabah Alliance, on a ticket of pro-Malaysia, scored a massive victory. But still the Sultan of Brunei elected not to join the Federation.

With TNKU essentially crushed, military operations focused on mopping up the centres of the insurrection, arresting those involved and installing the civil authorities. Six officers and thirty rank and file were unaccounted for.

The rebels on the run had two main choices: surrender or retreat into the interior. But most were coastal strip dwellers and physically and psychologically unsuited to dealing with the rigours of living and surviving in the jungle dripping from heavy rain. Those who decided to seek sanctuary in Indonesia risked interception from a wide screen of irregulars blocking tracks and rivers. That they had the reputation of being headhunters added to the concerns of the evaders. Some disappeared, no doubt dying of starvation, disease and from the fatigue of surviving in the jungle. About 100 were captured. The Battle at Limbang was still in progress when Salleh bin Sambas and his brother left the town and used bicycles to cycle south to ferry across the river at Ujong Jalan into Temburong District. At Bangar they learnt that Limbang had been lost. Heading south by river, Sambas had his wounds dressed at Belaban and then they joined about forty rebels hiding in the jungle near Batang Duri. Food was short. Life was made more uncomfortable by the heavy rains that flooded the Limbang Valley. Meanwhile Security Forces patrols, often working on information, were progressively squeezing the TNKU into the open and on 17 January, Sambas, his brother and a guide used jungle tracks at night to reach the home of their father at Kampong Tebahan. Fed by his father, Sambas and his brother then hid on a hillside for the next month.

Psychological Operations using Voice Twin Pioneers and visits to *kampongs* flushed out rebels with invitations to surrender, and broadcast to the mothers and wives the futility of their husbands and sons going on the run. One Voice Twin Pioneer clocked up twenty-one hours of broadcasting. In an operation on the Panduran Road from 21 to 23 March 1963, Lance Corporal Raw and Trooper Moffat, of the Queens Royal Irish Hussars, persuaded a TNKU captain and lieutenant to surrender but four others who chose not to were killed. Leaflets and safe conduct passes were dropped by aircraft. Wanted posters offered rewards to anyone who supplied information that led to the capture of leading TNKU. In Brunei at the top of the wanted list were Yassin Affandi Rahman, two brothers of A.M. Azahari, Sheik Osman and Sheik Salleh, and Salleh Bin Sambas. Transistor radios donated by the Brunei Government were distributed to village headmen. An amnesty also offered rewards for the surrender of weapons stolen from police armouries. Psychological Operations developed into a Combined Services organization, its first commander being Lieutenant Commander Smith, who arrived in Brunei from the Ministry of Defence.

As the 'bush telegraph' about the rebellion spread, by 15 December about 2,000 irregulars had formed a wide screen sealing rivers and ambushing escape routes covering the south and west. The North Borneo authorities covered the east and ships patrolled the coast. In Fourth Division, Resident John Fisher had summoned Paramount Chief Temenggong by sending a boat flying the Red Feather of War and calling the Dayaks along the River Baram to assemble at Marudi. The local knowledge of Junior Agricultural Assistant Bujang anak Nyuin proved a valuable resource. By 11 December about 1,000 Kenyah, Kayan and Ibans had been formed into loose company groups and had been supplied with buckshot for their shotguns. Led by Mr N. Coysh, of the Sarawak Rubber Development Department, the irregulars moved west across the swampy Sibuti watershed and by 12 December were threatening Bekenu. A group of 120 led by Mr D. Reddish, of the Borneo Company, moved fast to Bekenu up the River Sibuti and, crossing the headwaters of the Setap, sealed escape routes. About 100 irregulars covered the mouth of the River Baram. Another similarly sized group assembled by Mr J. Bagley, of the Sarawak Medical Department, marched upriver collecting Iban and linked up with B Company, 1 Green Jackets intercepting rebels making their way south toward the border through farmlands on the edge of the lower Setap. On 15 December A Company patrols were dropped or abseiled into the jungle from 846 Naval Air Squadron Whirlwind helicopters flying from HMS *Hermes*.

In Fifth Division, Tom Harrisson, who had been invited to Brunei by the Government as an observer, summoned the Kelabits from the highlands around Bario, the centre of his wartime activities. In 1947 he had been appointed the Curator of the Sarawak Museum in Kuching. With his wife, Barbara, he had undertaken pioneering excavations in the West Mouth of the Great Cave at Niah during the 1950s and 1960s and had discovered a human skull dated about 40,000 BC but the findings were not academically published. The find was eventually vindicated by excavations between 2000 and 2003. Penghulu Ngang anak Bundan was instrumental in stabilizing security in Upper Limbang by organizing patrols. His irregulars captured eleven TNKU in an ambush. How they must have feared for their lives after being captured by tribesmen reputed to be headhunters! The Penghulu in Nanga Medamit was absent when the rebellion broke and so Gawan anak Jangga deputized by assembling over 300 armed Iban. On 11 December he trapped several TNKU in a boat and invited them to surrender, but when they said that a large force had left Limbang to rescue them Gawan refused to be intimidated and handed the insurgents over to Royal Marines. Mr Lian Tapan, a retired Sarawak Police Field Force corporal, gathered former Field Force and General Duties police constables in the Pumor area and formed a unit to defend Bario Airfield and organized ambushes on likely escape routes. Mr Pauk

Ho Huan, the Headmaster of Ba Kelalan School, rallied Murat communities and formed them into home guards and patrols to hunt for the rebels on some of the easier escape routes.

Keeping a close watch on the Panduran, Temburong and Batu Apoi rivers, 42 Commando dominated Temburong District. L Company remained in the general area of Limbang. K Company patrols based in *kampongs* in the hinterland dominated tracks crossing the hills and through the acres of sluggish mangrove swamps. M Company had arrived at Labuan on HMS *Alert* and was flown to Brunei, where it was instructed to clear the road from Limbang to Bangar, where several local officials held hostage had been murdered. When the Queens Royal Irish Hussars was instructed to support the Company, during the night 12/13 December, Sergeant Daly and Lance Corporal Holdsworth returned to Brunei from Tutong, where they had been supporting 1/2 Gurkhas to secure the town, and joined the Royal Marines waiting to be ferried to Limbang by three Z-Craft in the first phase of the deployment. Eventually, the *Sindaun* appeared out of the night and beached on to the road on the third attempt, to enable Ferrets to be loaded. They 'cast off' from the wheelhouse but five minutes later the boat had not moved an inch. Daly watched as 'a gentleman in white, obviously the skipper, came to the bow to investigate.' Seeing that the landing craft was half on the road and half in the water, the skipper arranged for an Army lorry to push his command into the water and then set course for the River Limbang. At about halfway, a naval stoker surfaced from the engine room and announced that seawater was pouring from cracks in the sun-rotted rubber linings of the ramp. As the Royal Marines began pumping the bilge pump, Daly noticed that their kit was floating around the Ferrets. Although the skipper cheerfully assured everyone that they would make it to Bangar, he advised Daly and Holdsworth, who were taking their turn on the pumps, to start the Ferret engines, which was done. But the sea water persisted on rising and it was only after Trooper Reilly, who was Daly's driver, jumped out of his Ferret and said that his engine had packed up that the skipper admitted, 'Good heavens, we're sinking. Turn the dammed thing around!' He then headed for a clearing in front of the Residency and grounded the landing craft several feet from the beach. The whispered commotion on board was challenged by the Queens Royal Irish Hussar Defence Section commanded by Corporal Sharpe protecting the High Commissioner but then, seeing the predicament of the two Ferrets, he sent Trooper Mackenzie to Squadron HQ to arrange recovery. Meanwhile, a Royal Marine had tested the depth of water and suggested it might be worth landing the Ferrets to lighten the load. Reilly, up to his neck in oily water, turned the ignition switch, more in hope, and astonished everyone when the comforting whine of the almost submerged Rolls Royce engine coughed into life. He slotted into gear, kicked the clutch and accelerated, only for the Ferret to roll off the ramp and splash into six feet of water. Lieutenant Commander Black on HMS *Fiskerton* remembers:

> The first message I got in my cabin was that both the landing craft had been sunk, which spoilt my day really. I sent Harry Mucklow, the Chawton CO, to have a look. He commandeered a three tonner and appeared probably two or three hours later, to tell me that they had not sunk and they had got into the shore. It was a memorable day which the Army has never forgotten. I get reminded of it from time to time – the day I sank the armour in North Borneo.

A Chinese man piloted the Z-Craft through the twenty-six miles of dark, twisting river until M Company landed and advanced through the wet and boggy jungle, during which the Royal Marines encountered bull leeches that wriggled through eyelets into boots and tried to grope their way into trousers. Breaking out of the jungle at dawn, the Company systematically cleared Bangar against no opposition. Most of the rebels had fled up the River Temburong. HQ 42 Commando then moved to Bangar and occupied several large houses abandoned by local officials who had fled to Brunei Town to escape the TNKU. The Intelligence Section was billeted in a house on stilts beside the river, including Marine Fyffe back to issuing maps and aerial photographs, collating situation reports and investigating and identifying prisoners. After his Limbang experiences he was, after all, considered to be an expert on the TNKU and was required to search the dead bodies.

Meanwhile, A Company, 1/2 Gurkha Rifles had handed Miri to 1 Green Jackets on 11 December. When reports circulated of a rebel force at Muara Lodge on 12 December, Major Tony Lloyd-Williams quickly assembled two forces. The Sea Group consisted of A Company on board a requisitioned ferry named the *Higgins*, and Tactical HQ and two platoons of B Company in two Customs launches under command of Major Bowring. The Land Group consisted of two B Company platoons and a D Company platoon commanded by Captain (GCO) Lalsing Thapa, the Regimental Signals Officer. The two B Company platoons had been recalled from the Thai border. The Battalion Armourer, Staff Sargeant Hayter, worked throughout the night to weld steel plates around the gunwales to offer some protection. The next day Lieutenant Peter Down was tasked with ferrying the Gurkhas:

> We struck off in fine form, somewhat more cautiously with the lessons of Limbang fresh in our minds. The Gurkhas put up with an uncomfortable roll for some hours as we coasted with a cross-swell. We looked at lots of beaches and several rocks before we found a gap on the required bearing from the headland, albeit without our half-expected guide. We turned into line abreast and in the best Errol Flynn tradition started to run in to the beach. The master plan had been to put down a kedge anchor when about 50yds off, but at 100yds off we grounded and, assuming that we had arrived, we dropped the ramp.

Second Lieutenant Bruce Jackman was on board:

> We chugged into the blackness towards the coastline all crouched down behind this steel plating. The sun rose, the Hunters came and went and didn't fire anything, and we were still at sea because the tide was going out faster than we were going in, so we were making no headway. Well, the tide turned and at about 11.00am, we made it to the beach. The ramps went down and there was a surge forward – which stopped. Major Lloyd-Williams screamed at everyone to get going, fought his way through to the front and threw himself into ten feet of water. We were actually on a sandbank and the first Gurkhas who had thrown themselves in had to be fished out.

Lieutenant Down's embarrassment was intense:

> I don't think I ever felt so lonely as when eighty pairs of large Gurkha eyes swivelled round to focus on me in the wheelhouse

> with the unspoken question 'What now?' Luckily the sailors were on form. Able Seaman Jan Booty, our top man par excellence, rescued the dripping soldier and we rigged lifelines to get the Gurkhas ashore. The gap turned out to be a false lead, but a mile up the coast was another rock and gap which looked more promising. The Gurkhas set off on a reconnaissance and we sailors spent the morning offloading the soldiers' heavy kit and humping it to the track. An enterprising soldier commandeered a bullock cart to collect their kit. There was no fighting at the refinery but the Gurkhas elected to return by road when their time was up. Aided by the launches and the hastily positioned kedge, we eventually got the lighter off the sand and returned to Brunei somewhat chastened.

The launches had proceeded faster than the *Higgins* and beating the tide put Major Bowring's group ashore at least two hours before those on the car ferry could wade ashore. The two groups met at the lodge unopposed and secured the place. There were clear signs that the rebels had been using the lodge, for instance the warm embers of a fire. The one prisoner, a fisherman casting his net on the landing beach, was handed to Second Lieutenant Jackman, because he was responsible for prisoners, and turned out to be totally innocent. The *Higgins* remained firmly embedded in the sandbank for years and eventually broke up. A Company now had responsibility for Brunei Town and Muara and provided guards for the Sultan's Palace and the prison camp holding important TNKU and Brunei People's Party suspects. It was later the Force Reserve. A platoon commanded by the Mechanical Transport Officer carried out a ten day patrol in a hired *prahu* and on foot from Long Sheridan to Nanga Meridan and found the loyalty of the local tribes untroubled.

On 12 December, in North Borneo, communications between Sindumin and Sipitang were poor; nevertheless, Superintendent Davis and Sergeant Salleh had arrested several suspects and seized documentation at Kuala Mengalong. Bangsul was also searched. Meanwhile, Plunkett and Ross left for Lawas in the launch *Sangitan*. During the day it had lurked off Mengalong supporting Davis' cordon and search but had been diverted to investigate reports of a boat in Kaminis Bay. Nothing was found. At Sipitang, Plunkett, Ross and Parry had agreed that, since the unrest in North Borneo had been undermined, the Security Forces should confine their activities to protecting the border. Plunkett and Ross stayed overnight in Labuan and, after an early morning start, they met Superintendent Millington and Captain Morris of K Company, 42 Commando, in Lawas and agreed that the *Sangitan* should continue to patrol Brunei Bay and, importantly, that the North Borneo Police could cross into Sarawak as far west as Merapok. A Police Mobile Force section of ten men and some volunteers, commanded by Inspector Jaikoh, was sent to Melaman to conduct long range patrols and ambush likely crossing points and reinforce border security. It was now becoming increasingly difficult for TNKU fleeing from operations in Sarawak to find sanctuary in the coastal area of North Borneo. Some volunteers under Parry's command were released.

On 14 December Superintendents Ross and Davis met Millington and Richard Morris and agreed to continue the policy of patrols and ambushes along the border, and that North Borneo Police could operate to Merapok. Five TNKU border-crossers arrested during the day were transferred to the Sarawak Police Field Force at Lawas. Meanwhile, the headman of Kuala Kangalang had reported to John Parry that a *prahu* containing two members of the Brunei People's Party had entered the River Ular, which was near the border. This was inside Ross' tactical area of operations but when Parry could not contact Ross and Davies, he despatched the indefatigable Sergeant Salleh with a mixed Police and volunteers patrol to investigate. They captured the *prahu* but, when the occupants could not be found, a major operation conducted by Davis from Pantai and Parry from Sipitang swept through the area and arrested the two men the next day. They admitted that they had been in the area since 12 December and were waiting for a shipment of arms promised from the Philippines. Both were from Kuala Mengalong.

By 15 December Parry's forces had been on continuous operations for five days and he decided that his men must rest. During the evening intelligence was received from Beaufort that about twelve TNKU, who had avoided being arrested in police operations in Lubok, were hiding in Tunggok or Sungau. The next morning Ross instructed Parry to mount an operation. Selecting a mixed force of seventy police, police reservists and volunteers, he divided them into a Road Group and the River Group. Parry drove to Weston where the Road Group used the road to Tunggok and then on to Sunggau, while the River Group set up a blocking position south to cover a river. Tunggok was found to be free of subversive activity but when the Road Group set off on foot to Sunggau it was a difficult cross-country march. The Group took up a position on a ridge north of the *kampong*. After one of his men fired a warning shot, Parry invited the villagers to assemble in the open with their hands raised but, when nothing happened, it was with reluctance that he ordered an assault. However, by his own admittance, it 'was somewhat badly managed'. But remember, the operation had been planned by a man with no military experience. The complexities of an assault require clear and simple orders so that everyone knows what to do, but there is a well known military saying that as soon as the first round is fired, the plan collapses. Parry placed his men to the north and south but did not cover the east and west. Parry and Sergeant Salleh led their sections into the *kampong* but were pinned down by 'blue on blue' fire from the River Group to the south; fortunately they fired high and the bullets smacked into roofs and tree trunks. Parry managed to order the River Party to cease fire and then he gingerly stepped into the open and walked toward the headman's house. A man who emerged from a house and ran toward the jungle was shot in the arm by an irregular and then whisked to hospital in Beaufort. It turned out that there were no TNKU in Sunggau; however, when the villagers found that they were surrounded by armed men, they were too frightened to leave their houses.

After apologizing to the head man and his council, Parry sent twenty-five men by land to Lubok with the aim of driving rebels hiding in the *kampong* to use *prahus* to escape while he and several men lurked in boats in a mangrove swamp in ambush. It also turned out that Lubok was empty of suspects and he returned to Sipitang empty-handed. Next day a patrol arrested a senior ARAS, who admitted that Jaya bin Hassan was the most important rebel leader still at large and that he was hiding in the jungle not far from Masapol and was probably armed. When Ross agreed that he could pursue him, the following day Parry placed ambushes on the main track and two other tracks from Sipitang. Hassan was captured on the Sipitang road by three irregulars but without the revolver he had lost in the debacle near the beach on 7 December.

Meanwhile Superintendent Ross in Pantai had received a report that uniformed men had been seen near Kota Klias, a *kampong* on a junction of the River Khas in low lying ground north-west of Beaufort. He despatched a Police patrol to the area, but found that, without his knowledge, the *Sangitan* had been sent to help them. This concerned him because he was hoping to use the launch to intercept the arms shipment from the Philippines mentioned by the two men arrested on 14 December and its departure left a gap in his defences. When Captain China in Merapok sent a message to Ross suggesting that rebels in the jungle were planning to attack the village, Millington sent a Sarawak Police Field Force detachment; however, the attack did not materialize and the detachment used Merapok as a patrol base. The next day, patrols followed up a report received on 14 December of a *prahu* from Brunei landing men by looking for the remaining four but there were no sightings.

On 17 December, B Company, 1/2 Gurkha Rifles flew to Kalebakan in Tawau District to help the North Borneo authorities address reports of Indonesian subversion. Major Bowring had very little Intelligence on the situation and fearing that Tawau had fallen into TNKU hands planned a rapid fly-in and disembarkation. Meanwhile, a welcoming party gathered at Tawau airstrip expecting to welcome Royal Marines; however, as the Beverley touched down, the rear doors opened and before the aircraft had come to a stop the ramp was dropped and, as B Company and a Land Rover hurtled out, the pilot gunned his engines and took off, an event that impressed the Resident and his colleagues.

By 18 December, the rebellion in North Borneo had been smashed. On the instructions of Police Headquarters in Jesselton Superintendent Ross returned to Sipitang and left Superintendent Davis at Pantai to wind up operations until he departed on long leave on 21 December. On the same day, a major police operation in Sindumin rounded up nine TNKU who had slipped back into North Borneo from Brunei by *prahu*. Parry returned to his desk in the District Office. In the 1963 Birthday Honours List, Parry was awarded Member of the British Empire (Civil Division) for gallantry. There is no doubt that he was instrumental in maintaining law and order in Sipitang, a suggestion neatly enshrined in a letter from Governor Goode:

> 'I congratulate you on the courage, initiative and shrewd tactical sense which you showed. I have no doubt that your fine leadership and energy frustrated plans for more serious trouble in Sipitang. I

appreciate that you could not have acted so effectively had you not had the loyal and willing support of many people in the district. I congratulate you on having won their loyalty and confidence.'

On 23 December, the *Sangitan* returned to duty hunting pirates on the East Coast. It was now a question of mopping up the remnants. Several detainees released back to their *kampongs* gave information that led to arrests and the police finding caches of weapons and documentation. Arrests continued with some patrols having crossed the border. On Christmas Day, eight ARAS surrendered to Weston Police Station and, during the course of an interview, one said that he had infiltrated back to North Borneo on 15 December when the *Sangitan* had left the patrol station that had been ordered by Ross to support the operation organized by the Beaufort Police, in response to armed men being seen near Kota Klias. Next day the suspect showed the police a Mark 5 .303 rifle, which, he said, he had used at Limbang, and a telescope and 108 rounds of ammunition. Several detainees released to their *kampongs* showed police the locations of caches of weapons and handed in documentation. Arrests continued, including of some who had crossed the border. On the strength of information extracted from Jaya bin Hassan, a leading activist was arrested.

In his post-operation report, Superintendent Ross estimated that in the Interior Residency 281 arrests were made and seventy-three people surrendered between 8 and 25 December, as follows:

	Arrested	**Surrendered**
Melaman	4	
Pantai	6	14
Sindumin	44	
Sipitang	155	51
Weston	72	8
Total	**281**	**73**

Eighteen shotguns, two .22 rifles and a Greener Gun and 237 rounds of ammunition were stolen. Of these, twelve shotguns, one .22 rifle and the Greener were stolen from Weston and the remaining six shotguns and a rifle, possibly a Japanese .303, were taken from Lingkungan.

The revolt in Brunei was also collapsing and reports began to circulate of unkempt and starving young men drifting back to their *kampongs*, although this was not the case in the centre of the rebellion in Limbang and Temburong. Second Lieutenant Bruce Jackman of 1/2 Gurkha Rifles reminded his men during an ambush on the house of Sambas that, although there was a considerable amount of livestock running free, under no circumstances were they to supplement their diets with fresh meat. For ten days the Gurkhas apparently resisted the temptation. It was only when the platoon returned to its base that a number of grunting piglets and squawking chickens emerged from packs and sacks. On another occasion, Jackman and his platoon sat in ambush covering a suspect house and were bitten by mosquitoes and preyed on by huge bull leeches. A pile of palm leaves that twitched and rumbled turned out to be a saltwater crocodile. In total, 1/2 Gurkhas had killed fifteen TNKU and had captured 783, some of whom had surrendered, at the cost of two killed and seventeen wounded

M Company, 42 Commando moved to Kampong Amoh in the Paunduran Valley and worked with the North Borneo authorities to prevent TNKU crossing the border. An L Company patrol led by Second Lieutenant Targett-Adams spent ten fruitless days ambushing rivers, streams and paths in the area of Kampong Riong, supplementing their rations with eggs from a *kampong* in return for administering first aid to the villagers. Commando Headquarters moved to Bangar. Soon after Reconnaisance Troop arrived on 14 December, at a rubber plantation estate at Labu in Temburong District after a long march from Lawas, a Twin Pioneer dropped three pallets of supplies, the last one hurtling straight through the roof of the mosque. Within ten days, the Troop had captured thirty-four TNKU as well as five completely innocent people. The Troop spent eight weeks in Labu and had a baby girl named after them – Royal Marina. The Haji mended the mosque roof. So far, 42 Commando had captured 265 TNKU and a large amount of military equipment, including a Bren gun.

On 13 December the Brunei State Executive Committee had appointed Brigadier Glennie to command British Forces, Brunei, pending the arrival of Major General Walter Walker, commander of the 17th Gurkha Division, then on an official tour of Nepal to pay his respects to the king, visit the Gurkha depot and greet Gurkha veterans. On the same day, Sultan Omar neutralized political opposition and labour disruption by replacing the Legislative Council with an Emergency Council. Outwardly, he was still attracted to the Malaysian Federation proposal.

Four days later, after being briefed by General Poett at Headquarters Far East Command, Walker caught the night train to Singapore and was welcomed by Glennie at Brunei Airport on 19 December as Commander, British Forces, Borneo and Director of Operations. On the flight, he scribbled a few notes of essential ingredients for success for the directive that he planned to issue:

> Jointmanship
> Timely and accurate intelligence i.e. first class intelligence machine
> Speed, mobility and flexibility of Security Forces, particularly Army.
> Security of our bases, whatever they may be, wherever they are, whether an airfield or patrol base or whatever.
> Domination of the jungle.

Walker reported to Commander-in-Chief, Far East Command, thereby bypassing the three commanders-in-chief in Singapore. Expecting the three senior Service commanders in British North Borneo to report direct to him, his command was an early example of Joint Service command, which is now called 'purple'.

Brigadier Glennie briefed Major General Walker on Operation Ale while acknowledging weaknesses in the Headquarters Far East Land Forces decision-making, in particular that 99 Gurkha Infantry Brigade should have commanded from the start. He highlighted that the Army lacked maps, the Royal Navy had little information on ports and the RAF did not know the locations of landing strips. The current activity remained hunting surviving TNKU.

Within three days Walker established the joint Headquarters, British Forces, Borneo in Brunei High School and emphasizing that there was no room for inter-Service politics also insisted representation must include civil authority and police components at all levels. Determined to flush out the remaining TNKU in time for the Federation of Malaysia in August

1963, Walker was convinced that the rebellion was a prelude to something more sinister from Indonesia but, in spite of the hawkish declarations, there had been no reports of military activity. The main internal threat in Borneo, in his opinion, was the Maoist Chinese Communist Organisation (CCO), who could provide bases and shelter for subversives and Indonesian infiltration. Founded in 1956, using typical communist methods, it organized picnics and recreational and cultural events to talent-spot potential members. Those selected underwent ideological training before swearing an oath to become a Party member. The CCO had successfully subverted labour movements but it now faced colonial authorities prepared to deport and detain using emergency powers. Interrogations of suspects were suggesting that the organization was in the advanced stages of planning an insurgency campaign and had rehearsed attacks on police stations and assassinations and intimidation.

Walker also expected the Governors of Sarawak and North Borneo to surrender military sovereignty to him. Three days after he arrived, Walker attended the first meeting of the Borneo Security Council chaired by Sir Dennis White, the High Commissioner for Brunei. With a membership of senior diplomatic, political, military and police officials from the five Divisions of Sarawak and Brunei, it was answerable to the Commissioner-General for South-East Asia and Commander-in-Chief, Far East Command. A military adjunct was the Brunei Operations Committee, which was chaired by Walker. When Walker announced that he planned to concentrate 40 and 42 Commandos in Brunei and North Borneo under command of 99 Gurkha Infantry Brigade and that HQ QRIH and a squadron would move to West Sarawak to protect Kuching and take advantage of the roads, he tabled his concept to create two tactical areas of operations:

> Western Sarawak (First, Second and Third Divisions) controlled by Military Commander West Sarawak (COMKUCHFOR) in Kuching in an area covering 36,000 square miles.
>
> Fourth and Fifth Divisions, Brunei and North Borneo to be controlled by HQ 99 Gurkha Infantry Brigade.

This operational format remained, in one form or another, throughout the Confrontation with Indonesia.

The Colonial Office members were not entirely in agreement with his proposals and, although Walker explained that the Cavalry were perfectly capable of fighting on their feet, the roads, tracks and distances in West Sarawak were more suitable for armoured cars and mounted infantry provided by the Queens Royal Irish Hussars, particularly as most of the roads ran parallel to the border and therefore a fast response was achievable using armoured cars. When Governor Waddell of Sarawak cited that he required infantry, not armoured cars wrecking his roads, Walker appealed to Sir Dennis, 'Chairman, I wish it to go on record as having been told that my official military advice is unacceptable to the Governor of Sarawak'. While a compromise was reached that the Hussars would deploy to West Sarawak as 'mobile infantry', Walker insisted that a minute be inserted that he was the military commander, not the Governors. From this first meeting Walker concluded that the political members believed that since the rebellion had been quashed, that was the end of the matter. Nevertheless, he had successfully emphasized that he was the military commander.

The next day, 40 Commando minus two companies landed from the commando-carrier, HMS *Albion,* at Kuching. A Company, which was known as Pug Force, disembarked at Miri while S Company provided Embarked Forces for 6th Minesweeper Squadron patrolling the rivers of West Sarawak. HMS *Albion* then sailed to Tawau where C Company and a tactical headquarters were to take over from B Company, 1/2 Gurkha Rifles, which rejoined its battalion on 19 December.

On 21 December, Sultan Omar created a committee to be responsible for the rehabilitation and administration in rural areas for outlying areas by supporting development projects. At the same time, he showed his concerns for the families of killed or detained rebels by giving them US$2.5 humanitarian relief. Ten days later, he suspended the Constitution and dismissed the State and District Committees and replaced them with an Emergency Committee that included the British High Commissioner and ten nominated members.

HQ 99 Gurkha Infantry Brigade remained deep in the seat of the rebellion with 1 Queens Own Highlanders in Seria and 1 Green Jackets at Miri. C Squadron of the Queens Royal Irish Hussars provided wide-ranging patrols. Supporting HQ 99 Brigade was an Intelligence Corps officer and four NCOs from 21 Intelligence and Security Platoon to convert information into intelligence and disseminate those who needed to know. It was accompanied by Captain Keith Burnett, of the Royal Artillery, who was on his way to join 28 Commonwealth Brigade as the MIO and had been redirected to Brunei. In early January, an Intelligence Corps captain managed the Interrogation Centre, reporting to Mr David St J. Forrer, Head of Special Branch and a former Intelligence Corps National Serviceman. Special Branch was strengthened by the Royal Military Police. Keenly aware of prisoner welfare, the captain was able, eventually, to convince a medical officer to see every prisoner weekly. A staff sergeant from 19 Intelligence and Security Platoon scrutinized interrogation reports and collected evidence for prosecutions. Another Intelligence Corps member in the area was an expert Photographic Interpreter and Japanese linguist, but he was the Garrison Administrative Officer on Labuan.

Insisting that 'rear' areas did not exist, just areas in depth to be defended, Walker rejected as 'too little, too late' a Headquarters Far East Land Forces suggestion to fly battalions from Singapore to meet an incursion. His first priority was to defend the 971-mile border with Indonesia and dominate a 100-mile deep sanitized zone so that every incursion and outbreak of civil unrest could be addressed quickly. A top priority was to familiarize himself with British North Borneo and, consequently, he spent as much time as possible getting to know his soldiers, visiting villagers and liaising with useful sources of information. One of these was Tom Harrisson and the two men established a firm relationship. An opinionated man who had never commanded troops in the field, Harrisson had clashed with officers whom he believed were using conventional European tactics to fight an unconventional campaign and were failing to use the inland tribes who knew the jungle. At the request of Walker, he wrote a booklet entitled *Background to a Revolt: Brunei and the Surrounding Territory* that outlined the history and anthropology of Brunei in a readable form so that all troops arriving in Sarawak were familiar with British North Borneo.

With no foreseeable role after the Malayan Emergency, 22 Special Air Service had been reduced to two squadrons by the disbandment of B Squadron and C (Rhodesian) Squadron. An internal debate had separated those who believed the Regiment should support NATO and those who believed it had a global role. When the Brunei Revolt broke out, the

Commanding Officer, Lieutenant Colonel John Woodhouse, a global role supporter, lobbied the War Office and by 11 December he was in Brunei. When A Squadron arrived three weeks later, Major General Walker intended to use it as a reserve and a reaction force of 'tree jumpers' to pursue those making incursions. 'Tree jumping' was a high risk technique, developed during the Malayan Emergency, of the parachutist falling through the canopy of trees until the parachute was snagged by branches; then the parachutist abseiled to the ground using a long rope. Woodhouse convinced Walker that the Squadron should spread along the border and report direct to him. Within days, four-man patrols were deployed covering a twenty miles frontage. Helped by Tom Harrisson in Sarawak and John Warne in Sabah, patrols were introduced to longhouse elders where common courtesy and a cast iron stomach were required.

CHAPTER FOURTEEN

The Beginning of Confrontation

In West Sarawak, the Queens Royal Irish Hussars had settled in to a mixture of mounted and foot patrols in First and Second Divisions despatched from government bungalows at the Troop locations of Serian and Simanggang. Sometimes they boarded minesweepers that took them along the River Rajang to meet local boatmen, who then steered and poled their canoes along shallow and twisting rivers and watercourses. The Regimental periodical *The Crossbelts* records that week-long foot patrols were always popular – 'Infantry we became, but we learned quickly and were proud of it.' They had every right to be so, considering the exposure of the Royal Armoured Corps to jungle warfare was very limited. As with every unit, the crisis did not stop the Regiment celebrating St Patrick's Day, an event that was filmed by National Broadcasting Corporation of America.

A month after he arrived, drawing heavily on his experiences during the Malayan Emergency and his study of the French experience in Indo-China, Walker added to his successes 'winning the hearts and minds of the people, and especially the indigenous people'. It had been vital in defeating the Communist Terrorists in Malaya. With the need for timely accurate information of border activity, Walker left the police to manage urban and coastal strip internal security and deployed infantry sections to several longhouses covering cross border tracks and navigable rivers where the British soldiers revelled in their new role. In the first stages of 'hearts and minds', the medics played a valuable role in treating illness, inoculating against diseases and in providing dentistry, and ensured that incursions were denied local support. These early days of 'hearts and minds' laid the foundations of loyalty and ensured that it continued throughout Confrontation.

On 27 December, M Company received a warning order from HQ 42 Commando:

> Warning Order. Long Range patrol. Ten fit and experienced men from your company. Officer will be Lieutenant van der Horst. Full heli support. Signals and Medical provided from this location. Briefing at this location 09.30 hours 28 Dec. Leave pm 29th or am 30th.

Next morning Rupert van der Horst was briefed that Brigade HQ believed that TNKU were setting up a stronghold on Bukit Pagon, a 6,070ft high mountain, some forty miles south of Bangar on the southern most tip of Brunei on the border with Sarawak, and that he was to investigate.

The mountain straddles the southern tip of Temburong District with Fifth Division.The patrol, named *Rupertforce*, was expected to last seven days. In addition to SBA Terry Clark, the medic, there were two signallers, Sergeant Barnes and Marine McGinnis, and two Iban Sarawak Rangers, Adjit and Bahru.

During the early evening of 29 December the patrol was delivered to a helicopter landing site and encountered its first problem – the map was inaccurate. For the next two days, amid frequent downpours, van der Horst followed a chilly river flowing north through a valley carved through 200ft jungle-covered cliffs. Their course then changed to clambering up and down steep, muddy hills. It was not unusual for someone to miss their footing, curse and hurtle down a slope. Rations were short, and to make matters worse, Adjit missed shooting a pig. After Commando Headquarters advised van der Horst to expect a supply drop, it took the patrol an exhausting day and a half to climb to a 4,000ft ridge, only to find it was a false ridge. Morale rose when a Belvedere delivered food, spare clothing, beer and cigarettes. Next day, they crossed a plateau of rocks coated with roots, moss and vegetation, which proved to be the worst going, and were then confronted by a cliff, which they climbed using vines, and reached the main ridge of Bukit Pagan. By now, cold was adding to the discomfort of permanently soaked clothes. Fortunately, the airdrop had included pullovers and, huddling together, the patrol extracted a little warmth at night underneath their *bashas*. Next day, Commando HQ advised van der Horst to expect another drop; however, this was cancelled because the Auster pilot could not find them. He was unaware that the patrol still had two days march before they reached the summit and searched the wrong place. It was depressing news, particularly as the patrol was running out of rations. When another airdrop was arranged, a Valetta made five passes over the patrol and then flying at 150ft dropped a pallet only 30yds from the target. As van der Horst later recorded, 'Well done, the RAF'.

As the troops had moved into the jungle to cut off the TNKU, air resupply became vital. Air despatch was built around HQ 3 Army Air Supply Organisation with HQ 55 (Air Despatch) Company RASC and two of its Air Supply platoons and 22 Air Maintenance Platoon fully engaged. One of the first reinforcements from the United Kingdom to be deployed to Brunei was 1 Army Air Supply Organisation, which was placed on seventy-two hours notice to move on 14 December. Within days, 11 and 13 Air Supply Control Section and A (Air Supply) Platoon from 47 (Air Despatch) Company were on their way to Singapore courtesy of British United Airways. By mid-January, 13 Air Supply Control Section had returned to the United Kingdom and A Platoon, 47 (Air Despatch) Company moved to Labuan, while 55 (Air Despatch) Company returned to Singapore.

The patrol searched Bukit Pagon but finding no evidence of the TNKU began the descent to a river, with the person carrying the Bren frequently losing his footing and bumping downhill out of control. A deer was shot and roasted over a fire, although most found the venison too rich for large helpings; nevertheless, the fresh meat was welcome. The next day the patrol learnt that helicopters assigned to collect them were on another task and that fog had ruled out an airdrop. Adjit and Bahru shot a pig and another deer. It was still raining very heavily and the river rose alarmingly. Commando HQ radioed that a helicopter would recover them the following day from a shingle beach, but when the patrol reached it the beach was flooded. Nevertheless, they waded into the river in the hope that the helicopter would be able to land but van der Horst received another depressing signal that low cloud had again forced them back.

Another unsuccessful recovery was made that afternoon and consequently the patrol resigned itself to another cold, wet and hungry night. Next day, the river had risen even more and, since there was no chance of a helicopter, they hacked out a drop zone for a supply drop. During mid-morning they attracted the attention of a Valetta by firing flares and watched as it settled into a low approach, climbed out of the valley and then returned at very low level. In the doorway, the loadmaster shoved out five pallets, all but one landing in the centre of the drop zone. The missing one was rescued from the river. The patrol had a relatively comfortable two days until it was lifted out by two Wessexes and flown to Brunei. Debriefed at Commando HQ, *Rupertforce* was sent on leave at the Shell Hotel in Labuan where its members were spoilt. This patrol was probably one of the most rigorous of the Brunei Revolt and Confrontation.

Marine Fyffe's boredom in the 42 Commando Intelligence Section at Bangar was temporarily relieved on 16 January as the worst floods in living memory spread along the valley of the River Limbang. For two weeks the weather had been dreadful and then the river rose 18ft in four hours and burst its banks, sweeping away houses and flooding *kampongs*. In some places the river was 30ft above normal height and a mile across. Internal security operations were shelved as Belvederes of 66 Squadron and naval Wessex helicopters and troops, who had been hunting the TNKU, rescued frightened and soaked people from the roofs of their shaky huts, houses and trees. Assault boats delivered food and medical supplies. The 42 Commando padre, the Reverend Wood, described how a stream near Bangar Hospital ran uphill, such was the force from the main river, and flooded the wards. From this natural disaster, the British exploited the 'hearts and minds' strategy by sheltering and feeding more than 1,000 homeless refugees. B Company, 1/2 Gurkha Rifles, established flood evacuation centres that distributed food and medical facilities. To the south, two D Company platoons at Nanga Medamit and the platoon at Danau performed miracles to rescue, feed, clothe and accommodate about 600 people, some of whom would have undoubtedly drowned had not assault boats manned by Royal Navy and Royal Marines coxswains and Chinese boatmen in canoes rescued them from the debris-filled and fast flowing river, islets of high ground and smashed houses. Eventually the situation at Danau became so bad that Major Waterton ordered the platoon to return to Limbang before it became isolated. He was awarded the Royal

Humane Society Bronze Medal for several acts of gallantry. The situation elsewhere was not so bad as in Temburong. In Tutong, C Company built a sandbag wall along the banks of the River Tutong opposite the Police Station and near the fish market in which Captain Lea had taken shelter during the early morning on 9 December. Lea also ensured that the road to Brunei Town was kept open.

For Fyffe the floods were a welcome distraction until it was time to go to the toilet. The only one above water, and therefore the only one still functioning, was in a building on high ground at the other end of Bangar. The Section acquired a *prahu* that was precariously unsafe for inexpert handlers and, as a lifeline to the toilet, it was named *The Bumboat*. According to Fyffe, the boat could tell tales of heroic charges, mad paddling, gallant victories and ignominious defeats. When a mild attack of dysentery struck Commando Headquarters, the paddling became more frenetic and the cries of despair and anguish more frequent!

Major General Walker was determined that the rebels would be flushed in time for the emergence of Malaysia in August 1963. Throughout the Brunei rebellion, Radio Jakarta had broadcast a series of inflammatory statements designed to destabilize British influence in the region and then on 20 January 1963 Foreign Minister Dr Subandrio declared that Malaya represented the 'accomplices of neo-colonists and neo-imperialist forces that were hostile to Indonesia' and from henceforth Indonesia would adopt a policy of *konfrontasi*. *Konfrontasi*, literally translated as confrontation, had been widely used in Indonesia for years as a term to refer to the diametrically opposed differences between conservative traditional and liberal modern modes of thought and cultural expression. Expression of political, economic, social and military confrontation was a familiar phrase to the Indonesians but far less so to foreigners, who usually regarded confrontation as a direct intervention or open hostilities. This was borne out when Radio Jakarta warned that volunteers were ready to help liberate the three protectorates of British North Borneo from colonialism. Although local populations had become impatient with the cordon-and-search operations and curfews, the problem for Subandrio was that the British response to the floods had convinced many that they had arrived not as oppressors, as broadcast by A.M. Azahari, but had brought stability to a country destabilized by rebellion and natural disaster.

At the beginning of February, 1 Kings Own Yorkshire Light Infantry, from 28 Commonwealth Brigade, took over from the 1 Queens Own Highlanders and deployed A Company to West Sarawak under command of HQ 3 Commando Brigade, while B Company guarded key points in Brunei Town. D Company deployed to Limbang to continue the pursuit of the TNKU; 16 Platoon spent fifty-seven days on patrol near the border with just two short breaks; and 1/7 Gurkha Rifles arrived on HMS *Albion* and took over from the 42 Commando in Temburong District. The Commando relieved 1/2 Gurkha in Brunei Town and Tutong and were able to relax during the Muslim festival of Hari Raya Haji. However, patrols in the marsh around Trusan were arduous. When intelligence then indicated possible Indonesian military infiltration, F Troop, 145 (Maiwand) Commando Battery was flown to Batong Duri with its 105mm Pack Howitzers. Part of 29 Commando Regiment, it had been scheduled to convert to a Blue Water surface-to-surface guided weapon regiment in West Germany until the project had been cancelled and it then reformed as field artillery to support 3 Commando Brigade. Leaving Southampton on the troopship SS *Oxfordshire* on 17 September, it found itself in Brunei in late December. E Troop then replaced F Troop and achieved two distinctions; the first, of firing its guns from the deck of HMS *Albion* and the second, in so doing, supporting 1/7 Gurkha Rifles by delivering the biggest concentration of high explosive since Korea by shelling suspect TNKU camps. Like F Troop, it also patrolled as infantry with 'one half of the Troop chasing the rebels back into the swamp while the other half tried to ambush them there.'

Meanwhile, 1/7 Gurkha Rifles kept up the tempo against the TNKU. In one of its first contacts on 5 February, within a week of arriving, a C Company patrol, led by Sergeant Lalbahadur Rana, pursuing rebels through thick jungle, watercourses and steep hills found a damp handkerchief drying in the sun on a rock. Lalbahadur deployed his men to cover him while he and two riflemen checked the area, but they were spotted by a sentry and a brisk firefight developed in which two TNKU were killed and their sergeant major had his shotgun knocked from his grasp by a close shot. He managed to escape. The month continued with patrols having almost daily success in rounding up TNKU or finding weapons and ammunition caches. Near the end, after a report was received that rebels were sheltering in a barn in the middle of a paddi field, an Assault Pioneer Platoon lance corporal carried out a close target reconnaissance of the barn and found evidence of occupation. The information was passed to Special Branch by the HQ Company commander, Major Denis O'Leary, as probably correct and he led his company, using the maximum cover through the sparsely populated country, to a position overlooking the barn. He then reconnoitred it and, finding that it had been occupied the previous night and several times previously, believed it to be a short term safe house. In order to deceive the local population into believing that the operation was complete, O'Leary sent the majority of C Company to the main road but left two small ambushes covering the barn. As dusk turned into night, four figures were seen moving stealthily toward the barn; however, O'Leary did not spring ambushes because he wanted to catch the rebels once they were inside and unable to escape. The ambushers watched the TNKU cook a meal and whiffed the cooking aromas drifting over the fields and then the men went inside. No sentries were posted. The Gurkhas then took fours to move silently to a spur overlooking the barn. And then from a range of about 15yds, O'Leary rushed the barn, fired into it and withdrew to wait for dawn. Next day, a patrol found two dead rebels and two wounded ones, one of whom died before he could be transferred to hospital. The survivor was the sergeant major.

In spite of the hawkish declarations from Jakarta, there had been no identified military activity of any sort from Kalimantan. Nevertheless, Major General Walker believed that the Brunei Revolt was a prelude to something more sinister and that it would originate from Indonesia. The problem was that his opinion was intuition and not hard intelligence supported by co-lateral. The Chinese Communist Organisation was a subversive threat to be monitored. When he was made to think about reducing his force levels, Walker suggested that in future Far East operations in which British Forces were committed HQ 17th Gurkha Division should be the regional strategic reserve, as opposed to the War Office preference of sending the 'fire brigade' Strategic Reserve units from the United Kingdom. The continued lack of threat from the Indonesians and the near destruction of the TNKU meant that, by the end of March, Walker's men were under orders to return to their barracks in Malaya, Singapore and Hong Kong.

Nevertheless, the rotations of the units left in Brunei continued. At the end of March, Lieutenant Colonel John Heelis brought 2/7 Gurkha Rifles from Singapore, having left Hong Kong a few days earlier. A

Company moved to Limbang while B Company, which was commanded by Major David Cutfield, led an uncomfortable existence on an island at the mouth of the Brunei River. Assisted by the Assault Pioneer Platoon, almost all its operations were waterborne and involved patrolling not only glistening beaches but also coastal scrub, tangled mangrove and swamp. C Company at Tawau conducted anti-piracy operations with the North Borneo Police Mobile Force and the Royal Navy. D Company deployed to Muara to guard TNKU prisoners of war as well as conduct normal internal security operations. Intelligence from informants and prisoners suggested that Affendi and about twenty hardline TNKU were in the mangrove swamps of north-west Brunei Bay, intending to remain concealed until the hunt was discontinued. Patrols dispatched into the area found several campsites.

Meanwhile, hostility from Indonesia and the perceived threat from the Chinese Communist Organisation led Headquarters Far East to prepare contingency plans to deploy Headquarters 3 Commando Brigade to British North Borneo in the event of increased threat. And then on Good Friday, 12 April, thirty Indonesian guerrillas attacked Tebedu Police Barracks in First Division of Sarawak some three miles from the border. Under cover of darkness they crawled along a monsoon ditch and underneath a 10ft high chain link fence surrounding the compound, and took the police completely by surprise. A corporal in the Charge Room was killed and two constables in the sleeping quarters were wounded. The most senior officer, Inspector Chimbon, took cover under a water tank. The raiders then scavenged the bazaar for food and left, scattering pamphlets suggesting the raid had been conducted by the TNKU. But several factors suggested external influence. The raid had been planned and executed by troops experienced in raiding and was led by a person with military competence. Suspicions fell on Indonesian marines supported by Communist sympathizers in Sarawak. Lieutenant Colonel John Strawson, Commander, Kuching and new Commanding Officer of the Queens Royal Irish Hussars, was so concerned about the attack that the next day he sent a 'Flash' signal to Headquarters Far East Land Forces:

> In view of likely further incursions from Kalimantan and probability of CCO insurgency, I have recommended to HE The

> Governor, who agrees with me, the instant despatch of a brigade of troops from Singapore to ensure the security of Sarawak.

Strawson assembled his only reserve, B Company, 1 Kings Own Yorkshire Light Infantry, from jungle operations in Brunei by sending a Voice Psychological Operations Auster to instruct the soldiers to assemble at a jungle landing site, from which they were lifted by Belvedere helicopters to Brunei Airport. Walker needed all available helicopters. When he heard that maintenance on six 845 Naval Air Squadron Whirlwinds at the airport would take a week, he instructed that they be ready for operations the next day to fly the infantry to Kuching, which they were. The following day, a Royal Marines and two armoured car Troops were defending Tebedu Police Barracks.

The urgency of military signals is determined by the grade: from 'Priority' to 'Immediate' to 'Flash'. 'Flash' is so rare that when Strawson sent the signal, it had an immediate affect. Within hours, the new HQ Far East contingency plans swung into action. HQ 3 Commando Brigade and 40 Commando were recalled from Easter leave and 2/10 Gurkha Rifles was placed on notice. Next day, Major General Wyldebore-Smith arrived in Kuching and, agreeing with Strawson's assessment, issued instructions for 40 Commando to deploy to First Division immediately. L Company, 42 Commando, which had left Brunei on 29 March, returned on 17 April. Two Troops of C Squadron, Queens Royal Irish Hussars and 12 (Minden) Battery, 20 Field Regiment were already patrolling Kuching and the surrounding areas. Into Second Division moved 2/10 Gurkha Rifles with two rifle companies and a C Squadron troop. Third Division was covered by the remainder of 2/10 Gurkha Rifles. HMS *Albion* brought the bulk of the reinforcements from Singapore. The Gurkhas were annoyed to be instructed to unload their weapons and place the ammunition in the ships' magazine, as peace time rules demanded. Off Kuching, helicopters flew the Battalion command groups ashore while the rifle companies landed from landing craft. One company was transferred to two minesweepers and HMS *Alert* and ferried up the River Rajang to Sibu, the capital of Third Division, its principal role being to disrupt the Chinese Communist Organisation, much to the irritation of the Resident and Divisional police commander in this tranquil backwater of West Sarawak. The town was the second largest town in Sarawak and although thought to be sympathetic to the Chinese Communist Organisation, the arrival of the soldiers was greeted with some relief.

Major General Walker formed two brigade tactical areas of operations.

- West Brigade – Headquarters 3 Commando Brigade. Brigadier Barton took over as Commander, British Forces, West Sarawak.
- East Brigade. Headquarters 99 Gurkha Infantry Brigade to continue anti-TNKU operations in Brunei, Fourth and Fifth Divisions and maintain security in North Borneo with a Gurkha battalion and 1 Kings Own Yorkshire Light Infantry, 1 Queens Own Highlanders and the 1 Green Jackets in rotation.

So began the gradual escalation of the British military presence in Borneo that, between 1964 and 1966, would develop into a Commonwealth alliance. Walker kept his headquarters in Brunei Girls' School but, as the remnants of the rebellion were rounded up and the tempo of operations decreased, it was now much smaller than it had been in the New Year. For the first time, HQ 3 Commando Brigade was supported by a hurriedly assembled ad-hoc Intelligence and Security Platoon provided by the Intelligence Corps. It was accommodated in the Palm Court Hotel in Kuching that was not only close to Police Headquarters, it also served as a resting place for the local call girls carrying on their trade in other hotels. In May, a more permanent Section was formed.

Meanwhile, the Security Forces were tracking down the remnants of the active TNKU. Sambas and five companions met a one-eyed officer who guided them to Yassin Affendi's hideout on Kibi Island in the mouth of the River Kibi. With Affendi were two brothers of A.M. Azahari and several senior political and military leaders. Continued Security Forces pressures forced the group to move and, on 31 January, they went by boat to Sundar on the River Aru, where they had been told there were no troops or police. Sambas had now been on the run for one and half months. Food stocks were very low and three men sent to Luagon to find supplies returned empty-handed, much to the annoyance of the irascible Sheikh Osman Azahari. The next day, S Company ran into a lieutenant and ten men looking for food at Sulliman and captured him and one man. Under interrogation at Sundar and Limbang, the officer mentioned a few names but not the location of the hideout. Another party of seven returned to the Pandaruan area to find food and then rendezvous with the six rebel leaders on the River Garong. The leaders spent four days waiting for the six to return and then moved to Tanjong Kindanah on the River Gulang Gulang where they met two supporters, who fed them their first decent meal in two weeks. A fortnight later, Affendi decided to make evasion easier and split his group into two small parties. His group included Sambas and his father. Supported by the two men, the group lingered in the area for about three weeks before returning to the River Gulang Gulang. The second party of four, which included Azahari's two brothers, had become so fed up with evading that they persuaded a gravel boat skipper to take them to Kampong Bunut to the south-west of Brunei and sheltered with sympathizers. But a tip-off to Special Branch led to Pipes and Drums, 2/7 Gurkha Rifles, which was attached to B Company, surrounding the two houses in which they were hiding. Shortly before midnight on 17 April, the platoon led by Captain Michael Smith cordoned a house and encountered automatic fire from a Sterling. Nevertheless, both houses were overrun but as Captain Burnett, the Military Intelligence Officer, climbed into the loft to search he was killed. The Gurkhas fired into the ceilings; and the very seriously wounded Sheikh Osman stepped into the headlights of a Land Rover. He died in hospital a few days later. Burnett's family were already en route to Singapore. The following day, Sheikh Salleh was arrested. The Bunut operation was significant for it demonstrated that some of the hard-line TNKU had become fed up with living in the jungle.

On 17 December, the Sarawak Emergency Committee sought military assistance to enforce an amnesty to collect an estimated 8,514 shotguns held on the firearms register. Operation Parrot began two days later and netted 7,188 licensed firearms. A 2/10 Gurkha Rifles patrol stumbled on twenty Chinese youths doing physical training in a jungle clearing in the middle of the night. Three days later, eight guerrillas attacked the Police Field Force post at Gumbang, which was only 200yds from the First Division border. It had been reinforced by a B Company, 40 Commando section commanded by Corporal Radford and he personally accounted for two raiders. His leadership gained him the MM. Although documents again suggested TNKU responsibility, blood trails leading across the border strongly suggested Indonesian complicity. Brigadier Barton imposed a 'shoot-on-sight' curfew between 8.00pm and 4.00am five miles in depth along the border and ordered Operation Falcon Strike in which L Company, 42 Commando reinforced the First Division Sarawak Police Field Force detachments and were present in fifteen forts near *kampongs* covering likely crossing border points. Nevertheless, on 27 April, Tebedu Police Barracks was again attacked, this time by three raiders who crawled to within 20yds of the compound, cut the alarm system, removed *punji* sticks and opened fire with a shotgun and a Bren gun. A half-section from C Company, 40 Commando, returned fire but a dog tracker team had little success when the spoor was weak.

Affendi's group and the third party met at Kampong Serdang and after staying in the area for about a month then moved to a small island nearby. Intelligence assessments suggested that the core of TNKU leaders had moved to the coastal area east of Brunei Town. The arrest of two supporters led to the surrender of three rebels and the arrest, on 17 May, of a youth regularly supplying food to the TNKU hiding on the island. His information provided collateral to an air photograph that showed a small camp among a tangle of mangrove, muddy streams, grass-edged swamp and pockets of mosquito-ridden high ground measuring 2,000yds long and 800yds wide. Time was of the essence because, once the rebels realized their supplier had been arrested, they would move. The food supplier agreed to guide a patrol to the camp on his next scheduled supply run on 20 May. Lieutenant Colonel Alan Seagrim, the 2/7 Gurkha Rifles Commanding Officer, selected B Company to make the attack. When the food supplier said that access to the island was best at high tide, Major Cutfield decided on an early morning attack and divided his Company into three:

- 4 Platoon to provide ten Gurkhas for the Assault Group. The rest were in reserve.
- 5 Platoon to remain on Serdang island.
- 6 Platoon to form a block on the north-east extremity of the island.
- The attached Assault Pioneers were to patrol the river in boats so that the noise of their engines would screen noise made by 4 Platoon.

Joined by a Military Intelligence Officer, Inspector Gregory, a sergeant from Special Branch and the food supplier, and using a boat, at 6.45am, the Assault Group used a light beacon as a navigational aid to find a stream flowing through the swamp indicated by the guide. However, it became so narrow that they had to slip over the side and wade through the glutinous mangrove mud. After about one and a half hours, it was clear that the youth was lost and so the Group returned to Serdang where the police requisitioned two canoes. Cutfield, the youth, the Military Intelligence Officer and the Special Branch officers used one canoe, while four Gurkhas used the second one. The remaining six riflemen used the small boat. At 9.30am, the group re-entered the swamp and paddled up a narrow stream until the guide indicated that the rebel camp was no more than three minutes away. It was about 10.45am. Cutfield and the two Special Branch slipped into the water and slowly waded until they spotted a towel and the outline of a shelter and then heard voices. Believing they had been seen, the three opened fire and then the Special Branch sergeant invited the TNKU to surrender. Abdullah bin Jaaffat, the Tutong/Belait Area Commander, immediately replied, 'It's alright. I won't run away'. He said that nine rebels had fled and they were unarmed. The ten Gurkhas picked up the spoor and noted that they had split, with one group heading north and the other west toward 6 Platoon.

The latter had lain in ambush for nearly four hours when they heard the shots. Rifleman Nainabahadur Rai was standing by a tree in a clump of overgrown rubber when a movement he saw about 75yds away materialized into four men, with the leader carrying a drawn pistol. Nainabahadur held his fire, in case the Assault Group were in pursuit. The leader was about 30yds away when he saw the Gurkha and charged. At a range of about 15yds, Nainabahadur fired, his bullet mortally hitting the leader in the chest and passing through to hit the second rebel. The remaining two, also wounded by Nainabahadur, dropped into cover but were quickly found by him. One was Yassin Affandi Rahman. The second group also ran into 6 Platoon and were captured after a hopeless firefight with two Gurkhas. They were Salleh bin Sambas, who had been wounded in the thigh, and his father. Another man was captured the next day. A search of the camp revealed three .38 police revolvers, a .45 Browning automatic pistol, three shotguns, a police Mark V .303in rifle, *parangs*, a transistor radio, 50lbs of rice and 10lbs of sugar. The prisoners were taken to Limbang where British and Gurkha soldiers gave blood to keep bin Sambas alive. Cutfield was awarded the Military Cross. Nainabahadur was awarded the first of two Military Medals he won during Confrontation. He was selected by the British Council for Rehabilitation of the Disabled as 'Man of the Year' and travelled to London to receive his award, amid considerable publicity.

By 19 January 1963, fifty-five TNKU had been killed and 3,288 captured, of which thirty-three had been wounded in actions with the Security Forces. Belait District had the largest number detained of 692, of which only fifty were released. As retribution followed the rebellion, the majority of low level TNKU were quickly released from the prison camps and permitted to return home. Mostly held in a detention centre at Berakas, although some of the hardcore were shipped to Hong Kong, the morale of the majority was, inevitably, low. While there is nothing wrong in opposition, armed rebellion is extremely serious, but they had been abandoned by their leaders, who they blamed for the failure of the rebellion, which had suffered from poor leadership and ineffective organization. Confined with their colleagues and supplied with reasonable food, shelter, and medical support, morale soon rose and some said that they would succeed next time. Others were contrite and ashamed and not looking forward to a period of detention. By January, 794 were released after capture after giving an oath of loyalty to Sultan Omar, leaving 2,494 detained. Trials saw some sentenced up to one year and six months. For the hardcore and commanders, most were jailed for between eleven and fifteen years. After his capture Salleh bin Sambas was taken to Brunei Police Headquarters and spent four weeks under interrogation by the police collecting evidence and by the British seeking military information that may affect the internal security of Brunei. He was then sent back to Limbang where he stood trial and received fifteen years – five years for his involvement in a rebellion against the Government of Brunei; seven years for the illegal possession of firearms; and three years for his membership of the TNKU and his position as a commander in the organization. He served his sentence in Limbang. In 2004, he was interviewed in Martin Spirit's Brush Fire Films documentary *Return to Limbang* and was introduced to Major General Jeremy Moore and Brian Downey of 4 Troop at Limbang. It was a moving meeting.

On 12 July 1973, the Sultan's birthday, apparently with Malaysian complicity, twenty detainees broke out of Berenkas Prison and reached

East Malaysia, where they were given sanctuary throughout the 1970s. It was only in 1990, after pressure from Amnesty International, that the process to release the rebels began. Most of those who took part in the escape returned during the mid-1990s and, although re-arrested, were generally quickly released after taking an oath of loyalty. Several were invited to join the Brunei government. One was Dr Haji Ahmad Zaini, who had been the Vice President of the Brunei People's Party. A trusted lieutenant of A.M. Azahari, he had been with him in Singapore when news of the rebellion broke out. A.M. Azahari died in exile in 2002. Yassin Affendi, still battling for democracy, has formed the Brunei National Solidarity Party.

CHAPTER FIFTEEN

Brunei and Confrontation

As Confrontation gathered pace after the Tebedu attack, politically, the British could do little except defend the 970-mile border by developing an efficient intelligence system and countering the incursions with ambushes.

Brunei was not markedly affected by the fighting because of its distance from the border, however internal security operations continued to ensure the country remained on side. If there was one subject that was persistently mentioned, it was the frequent reference to the TNKU. Foreign Minister Subandrio and his Central Intelligence Bureau had supported the revolt and claimed to have enlisted about 1,000 TNKU exiles and other 'volunteers' into the Brunei Regiment and raiding companies with such stirring titles as 'The Thunderbolts', 'Night Ghosts' and 'World Sweepers'. Interrogations late in Confrontation established that the 'volunteers' were largely former Indonesian Army, convicted criminals and pirates cajoled into the militias. During the revolt, General Yani, the Army commander, had declared 'fullest moral support' to the TNKU and assured that his 'troops were awaiting orders' but no more. So far as the Army commanders were concerned, Subandrio's intervention was a welcome distraction. Colonel Hassan Basri, a Kalimantan Inter-Regional Command intelligence officer, had established links with Chinese refugees from Sarawak, however, at no time did Sukarno insinuate that Malaya was under a communist threat. The British collectively nicknamed the insurgents as Indonesian Border Terrorists (IBT).

The Federation of Malaysia Agreement was signed in July 1963, however Sultan Omar opted out for two principal reasons. First, he was not prepared to accept that, after ten years, the oilfields would become a taxable Federation resource and Brunei was likely to lose out. Second, as head of a sovereign state, he objected to being the last in the hierarchy of the Council of Rulers in which the other members were sultans as heads of Malaysian provinces within the state of Malaysia. Politically, his decision prevented Malaysia from applying pressure to establish democracy in Brunei and lift the State of Emergency. Within days of the declaration, there was a surge of huge anti-British feeling in Indonesia and the British Embassy was sacked, an action most probably officially supported. Nevertheless, Sukarno found himself not only isolated but that the Commonwealth nations were helping Malaysia to defend East Malaysia, which now consisted of Sarawak and Sabah, formerly North Borneo. The US-brokered Bangkok Talks collapsed when a ceasefire broke down.

Increased incursions into East Malaysia led Major General Walker to develop Operation Claret in which Commonwealth infantry units, usually a company, crossed the border, under the severe restrictions of Walker's 'Golden Rules'. The aim was to destabilize Indonesian operations by attacking camps ambushing lines of communications, initially to a depth of 5,000yds south of the border, later 10,000 yards. One of the deepest penetrations was achieved by a Gurkha battalion. Brunei was a sovereign state needing to defend itself and in the spring of 1964, Sultan Omar recalled the Brunei Malay Regiment from Siginting Camp in Malaysia. The 463-strong regiment disembarked from the Straits Steamship Company coaster *Auby*, which was well known to British troops, and paraded in Brunei Town on 6 May. Now commanded by a British officer supported by other Loan Service officers and NCOs in key positions, the Regiment moved into its new barracks at Berakas and, after local training, took responsibility for the internal security and defence of Brunei.

In August 1964, Sukarno widened Confrontation by landing troops and paramilitary police by parachute and from the sea in south-west Malaysia. Most were dealt with quickly. Meanwhile, the shallow raids in Operation Claret were forcing the Indonesians onto the defensive. Sukarno could not complain without being accused of sending troops into Malaysia. In the Battle of the Rivers, Operation Claret attacked riverine lines of communications. In early 1965, Harold Wilson's Labour Government published its White Paper on Defence in which the separate Service ministries were to centralize into the Ministry of Defence and that the priority strategic emphasis was the defence of Europe. In mid-1965, the Communist Party of Indonesia took advantage of the ill-health of Sukarno to launch a *coup d'etat* but when six senior generals were murdered, General Suharto used the Army to decimate the Communist Party and, in so doing, gained a powerbase. Stronger peace feelers were initiated by Indonesia. By the beginning of August 1966, Confrontation was edging to a mutual conclusion and British Forces, Borneo reverted to internal security and guarding the East Malaysian border. Nevertheless, hardline Indonesian officers continued to send special forces and TNKU across the border to gather intelligence on Commonwealth military activities and stir up subversion among the Chinese, particularly during further Bangkok Talks ceasefire discussions. The only incursion to threaten Brunei occurred during this period and was significant because of the depth it achieved.

When 1/7 Gurkha Rifles arrived on its fifth and final tour, intelligence reports were suggesting co-ordinated incursions by two groups into Fifth Division and the Interior Residency of Sabah, with the aim of sabotaging the Seria oilfields and destabilizing peace talks. The Intelligence Corps Field Intelligence Corps Officers, all NCOs, and the Border Scouts network were alerted to collect information from traders. A prisoner then claimed that at Long Bawang, Assistant Lieutenant Sumbi was selecting about fifty men for the operation. Major Alan Jenkins, the B Company Commander at Ba Kelalan, also learnt from an Indonesian battalion commander, who had been pushed deep into North Kalimantan by Operation Claret, that his unit had been replaced by a mixed bag of the para-commandos, Sukarno fighters known as 'Sukarnolewan', Diponegoro Division deserters and hardcore TNKU.

By 7 July, Sumbi had briefed his men that their mission was to train dissidents in Temburong District and attack the oil refinery at Seria. Five days later, his last supply air drop was reported by a Field Intelligence Officer and then nothing was heard until 25 July, when Major Jenkins was told that Sumbi had crossed the border two days earlier. Six days later, a Gurkha Independent Parachute Company patrol on exercise followed five-day-old tracks of thirty men four miles north of Ba Kelalan, heading north and eleven miles inside Brunei, then found a bivouac littered with abandoned British canvas jungle boots and sacking; the sacking had probably been wrapped around boots to avoid leaving footprints. During the evening of 3 August, a 2/7 Gurkha Rifle patrol attacked a camp in which Sumbi had been seen and then laid a communist-style annihilation ambush along the River Kelalan to trap the Indonesians, but they disappeared. Under the Bangkok Agreement, Confrontation was concluded on 11 August 1966 and British Forces, Borneo ceased offensive operations, which included the pursuit of Sumbi. Nevertheless, 1 Queens Own Buffs lost Private Mark Barton, of C Company, killed in a brisk battle three days later.

And then on 12 August, a month after the incursion was first reported, a bedraggled Indonesian staggered into Long Lopeng and admitted that Sumbi was camped two miles to the west. He had been so unsettled by the 3 August ambush, although he believed that he had not been detected, that he had divided his force in the hope that some would reach the Temburong dissidents. Two other prisoners then said that Sumbi was aiming for the 6,070ft high Bukit Pagon, the same feature that had tested Lieutenant van der Horst's 42 Commando patrol in January 1963. Below it the River Pasia flows north into Brunei Bay. If Sumbi reached it, boats could quickly take his force to relative safety among sympathizers. On 20 August, 1/7 Gurkha Rifles was ordered to continue the pursuit and, the next day, Major Jenkins and two platoons were inserted to the east of Bukit Pagon where they found the going very difficult – steep, mountainous slopes, thick jungle rivers in full flow and persistent heavy rain, but no evidence of Sumbi. As the search focused on the River Parsai valley, eight exhausted prisoners were captured. Shortly after Jenkins' men, also exhausted, had been reduced to one patrol, during the evening of 2 September his lead scout saw a small bivouac across a shallow river. Jenkins ordered a 'quiet' camp and, next morning, the patrol passed through the bivouac and then challenged four Indonesians ahead to surrender. One was about to resist until dissuaded by his colleagues. It was Lieutenant Sumbi.

Forty-three of Sumbi's men had been accounted for, the missing being three Indonesians and four TNKU. In the third week of September, A Company, 1/7 Gurkha Rifles captured the Indonesians in the lower reaches of the Trusan. When, on 7 October, some Iban reported to

Lieutenant Colonel Cross, the officer who had formed the Border Scouts and the Gurkha Parachute Company, that four starving Indonesians had wandered into a longhouse and were now sheltering in a hut near a prominent tree in a gully, he contacted the Royal Brunei Malay Regiment. Major J.R.E. Lloyd, commanding C Company based in Bangar, led two platoons commanded by Lieutenants Husain and Musa to the area and placed one in ambush positions while the second one swept through the area to flush out the enemy but failed to find the hut. Major Lloyd then joined the platoon and was about to conduct another sweep, when four bedraggled men emerged from the jungle and led the soldiers to the hut, where they surrendered their arms and ammunition. Two were from Brunei.

Apart from the 3 August ambush, no shots had been fired during the six week pursuit. It was a remarkable operation. Major Jenkins was awarded a MC, not for gallantry but for leading a relentless and potentially hazardous pursuit resulting in the capture of twenty-four Indonesians. He achieved fame in the 11 November 1967 edition of *The Hornet* when the operation was depicted, although the article appears to include material from Borneo citations listed in the London Gazette. On 28 August, 1 Royal Hampshires laid several ambushes in west Sabah in response to an incursion directed at the Interior Residency. When intelligence emerged of subversive interest in several security bases, on 2 September three platoons searched 12 Mile village and arrested a Chinese man who could not satisfactorily account for 100lbs of rice. When these operations sparked more sightings, including barefoot, armed men in the jungle, the Intelligence Section made five crucial conclusions:

- The incursion was directed at Kalabakan where there had been a large Indonesian workforce in the forestry since before the Brunei Revolt.
- The enemy strength could be estimated.
- Equipment had been identified.
- The enemy were short of food.
- The enemy were lost.

In an operation not dissimilar to that mounted by 1/10 Gurkha Rifles in January 1964, in the Brantian area, Lieutenant Colonel Wilson denied the incursion food, shelter and tranquillity by ambushes, harassment, responding quickly to sightings, and guarding villages and towns. Several disconsolate and starving IBTs were captured.

In 1971, under Sultan Haji Hassanal Bolkiah, Brunei assumed full responsibility for internal government, except for external defence, which remained with Great Britain but was funded by Brunei. A battalion of Gurkhas, based in modern barracks at Seria gifted by the Sultan, rotated with one of the battalions in Hong Kong. One of its duties was to provide the Demonstration Platoon to the Jungle Warfare School outside Tutong on the banks of the River Tutong and close to a beach. The School had previously been in Malaysia. The British continued to support the Regiment with Loan Service officers and other ranks in a wide range of appointments, including contributing to the Intelligence Section. The Gurkha Reserve Unit was formed in the early 1970s to protect key points.

Was Operation Ale an operational failure? Considering the plan had been in existence since 1953, it appears that nothing had been done by successive commanders-in-chief to add flesh to the contingency plan. Indeed, there are similarities between the Revolt and the Falklands War twenty years later. Intelligence seems to have been almost non-existent. There were no maps of Brunei and those initially issued to the Falklands Task Force were ungridded. The RAF did not know about airstrips and the Royal Navy did not know about ports, harbours and navigational hazards in both instances. In 1962, the RAF came to the rescue by mobilizing aircraft to fly in ground forces within eighteen hours and in 1982, the Royal Navy assembled a Task Force. Without them, in both cases, the Army was going nowhere.

Was the Revolt an intelligence failure? Well – what is intelligence in the military context? In its basic format, it is the conversion of information about an enemy, and indeed a friend, in a timely format for commanders to consider. Operational, in effect battlefield Intelligence sources include documents, people (such as prisoners and refugees), ground and air imagery, topography and intercepts of communications. Allied to Operational Intelligence is Protective Security, sometimes called Field Security, of counter-intelligence to defend people, information, infrastructure, arms and equipment against espionage, sabotage, subversion and terrorism. A key feature in both skill sets is the Intelligence Cycle of the continuous collection, evaluation, analysis, collation and timely dissemination of reports, summaries and assessments, each graded for reliability of sources and co-lateral to other information. When intelligence is presented it should be presented without bias and without being tailored to please the decision-maker, who should, in turn, consider the conclusions dispassionately. But intelligence has one major problem. Some sources are considered so precious that the intelligence gained is not shared on the need to know basis. Not infrequently, this cost lives, a good example being the protection of Enigma information during the Second World War. Government security and intelligence organizations are equally secretive. Commercial organizations have a right to hold on to their resources except where national security might be involved. So were the intelligence signals missed in Brunei?

At first glance, this appears to be the case. The first indication that something was up emerged in April 1962 and then there had been increasing evidence of planned insurrection in November. However, this information had been collected by the Sarawak and North Borneo Police and passed to the office of the Commissioner General for South East Asia. Brunei was a Protectorate but its Special Branch was inexperienced and seemed to have missed the indicators of armed rebellion, not that there were expectations of one.

According to Alastair Ker-Lindsay, there can be no doubt that British Shell Petroleum had an intelligence system which appears to have been used effectively. Its Managing Director, Mr Linton, and Director of Security, Mr Griffiths, were both aware that something was up. This was hardly surprising. Brunei was in a period of instability and it was inevitable that the Shell work force would be full of innuendo, rumour and political conversation. Ker-Lindsay found Griffiths locking up the armoury of the Oilfield Security Force. But there are questions. Where had the fixed-wing aircraft usually parked at Anduki gone? Why was a Shell launch loitering outside Sultan Omar's Palace during the night of 8/9 December? From where and when did Mr Linton receive reliable information that he passed to Assistant High Commissioner Park that a revolt was planned for early on 8 December? How much information acquired by Shell was passed to Special Branch? Indeed, how strong was the relationship between Shell and Special Branch?

And interestingly, what was the role of British Intelligence Services and why were they involved in running covert operations with the US Central Intelligence Agency to ensure that countries and individuals friendly with the West remained in power? The author Greg Poulgrain, in his book *Konfrontasi,* and in communications with the author, suggests that the inner circle of the People's Party of Brunei had been penetrated by British Intelligence and it was British Intelligence that had precipitated the outbreak of the insurrection, the strategy being to 'invite' an Indonesian response, which would then persuade Sarawak to 'jump into the lap of the British colonization plan' of establishing Malaysia, but with the oilfields in Brunei remaining separate. Which is exactly what happened in 1963.

The one organization that seems not to have been aware of a potential threat in Brunei was Far East Command, otherwise surely General Poett would not have visited the Philippines, unless he was encouraged not to change his diary dates. When Speaker Harley said in 1704 that 'Information is the soul of business', he could have said the same of 'Intelligence of military operations' except that, in 1962, the Army still did not consider Intelligence to be a priority operational activity in peacetime. Indeed, during the 1920s, Field Marshal Douglas Haig had said 'Intelligence is a rather special kind of work and has a very small place in the Army in peacetime'. The antipathy was neatly summarized by Brigadier Brian Parritt, a future and influential Director of the Intelligence Corps, in his book *The Intelligencers:*

> The British Army has never liked or wanted professional intelligence officers. It has continually been held that the best man to help a commander assess the capabilities of enemy infantry is an infantryman, the best man to judge the potential threat of cavalry is a cavalryman. To have an officer devote his military career to Intelligence was, in most Generals' opinion, a short-sighted policy which would lead to the officer having a specialised and narrow outlook to problems which require a wide and practical background of military experience.

The consequence of this attitude was that when the British were not fighting, intelligence was not collected and neither was it shared by others on a need to know basis. The post-1945 campaign list is littered with examples – Palestine, the Malayan Emergency, the Cyprus Emergency, Confrontation, Northern Ireland, the Falklands and the Gulf War. And yet, in 1962, Far East Command had been exposed to an ideology that was affecting the Far East – communism. The Korean War had been concluded in 1954. Chin Peng and his Communist Terrorists had been driven from Malaya by 1959. The French had been ejected from Indo China and the Americans were beginning to take an interest in the region. The Communist Party of Indonesia, albeit nationalist in nature, was exerting considerable influence. And there had been attempts by Indonesia to encroach into Sarawak on several occasions. One problem that the Army faced was the Intelligence staff appointments were filled by officers from any Arms and Service, usually on two-year postings, and therefore there was little continuity and expertise. The re-organization of the Intelligence Corps, after the cessation of National Service, to include Operational Intelligence, in addition to Field Security, or Protective Security, as it was known, helped to provide some collection and collection expertise. Previously, this had been carried out by intelligence clerks posted from within armies, corps, divisions and brigades.

And what about the Indonesian connection? If we accept that ambitious countries, political parties and commercial organizations have aspirations of expansion to increase their sphere of influence, then one method is a takeover of a weaker body. When Rajah Vyner Brooke ceded Sarawak to be a British colony in 1946, he thought it in the best interests of the state. But the decision was not without significant dissent against the transfer from a benign government to the formality of a governor accountable to London, and therefore the Colonial Office was content to see the murder of the second Governor, Sir Duncan Stewart, three years later blamed on anti-secessionists. A recent investigation in the radio documentary *Documents: The 1949 Assassination of British Diplomat Duncan Stewart* (BBC Radio 4; 12 March 2012), suggests that the assassins, far from returning the Rajah dynasty to power in Sarawak, were part of a political movement that intended to help Indonesia take over Sarawak. The rationale for deflecting the blame onto Anthony Brooke was to avoid the second conflict with Indonesia within three years, particularly as the Malayan Emergency was gathering pace. Equally, Indonesia took a back seat because it could not be seen to have been involved with the murder of an official of the most powerful influence in the region, although President Sukarno continued to press for increased regional influence that included British North Borneo. The next opportunity emerged when A.M. Azahari made his bid for power on the ticket of a federation of North Borneo and, in much the same way that Sarawak had been destabilized by secession, so was that upheaval in Brunei presented as an opportunity to overthrow Sultan Omar III and gain a profitable foothold along the northern shore of Borneo. There is concrete evidence that Indonesian intelligence officers in Kalimantan Combat Command had trained Bruneans and, by implication, the People's Party of Brunei and TNKU. When the rebellion broke out, broadcasts of support by Indonesian leaders undoubtedly gave the TNKU the will to rebel; indeed, such was their certainty that in several instances, British aircraft were believed to be Indonesian.

And the Sultanate of Brunei? The throne was not overthrown and while the state may not have had the territorial influence it had during its heyday, the Seria oilfields made it one of the richest in South East Asia. The possibility of an autonomous federation of North Borneo, in itself susceptible to communist and nationalist influences, had been pushed aside. The Sultan could be assured that it was defended by powerful armed forces until the Brunei Armed Forces were trained and ready. Politically, the Sultan remained master of the destiny of Brunei without having to account to Malaysia.

Bibliography

Hooker, Virginia Matheson; *A Short History of Malaysia*; Allen & Unwin; Crows Nest (Australia); 2003

Hajid, Harun Abdul; *Rebellion in Brunei: The 1962 Revolt, Imperialism, Confrontation and Oil*; IB Tauris; 2007

The Berwickshire News; *Coldstream Woman's Husband (Herbert Blanche) Was Used as Human Shield by Rebels*; 8 January 1963

Pocock, Tom; *Fighting General: The Public and Private Campaigns of General Sir Walter Walker;* Collins, London; 1973

Van der Bijl, Nick; *Confrontation; The War with Indonesia;* Pen and Sword, Barnsley; 2007

Index

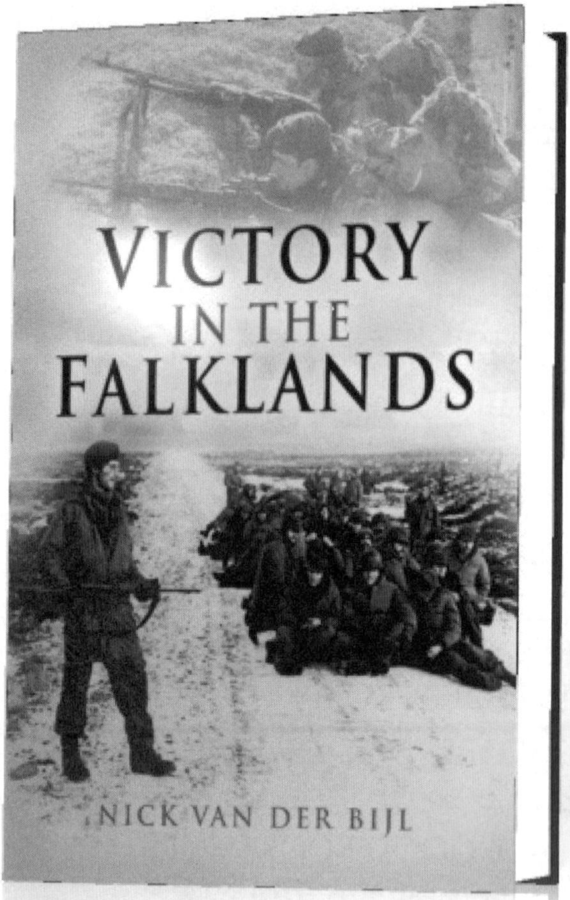

9781844154944 • 256 pages •
16 B&W plates • HB • £19.99

The hundred days of Spring 1982 that witnessed the robust British response to General Galtiere of Argentina's invasion of the Falkland Islands are for many the most remarkable of their lives. The anger of seeing foreign troops on British soil; the anxious waiting as the Task Force headed South; the shock of the loss of ships, aircraft and life; and, finally, elation over a stunning and complete victory. All these emotions and more were experienced by a nation unfamiliar with war.

While there are many books on the War, *Victory in the Falklands* stands out as a superb overview of the conflict, covering all the military phases, be they land, sea or air, as well as the political context and manoeuvrings. The copious use of firsthand accounts brings an immediacy to the story and we gain a real impression of what it felt to be part of the tri-service team that won so great a prize. *Victory in the Falklands* is a stirring story, which will revive many a memory for some and give a greater understanding for others.

WHAT THE CRITICS SAID:

'*Victory in the Falklands* is a stirring story, which will revive many a memory for some and give a greater understanding for others.'
The Officer

'A stirring account.'
Pennant

'Nick Van Der Bijl's splendid book stands out as a balanced yet thoroughly readable account of the struggle.'
Eastern Daily Press

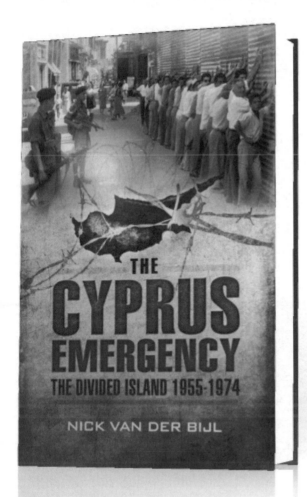

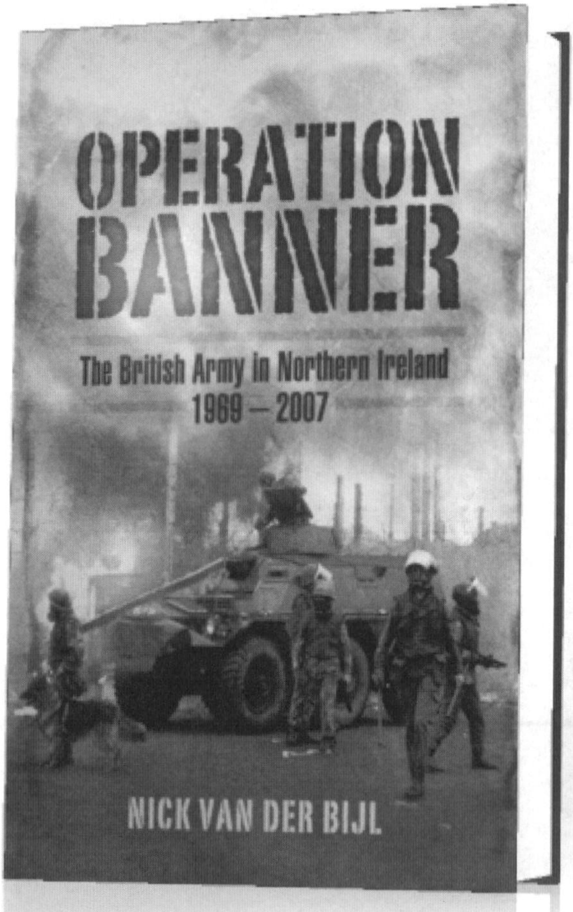

9781844159567 • 288 pages • 16 B&W plates • HB • £19.99

In summer 1969 the annual Loyalist marching season sparked violence in Londonderry which spread rapidly. After three days of violence the British Government deployed troops in support of the Royal Ulster Constabulary. Initially the Catholic community welcomed the Army's presence but this was to change over the years.

The first soldier was killed in 1971 and a further 48 died that year. January 30 1972 – Bloody Sunday – galvanised IRA recruitment and the British Embassy was burnt in Dublin. The Official IRA bombed Aldershot HQ of the Parachute Regiment and in August 1972 the Army launched Op MOTORMAN to clear No Go areas. Internment followed and the Province was firmly in the grip of sectarian violence. The next 30 years saw a remorseless counter-terrorist campaign which deeply affected the lives of all the people of Northern Ireland and several generation of the British Army.

The Peace Process ground on for over ten years but the campaign formally ended in 2007 with the establishment of hitherto unimaginable power sharing.

WHAT THE CRITICS SAID:

'The 16 pages of monochrome photographs are very revealing... As such, it is well worth the cover price.'
MEDAL NEWS

'For anyone wanting a sharp account of when and where things happened, this is like cut glass.'
DEFENCE FOCUS

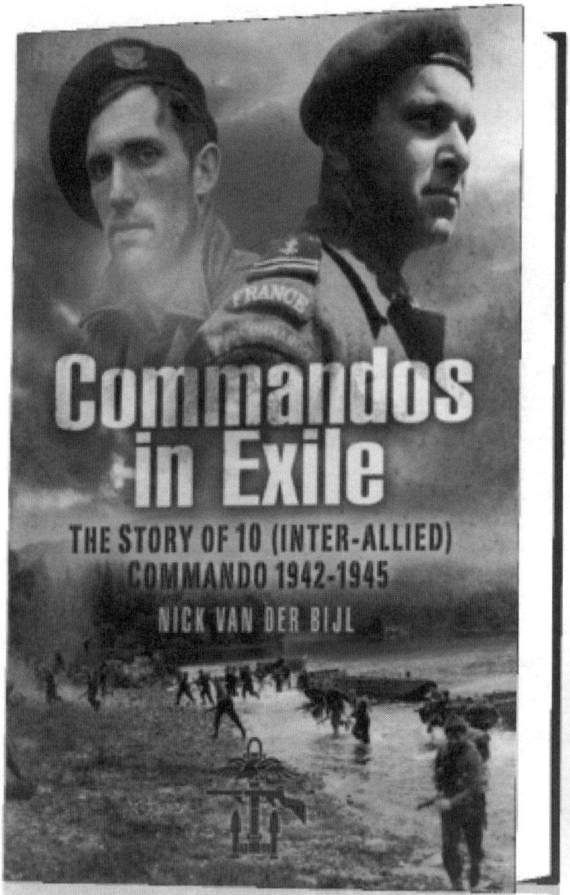

9781844157907 • 256 pages • 16 B&W plates • HB • £19.99

Commandos in Exile is the story of one of the least known and most unusual units in the Second World War.

This Commando comprised members of French, Dutch, Belgian, Norwegian, Polish and Yugoslav Free Forces who had escaped from German occupation. All members of this multi-national Commando had to pass the Green Beret commando course at Achnacarry in Scotland and the book begins by describing this training. In addition to the six national contingents, the author reveals that there was a secret additional troop, drawn mainly from East European Jews who had either been exiled or had escaped Nazi occupation and persecution.

10 Commando never fought as an entity but loaned troops for specific operations relevant to their origins. For example One Troop (French) took part in the Dieppe Raid, 2 Troop (Dutch) fought at Arnhem and 5 Troop (Norwegian) raided the Lofoten Islands. At other times members played key intelligence roles questioning POWs, translating captured documents, conducting reconnaissance patrols and gathering intelligence on the D-Day beaches.

With its full accounts of 10 (Inter-Allied) Commando's action and intelligence operations, *Commandos in Exile* is a fascinating and revealing read.